Tariff Structure, Intermediate Goods, and China–U.S. Trade Friction

Focusing on the interconnection of tariff structure, international trade, and welfare evaluation, the book investigates the characteristics of tariff structures of China and the U.S. in recent years and measures the impact of the Sino–U.S. trade friction that started in 2018.

The first part of the book discusses levels and evolution trends of the tariff systems of China and the U.S. from 2000 to 2014 and makes a comparison between the two countries' tariff structures. The second part centers on the Sino–U.S. trade friction in 2018, analyzing its development, overall impact on welfare, and relevant impact mechanisms. The author draws on the quantitative analysis method currently prevailing in the field of international trade, taking global value chains, intermediate goods, and variable markup into consideration. In contrast to the research conclusion applying standard trade theory, the result indicates that either unilateral imposition of additional tariffs or bilateral tariff friction will give rise to the deteriorated welfare level of both countries.

The book will appeal to academics and policy makers interested in international trade, China–U.S. relations, and the trade friction.

Haichao Fan is Professor of Economics in the Institute of World Economy, School of Economics, at Fudan University, China. He specializes in international trade and Chinese Economy.

China perspectives

The *China Perspectives* series focuses on translating and publishing works by leading Chinese scholars, writing about both global topics and China-related themes. It covers Humanities & Social Sciences, Education, Media and Psychology, as well as many interdisciplinary themes.
This is the first time any of these books has been published in English for international readers. The series aims to put forward a Chinese perspective, give insights into cutting-edge academic thinking in China, and inspire researchers globally.
To submit proposals, please contact the Taylor & Francis Publisher for China Publishing Programme, Lian Sun (Lian.Sun@informa.com).
Titles in economics partly include:

China's Economic Reform and Development during the 13th Five-Year Plan Period
Lin Gang, Wang Yiming, Ma Xiaohe, and Gao Debu

Cultural Economics
Li Yining

Technological Innovation and Economic Development in Modern Japan
Guan Quan

Resources, Power, and Economic Interest Distribution in China
Zhang Yishan

Industrial Development in Modern China
A Quantitative Analysis
Guan Quan

Tariff Structure, Intermediate Goods, and China–U.S. Trade Friction
Haichao Fan

For more information, please visit https://www.routledge.com/China-Perspectives/book-series/CPH

Tariff Structure, Intermediate Goods, and China–U.S. Trade Friction

Haichao Fan

Routledge
Taylor & Francis Group
LONDON AND NEW YORK

First published 2021
by Routledge
2 Park Square, Milton Park, Abingdon, Oxon OX14 4RN

and by Routledge
52 Vanderbilt Avenue, New York, NY 10017

Routledge is an imprint of the Taylor & Francis Group, an informa business.

English Version by permission of Fudan University Press.
British Library Cataloguing-in-Publication Data
A catalogue record for this book is available from the British Library

Library of Congress Cataloging-in-Publication Data

Names: Fan, Haichao, author.
Title: Tariff structure, intermediate goods, and China-U.S. trade friction / Haichao Fan.
Other titles: Guan shui jie gou fen xi, zhong jian pin mao yi yu Zhong Mei mao yi mo ca. English
Description: Abingdon, Oxon ; New York, NY : Routledge, 2021. | Series: China perspectives | Includes bibliographical references and index. |
Identifiers: LCCN 2020044462 (print) | LCCN 2020044463 (ebook) | ISBN 9780367706968 (hardback) | ISBN 9780367707064 (paperback) | ISBN 9781003147626 (ebook)
Subjects: LCSH: China--Commerce--United States. | United States--Commerce--China. | China--Foreign economic relations--United States. | United States--Foreign economic relations--China. |
Tariff--China. | Tariff--United States.
Classification: LCC HF3838.U6 F3613 2021 (print) | LCC HF3838.U6 (ebook) | DDC 382/.70951--dc23
LC record available at https://lccn.loc.gov/2020044462
LC ebook record available at https://lccn.loc.gov/2020044463

ISBN: 978-0-367-70696-8 (hbk)
ISBN: 978-0-367-70706-4 (pbk)
ISBN: 978-1-003-14762-6 (ebk)

Typeset in Times New Roman
by MPS Limited, Dehradun

Contents

Figures

Tables

Acknowledgments

I would like to express my special gratitude to my wife, my son, and my daughter for their encouragement and full support!

I would like to thank my students, Lina Zhang and Guangyuan Guo, for their excellent assistance in this project.

My sincere thanks also goes to Jiayue Cheng, who helps to do translation work.

As always, the responsibility for any errors remains my own.

Haichao Fan

Introduction

Since China's entry into the World Trade Organization (WTO) in 2001, tariffs on most Chinese imports have been substantially lowered or exempted. That makes it more difficult to achieve the expected goal of "promoting growth and adjusting structure" by formulating corresponding policies simply focused on the overall tariff levels. In 2015, Afghanistan became the 164th member of the WTO, covering most of the world's countries and regions. From a global perspective, although the tariff levels of different members in WTO have been significantly reduced, the differences in tariff levels and tariff structures of different countries (regions) are still quite striking, which will have a very important impact on international trade.

According to the research of Rodriguez (1998), the tariff structures of developed countries have not experienced fundamental changes in the past three decades. Although most countries still implement cascading tariff structure[1], in some countries, such structure is not adopted in reality (Liu & Wu, 2007). So, is China still adopting a cascading tariff structure? How different is its impact on different products? For different products, is there certain regularity in tariff characteristics, changes, and distribution? What's the policy implication for China? These are the key questions that this book will focus on.

De-globalization and trade protectionism rose since 2016, with the U.K.'s withdrawal from the E.U., Trump's successful election as U.S. President, the end of the Trans-Pacific Partnership (TPP), and increasing inter-country and interregional trade frictions.[2] The frequent occurrence of these de-globalization events adds to the uncertainty of global economic development, among which, the Sino–U.S. trade friction is the most typical one. In August 2017, U.S. President Donald Trump signed a Presidential Memorandum, instructing the Office of the United States Trade Representative to initiate a Section 301 Investigation against China, which kicked off a new round of trade friction between China and the U.S. (Yu et al., 2018). On April 4, 2018, the U.S. announced that it would impose a 25% tariff on a number of products, with a total value of 50 billion U.S. dollars imported from China, and proposed an additional tariff list. In the afternoon of the same day, in response, China decided to impose a 25% import tariff on $50 billion worth of goods originated from the U.S. (Fan & Zhang, 2018).[3]

As the world's two largest economies, trade friction between China and the U.S. is bound to have a huge impact on the well-being of both countries and the rest of the world.[4] So how big is the impact? How can we construct an appropriate model to accurately evaluate this impact? This book attempts to provide solid answers for these questions, theoretically and quantitatively.

Specifically, based on the author's previous research, this book will mainly focus on the Sino–U.S. trade friction in 2018, analyze the related characteristics of the Sino–U.S. trade friction from the tariff structure differences between the two countries, especially from the perspective of tariffs on intermediate goods, and answer the aforementioned questions by adopting the quantitative analysis method that is currently used in the field of international trade. The book is divided into two parts: the first part mainly discusses the characteristics and evolution trends and summarizes the similarities and differences of tariff structure between China and the U.S., while the second part focuses on the Sino–U.S. trade friction in 2018 and analyzes its development process, potential impact, and relevant impact mechanism.

To be specific, the first part of this book focuses on the characteristics, evolution trends, and differences between the tariff structures of China and the U.S. from 2000 to 2014. Tariff structure generally refers to "tariff rate structure," that is, the correlation between the tariff rates of various commodities. In this book, the author explores the correlation between the tariff rates of various commodities, analyzes questions such as tariff distribution and possible changes in the distribution of different products (industries), and discusses tariff rates and evolution of products with different characteristics. The overall research mainly starts with the two dimensions of time and product, and the author studies the tariff levels, structure characteristics, and evolution trends of China and the U.S.

The second part of this book focuses on the trade friction between China and the U.S. in 2018. On the whole, the second part can be divided into the following three chapters: Chapter 3 summarizes the historical process and evolution of the trade friction between China and the U.S. in 2018, supplemented by relevant cases, and it briefly discusses the impact of this trade friction on Chinese and U.S. enterprises and possible long-term and short-term coping strategies; Chapter 4 starts with the classical trade theories and makes a brief theoretical analysis of problems, including tariffs, terms of trade, and welfare; and Chapter 5 analyzes the welfare impact of the Sino–U.S. trade friction in 2018 and its mechanism using the quantitative analysis method. In contrast to the research conclusion of standard trade theory, this book conducts a quantitative analysis that takes global value chains into consideration, and the result shows that the overall welfare for both China and the U.S. will worsen in both unilateral (the U.S. unilaterally imposes tariffs on imports from China) and bilateral trade friction (both countries impose tariffs on imports from each other).[5]

Globalization has always proved mutually beneficial for trade partners. On the 40th anniversary of China's reform and opening-up policy, the author compiled this book based on previous research, hoping to provide new evidence and directions for thinking for China's tariff structure and the Sino–U.S. trade friction.

Notes

1 This is specifically manifested in the incremental increase of tariff rates from upstream to downstream products, and also from primary to manufactured goods.
2 For example, after the election of Trump as the new President of the United States on November 9, 2016, the U.S. withdrew from the TPP negotiation and the North American Free-Trade Agreement (NAFTA). In the meantime, import tariffs werc significantly increased. On March 29, 2017, British Prime Minister Theresa May wrote to the E.U., marking the formal start of the "Brexit" process; on March 19, 2018, the E.U. and U.K. reached broad agreement on the terms of a 2-year transition period after the U.K. left the E.U. in March 2019, and on June 26 of that year, the Queen granted royal assent to the Brexit legislation, allowing the U.K. to leave the E.U. On March 8, 2018, President Trump signed a decree stating that tariffs would be imposed on steel and aluminum goods from all countries except Mexico and Canada.
3 So far, there have been three rounds of additional tariff lists mutually announced and implemented by China and the U.S. The first round (which came into force on July 6, 2018) involved 545 products announced by the Chinese side and 818 by the U.S. side. Both sides have announced additional tariff rates of 25%. The second round of the tariff lists related to products worth about 16 billion U.S. dollars imported by each side from the other country, and it took effect on August 23, 2018. The additional tariff rate was 25%, with the Chinese list covering 333 items and the U.S. list covering 279 items. The third round of the tariffs list, on the other hand, came into force on September 24, 2018, and the U.S. announced a tariff list covering 5,745 products from China worth 200 billion U.S. dollars at an additional tariff rate of 10%, which would be increased to 25% as of January 1, 2019. The tariff list announced by China involved 60 billion U.S. dollars of products imported from the U.S., with tariff rates ranging from 5% to 10%. The information is compiled from people.com, the announcements from Customs Tariff Commission of the State Council and the United States Trade Representative (USTR). See Appendix 1 of this book for a detailed list.
4 Unless otherwise noted, all Sino–U.S. trade frictions mentioned in this book refer to the Sino–U.S. trade friction in 2018.
5 Studies in standard trade theory show that when large countries impose tariffs, their terms of trade will improve; other things being equal, their welfare level will increase correspondingly.

Part 1

Characteristics of tariff structure of China and the U.S. and evolution differences

A tariff is generally a tax levied on imports.[1] Tariff structure refers to the correlation between the tariff rates of various commodities. Back in the 1960s, the statistical analysis of Balassa (1965) and other scholars found that many countries were adopting a cascading tariff structure, which was manifested in the incremental increase of tariff rates from upstream to downstream products and also from primary to manufactured goods.[2] Scholars such as Corden (1966) conducted further research and concluded that one of the reasons why the cascading tariff structure was mostly adopted was for its effect on protecting the domestic market and related industries of importing countries. So, do countries in the current world still adopt the cascading tariff structure? What are the characteristics of China's tariff structure? Does it have any marked difference from that of other countries? This part will focus on these issues.

In recent years, a number of scholars have, from the perspective of welfare, further explored the relationship between a country's tariff structure and its welfare and economic growth. For example, Takashi Fukushima (1979) has extended Hatta's (1977) study and demonstrated that when tariffs on all high tariff products are lowered in equal proportions, the level of welfare and utility in importing countries will go up. A study by Anderson and Neary (2007) finds that changes in import tariffs can affect market access and thereby influence the level of welfare of importing countries. By extending the Grossman-Helpman "Protection for Sale" model and looking into the economic prospect of importing countries, Nunn and Trefler (2010) have examined the relationship between the "skill-bias" of tariff structure and the long-term economic growth of a country. A high degree of positive correlation between the two is found in their study.

These studies have further shown that to better formulate its national development strategy, tariff guideline, and policy, a country should be fully aware of the evolution trend and characteristics of its tariff levels and tariff structure, and their similarities and differences in contrast to those of other countries. However, few studies in the existing literature focus on a country's tariff structure and explore the specific characteristics and evolution of a country's tariff structure.

In view of this, based on the previous research results, the author analyzes the characteristics and evolution of the tariff structure of China and the U.S., and compares their differences from the following three levels:[3]

1. At the overall level, this book mainly discusses the trends and specific characteristics of three indicators over time, including the means, variances, and peaks of imported product tariffs of China and the U.S. at the HS2 chapter level from 2000 to 2014.
2. At the industry level, from the perspective of specific product characteristics, this book exhibits the tariff evolution and distribution in the two countries by exploring the tariff characteristics and changes of different imports. Two key indicators are selected, namely, the U.N. Classification by Broad Economic Categories (BEC) and elasticity of substitution of imports. These indicators depict the features of imported products in terms of their uses and correlation with their domestic counterparts, which can basically reflect the main characteristics of imported products.
3. At the tariff evolution level, from the two extreme tariff levels (the highest and the lowest), this book discusses the product's characteristics and its evolution under different levels of tariff protection. Through a comparative analysis of the differences of all aspects among the products at different tariff levels, this book further explores the trade protection effects of tariff on specific products and industries.

In terms of research data, this study uses the Most-Favored-Nation (hereafter abbreviated as MFN) Rate of Duty, covering the period from 2000 to 2014.[4] These data are selected mainly for the following three reasons:

1. At present, most countries in the world are WTO members, and the MFN rate of duty is adopted by the majority of them, so it can basically represent the actual tariff levels among the countries.[5]
2. Compared with the bound tariff, the MFN rate of duty is better at reflecting the actual tariff levels.[6]
3. The MFN rate of duty is easier to come by, and its data samples are more comprehensive.

Considering that the trade weighted value of tariff levels may obscure the true tariff situation of commodities, this book uses a simple average method to integrate tariff data for representing the average tariff level of that industry (country).[7] Of course, this study also takes the impact of import volume into account.

1 Characteristics and evolution trends of China's tariff structure

1.1 Characteristics at the overall level

Anderson and Neary's (2007) study suggests that the changes in the average and variance of tariff in one country can provide a comparatively adequate picture of the changes in its tariff structure and the impact of such changes on its welfare level. This chapter depicts and studies China's overall tariff level from the perspective of averages, variances, and peaks of the country's tariff.

1.1.1 Average tariff

Figure 1.1 depicts the trend of China's average tariffs from 2000 to 2014 at the HS2 industry level. It can be learned from the figure that, in the course of time, the average value of China's import tariff shows a sharp decrease, especially from 2000 to 2004 when its tariff level almost registered a straight-line decline; and from 2004 to the present, although its tariff level is still following a downward trend, the pace has slowed down significantly. On the one hand, this shows that China's tariff structure is influenced not only by the declining overall tariff level in this period, but also by the adjustment at the industry (product) level which has started playing a relatively dominant role. On the other hand, it suggests that in the new context, there is an urgent need to explore innovative and more effective tariff restructuring measures to facilitate the realization of China's trade and industrial policy goals.

1.1.2 Tariff variance

Table 1.1 shows the changes of China's tariff variance during the sample period. From 2000 to 2014, the tariff variance at the HS2 level dropped from 8.77 to 4.47, down by nearly half. After 2005, although the tariff variance in China was still decreasing, its pace gradually slowed down, and the value basically remained between 4 and 5. In other words, during the sample period, China's tariff structure gradually became more centralized and less volatile, and the overall structure grew increasingly stable over time. From a

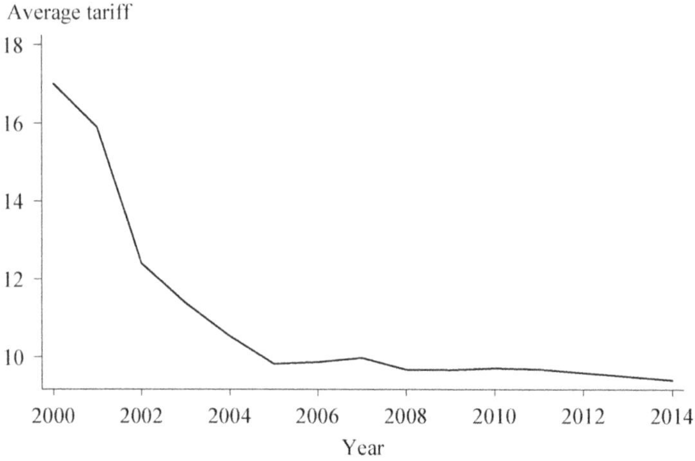

Figure 1.1 Average tariff change over time in China (2000–2014).

Table 1.1 Tariff variance changes in China during 1992–2014

Year	*2000*	*2001*	*2002*	*2003*	*2004*	*2005*	*2006*
Variance	8.77	8.21	6.42	5.68	5.11	4.47	4.73
Year	*2007*	*2008*	*2009*	*2010*	*2011*	*2014*	
Variance	4.76	4.80	4.81	4.78	4.78	4.47	

comprehensive view, compared with the period when it first joined the WTO, China has seen its tariff distribution deviated and changed considerably in the following 14 years. Since 2004, China has formed a relatively stable tariff structure, both in terms of the overall tariff level and in the degree of change deviation in the structure.

1.1.3 Tariff peaks

Tariff peaks, as defined in the WTO Glossary Terms, are relatively high tariffs of specific categories of products amid generally low tariff levels.[8]

Based on this definition, as shown in Table 1.2, the author has collected China's tariff peaks from 2000 to 2014. In the table, column 2 (HS2 code) shows the HS2 codes corresponding to the industries with the highest tariffs of the year, column 3 (highest tariff) represents the value of import tariff of the industries with highest tariffs, column 4 (quantity) reflects the number of industries with tariff peaks for the year, and column 5 (proportion) depicts the share of the number of tariff peak industries in the total number of import industries that year.

Table 1.2 Situation of tariff peaks in China (2000–2014)

Year	*HS2 code*	*Highest tariff (%)*	*Quantity*	*Share (%)*
2000	22	56.79	35	36.46
2001	10	54.34	34	35.42
2002	24	39.33	35	36.46
2003	24	34.44	32	33.33
2004	10	32.03	30	31.25
2005	24	30.67	31	32.29
2006	10	30.47	32	33.33
2007	24	30.67	31	32.29
2008	24	30.67	29	30.21
2009	24	30.67	29	30.21
2010	24	30.67	29	30.21
2011	24	30.67	29	30.21
2014	24	29.72	29	30.21

Through analysis of the figures in Table 1.2, we've found that the quantity of tariff peak industries in China, in the years between 2000 and 2014, dropped from 35 to 29 at the HS2 industry level, showing a significant decline over time; in the same period, the highest tariff over the years also registered a considerable decrease. However, as of 2014, nearly 30% of China's imports listed in HS2 chapters still belonged to tariff peak industries, which are subject to higher import tariff.

In terms of the categories of industries with the highest tariffs, the industries to which highest tariff products belong remained largely unchanged; they are mainly the industries of Chapters 10, 22, and 24, namely, cereals (10); beverages, spirits, and vinegar (22); and tobacco and manufactured tobacco substitutes (24). In other words, China may have a certain degree of import restrictions on these three industries.

Table 1.3 presents the corresponding HS2 chapter codes of all tariff peak industries in China in 2014. In this table, the starting year denotes the year in which the industry first appeared in the rank of tariff peak industries between 2000 and 2014. For example, the corresponding starting year for Chapter 2 industry is 2000, which indicates that tariff peak industries are listed since 2000. According to Table 1.3, 24 of the 29 tariff peak industries in 2014 had been included in China's tariff peak industries since 2000, with the latest one becoming one of them in 2005. It is noteworthy that most of these tariff peak industries have essentially remained so since they first entered the rank.[9] In other words, from the perspective of industry categories, China's tariff peak product categories show little change and strong stability. And from the view of specific sectors, China's historical tariff peaks are concentrated in the following sections: live animals, animal products (2/5); vegetable products (4/8); animal or vegetable fats and oils and their cleavage

Table 1.3 Tariff peak industries in China in 2014

HS2 code	*Starting year*	*HS2 code*	*Starting year*	*HS2 code*	*Starting year*
2	2000	21	2000	65	2000
4	2000	22	2000	67	2000
8	2000	24	2000	68	2005
9	2005	42	2000	70	2004
10	2000	43	2000	87	2000
11	2000	57	2000	91	2002
15	2000	61	2000	92	2000
17	2000	62	2000	93	2005
19	2000	63	2000	96	2000
20	2000	64	2000		

Note
Please refer to Appendix 2 at the end of the book for the complete table for 2000–2014.

products (1/1); prepared food stuffs, beverages, tobacco, and manufactured tobacco substitutes (6/9); raw hides and skins, leather, fur skins, and article thereof (2/3); textiles and textile articles (4/8); footwear, headgear, umbrellas, etc. and parts thereof (3/4); and articles of stone, plaster, cement, glass, or similar materials (2/3).[10] These industries are concentrated in the first 13 of the 22 industry sections and are mainly in Sections 1–4, 8, and 11–12, while most of the new industries also belong to Sections 1–4.

High tariffs are often believed to discourage import of related goods, which will in turn create trade barriers. In 2014, for example, by mapping the proportion of import trade of tariff peak industries (see Table 1.4), it is easy to see that this situation is corroborated by the data from China. What Table 1.4 illustrates is the import situation of 29 tariff peak industries in China in 2014. In the table, column Share shows the percentage of imports of tariff peak industries to the total imports of that year, while the ranking column refers to its corresponding ranking in the rankings of all industries from bottom to top after calculating their proportion of imports of the year. As can be seen from the table, nearly 2/3 of the tariff peak industries had a low proportion of imports. Meanwhile, the total imports of tariff peak industries accounted for only 12.35% of total imports of the year, which means that the tariff peak industries that accounted for 1/3 of the total industries only had a proportion of imports of approximately 10%.[11] This further indicates that China has indeed posed considerable import restrictions on imports in these industries.[12]

Summary

Through the aforementioned study, three main features of the change in China's import tariff structure from 2000 to 2014 can be roughly identified:

Table 1.4 Import characteristics of tariff peak industries in China in 2014

HS2 code	*Share*	*Ranking*	*HS2 code*	*Share*	*Ranking*
93	0.001%	2	64	0.114%	43
65	0.003%	4	43	0.116%	44
57	0.013%	10	17	0.122%	46
67	0.016%	12	91	0.140%	49
92	0.023%	14	19	0.168%	51
9	0.023%	16	62	0.199%	55
63	0.028%	20	22	0.204%	57
20	0.046%	22	8	0.309%	66
96	0.052%	26	10	0.338%	67
24	0.071%	29	2	0.371%	69
42	0.075%	31	4	0.388%	70
11	0.078%	33	70	0.402%	71
21	0.093%	36	15	0.523%	75
68	0.095%	37	12	2.624%	86
61	0.103%	40	87	5.608%	92

Note
Please refer to Appendix 2 at the end of the book for the complete table for 2000–2014.

1. The overall tariff level shows a trend of a sharp decrease over time.
2. The overall tariff structure tends to be centralized, and the basic tariff structure has been formed and remains relatively stable.
3. Although China's overall tariff is already at a relatively low level, the quantity of tariff peaks remains high, and import restrictions exist extensively in China.

1.2 Characteristics at the industry level

The previous section focuses on China's general tariff structure, but since 2005, the level and overall structure of its tariff have not changed much, so it is necessary to explore the precise characteristics of its tariff structure at the specific industry level. This section further demonstrates the development and evolution characteristics of China's tariff structure at the industry level mainly from the perspective of imported goods and their own features. Two indicators, the U.N. Classification by Broad Economic Categories and elasticity of substitution of imports, are primarily selected to further study the characteristics of China's tariff structure at the industry level in terms of both the use of imported goods and the impact of such goods on the demand of similar domestic counterparts.

1.2.1 Use of imports

According to the U.N. Classification by Broad Economic Categories (hereinafter abbreviated as Classification by BEC), goods traded by a

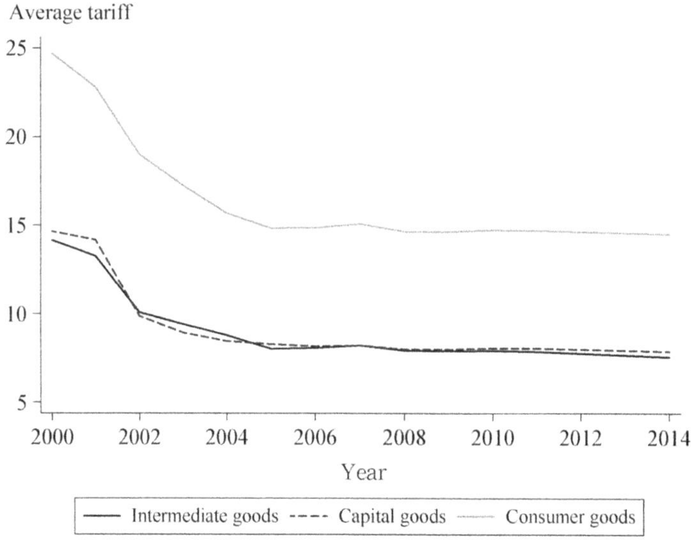

Figure 1.2 Changes of average tariffs of three categories of imports in China during 2000–2014.

country can be divided into three categories: capital goods, intermediate goods, and consumer goods, among which capital goods and intermediate goods are normally used as intermediate inputs to the production process in the importing country, while consumer goods are generally used for domestic final consumption. The tariff generally varies for goods for different uses; meanwhile, the tariff and volume of the imports for different uses can basically reflect the specific import tariff structure of the country and the degree to which the cascading tariff structure corresponds.

Figure 1.2 shows the line chart of tariff changes of various goods in China from 2000 to 2014 after classifying the various imports based on the Classification by BEC. It can be learned from this figure that similar to the change trend of China's overall tariff level over time, the average tariff levels of products of all the three categories have shown a substantial decline. Comparing to the goods of the other two categories, tariffs on consumer goods are consistently higher, while those on intermediate and capital goods remain at lower and closer level. In other words, on the whole, China's current tariff structure displays a relatively obvious feature of cascading tariff structure; that is, among imported goods, tariff rates of manufactured goods are significantly higher than those of intermediate inputs and primary goods.

Further mapping of the import shares of various products in the past years is shown in Figure 1.3. Combined with Figure 1.2, the import share of intermediate inputs continues to be the highest—although the average tariff

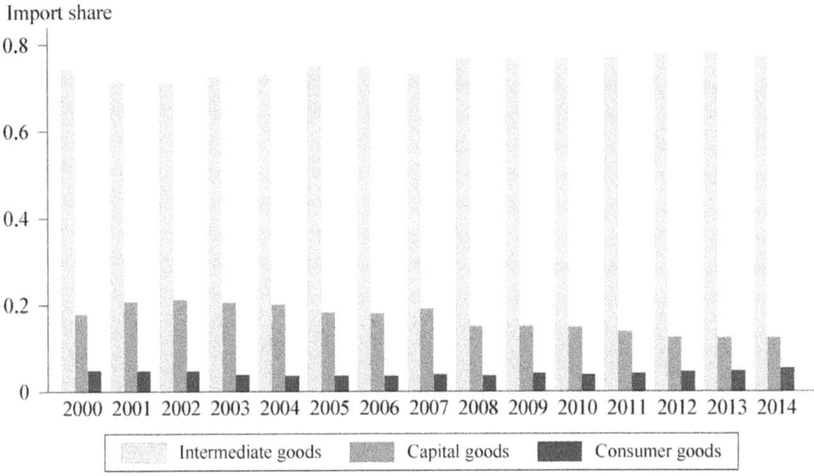

Figure 1.3 Change of total import shares of three categories of products in China during 2000–2014.

level of consumer goods in China is consistently higher than that of intermediate inputs. On average, in terms of the import structure, more than 70% of China's imports are intermediate goods, while the import share of capital goods is about 20%, and that of consumer goods is less than 10%. If capital goods are also considered to be an intermediate input, China's share of imported intermediate inputs makes up for over 90%. In other words, intermediate goods account for the vast majority of China's imports, and their share is significantly higher than that of consumer goods.

1.2.2 Elasticity of substitution of imports

Figure 1.4 plots the correlation between the elasticity of substitution of imported products and the tariff levels at the HS2 level. In relative terms, the greater the elasticity of substitution of an imported product, the greater the import tariff imposed by China on it, and the two show a relative significant positive correlation.

According to the value of the elasticity of substitution of imported goods over the years, products are further classified into two categories, that is, products with high and low elasticity of substitution, and the trends in the average tariff of the products over time are shown in Figure 1.5.[13] In the figure, the solid line represents products with higher elasticity of substitution (above the median), and the dotted line represents those with lower elasticity of substitution (below the median). According to the figure, the average tariff values of both of China's high and low elasticity of substitution

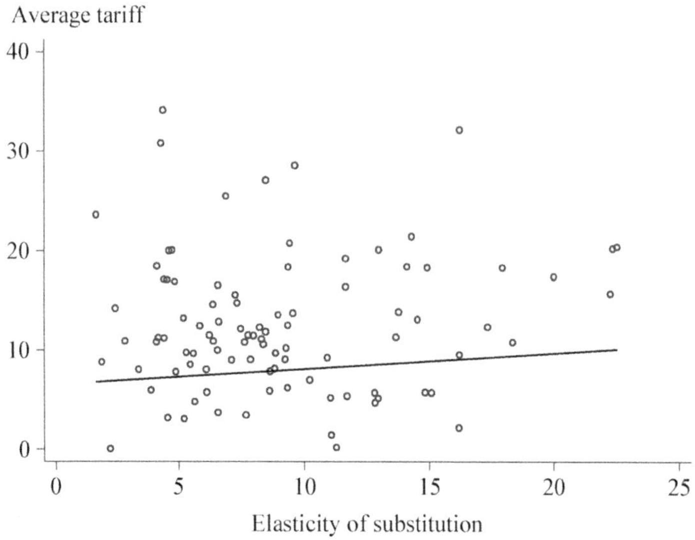

Figure 1.4 Correlation between elasticity of substitution and average tariff (China).

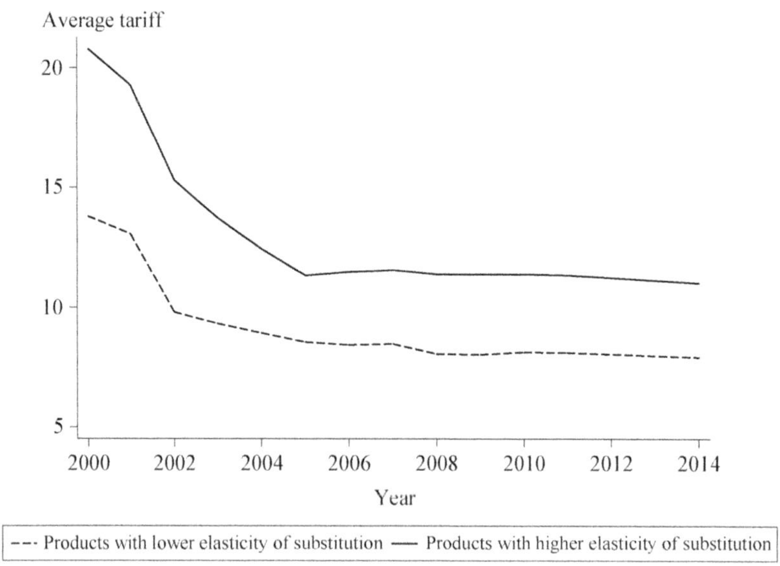

Figure 1.5 Tariff changes over time of products with high and low elasticity of substitution (China).

Table 1.5 Variance changes of imported products with high and low elasticity of substitution during 2000–2014 (China)

Year	*2000*	*2001*	*2002*	*2003*	*2004*	*2005*	*2006*
Low elasticity of substitution	7.50	7.23	6.09	6.23	6.10	5.63	5.74
High elasticity of substitution	14.88	14.16	10.01	9.10	8.76	7.36	8.31
Year	*2007*	*2008*	*2009*	*2010*	*2011*	*2014*	
Low elasticity of substitution	5.53	5.23	5.24	5.35	5.34	5.10	
Low elasticity of substitution	8.35	8.33	8.30	8.29	8.30	7.27	

products show a decreasing trend over time, and the tariff levels of higher elasticity of substitution products are always larger than those of lower elasticity of substitution products.

Why does China levy higher tariffs on products with higher elasticity of substitution and lower tariffs on those with lower elasticity of substitution? The following two reasons may explain this. First, products with higher elasticity of substitution are easier to be substituted by foreign products, and tariff adjustments of the same magnitude are more likely to induce shocks to the demand for the same domestic products. Therefore, importing countries generally tend to impose higher tariffs on products with higher elasticity of substitution. Second, domestic producers of products with higher elasticity of substitution are more willing to lobby governments in various ways to raise tariffs on such imports so as to increase the competitiveness of the same domestic products in the domestic market. Thus, on the whole, products with higher elasticity of substitution are subject to higher tariffs and those with lower elasticity of substitution to lower tariffs.

Next, from the mapping of the changes in the variances of import tariffs of products with high and low elasticity of substitution over the years (see Table 1.5), it can be found that, consistent with the change trend of China's overall tariff levels, for both products with high and low elasticity of substitution, their tariff variances are declining, but on the whole, the tariff variances of products with higher elasticity of substitution are decreasing more than those of products with lower elasticity of substitution. Meanwhile, the tariff variances of products with lower elasticity of substitution have remained smaller than those of products with higher elasticity of substitution. This indicates that, in terms of import elasticity of substitution, both of the tariff structures of imported products with high and low elasticity of substitution in China tend to be centralized. In contrast, the tariff distribution of products with low elasticity of substitution is more centralized and stable, while that of products with high elasticity of substitution is more decentralized.

Summary

In general, from the perspective of characteristics at the industry level: (1) At present, China presents relatively obvious characteristics of cascading tariff structure. Of imported products, the tax rate on manufactured products is significantly higher than that on intermediate inputs and primary products. (2) Among China's imports, intermediate goods account for an overwhelming majority, and the import share of consumer goods remains small. (3) The greater the elasticity of substitution of China's imports, the higher the import tariff charged on that product, and the two display an obvious positive correlation. Meanwhile, tariff levels of products with higher elasticity of substitution are always greater than those of products with lower elasticity of substitution. (4) As time progresses, both of the tariff structures of imported products with high and low elasticity of substitution in China tend to be centralized, and the tariff distribution of products with low elasticity of substitution is more centralized and stable, while that of products with high elasticity of substitution is more decentralized.

1.3 Characteristics of tariff change

From the perspective of China's tariff change, this section focuses on the characteristics of products with lowest and highest tariffs at the HS2 industry level over the years. Specifically, products with the lowest (highest) tariffs are selected in the following way: First, average the tariff of HS6 products over the years to HS2 level. Next, arrange them in ascending order. Then, select the top (bottom) ten products as the lowest (highest) tariff products and record their corresponding HS2 industry codes. In some individual years, some products have equal tariff values, so in those years, there are more than ten product categories.[14]

1.3.1 Lowest tariff products

Figure 1.6 reflects the changes in the categories of the lowest tariff products in China over the years from 2000 to 2014, where the horizontal axis represents the year and the vertical axis represents corresponding HS2 industry codes of the product. The position of each HS2 code on the vertical axis is fixed, so the changes in the position of the blocks in the figure reflect the evolution of the HS2 code product categories over time. Figure 1.6 shows that in the period 2000–2014, the categories of top ten lowest tariff products in China merely changed and generally displayed a relatively stable trend. Moreover, most of these products underwent minor changes and adjustments within the comparatively fixed HS2 code range. This means that the broad industry categories to which the lowest tariff imports in China belong are relatively constant and have not changed significantly. The HS2

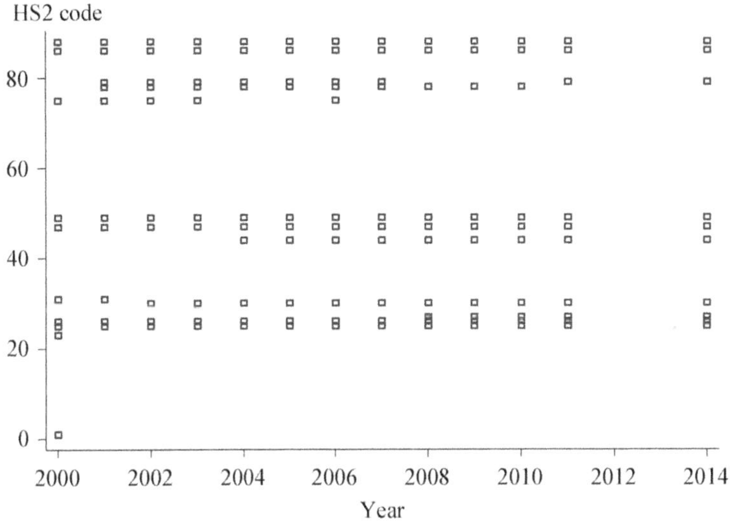

Figure 1.6 Changes in categories of the lowest tariff products in China during 2000–2014.

industry codes of the lowest tariff products in 2000 and 2014 and the corresponding product characteristics are shown in Table 1.6.

In Table 1.6, figures in column 2 represent HS2 industry codes of the products, where the boxed figures represent the products shared by 2000 and 2014. It is easy to see that 2000 and 2014 share six categories of lowest tariff products; that is, in terms of product categories alone, those of China's lowest tariff imports have not changed much and are relatively stable. However, as for the values of product tariffs, even for the same product, the tariff value still shows a clear downward trend. For example, products in Chapter 47 were subject to an average tariff value of 1% in 2000, which was at a fairly low level, but in 2014 the tariff level dropped straight to zero.

In terms of specific characteristics at the industry level, on the whole, the characteristics of lowest tariff products imported by China have not changed significantly. Most of its lowest tariff imports in 2014 were intermediate goods and products with high elasticity of substitution, and among the lowest tariff products imported in 2014, these two categories of products still accounted for a large proportion.

In order to prevent the impact by some year-specific effects of 2000 or 2014 on the universalism and generality of the conclusions of the above studies, we list all HS2 industry codes and product characteristics of the top ten lowest tariff products for the period 2000–2014. The detailed results are presented in Appendix 3 at the end of the book. The analysis of the appendix shows that from 2000 to 2014, the above characteristics are

Table 1.6 Characteristics of China's top ten lowest tariff products in 2000 and 2014

Year	*HS code*	*Average tariff (%)*	*Classification by BEC*	*Classification by elasticity of substitution*
2000	1	5.54	Intermediate good	High elasticity of substitution
2000	23	5.98	Intermediate good	High elasticity of substitution
2000	**25**	4.30	Intermediate good	Low elasticity of substitution
2000	**26**	1.85	Intermediate good	High elasticity of substitution
2000	31	5.00	Intermediate good	Low elasticity of substitution
2000	**47**	1.00	Intermediate good	High elasticity of substitution
2000	**49**	5.25	Consumer good	Low elasticity of substitution
2000	75	6.22	Intermediate good	High elasticity of substitution
2000	**86**	5.42	Intermediate good	Low elasticity of substitution
2000	**88**	3.47	Intermediate good	High elasticity of substitution
2014	**25**	2.67	Intermediate good	Low elasticity of substitution
2014	**26**	1.08	Intermediate good	High elasticity of substitution
2014	27	3.89	Intermediate good	High elasticity of substitution
2014	30	4.21	Consumer good	High elasticity of substitution
2014	44	3.89	Intermediate good	High elasticity of substitution
2014	**47**	0.00	Intermediate good	High elasticity of substitution
2014	**49**	2.59	Consumer good	Low elasticity of substitution
2014	79	3.78	Intermediate good	High elasticity of substitution
2014	**86**	3.94	Intermediate good	Low elasticity of substitution
2014	**88**	2.07	Intermediate good	High elasticity of substitution

Note

Boxed figures in column 2 indicate products shared by 2000 and 2014.[15]

indeed present in China's low tariff imports. At the same time, most of the new products are products with low elasticity of substitution and consumer goods.

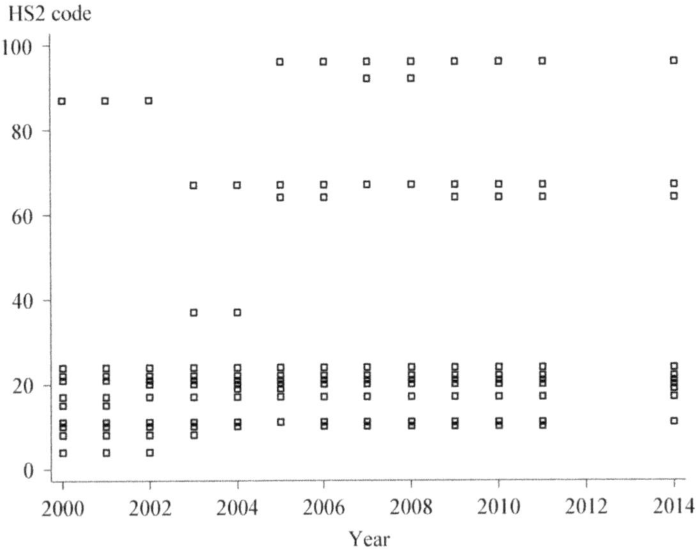

Figure 1.7 Changes in categories of the highest tariff products in China during 2000–2014.

1.3.2 *Highest tariff products*

Similar to the study of the lowest tariff products, Figure 1.7 reflects the change diagram of the industry categories to which China's top ten highest tariff products belong over the years between 2000 and 2014. As can be seen from the figure, in contrast to the lowest tariff products, compared with 2000, the categories of China's top ten highest tariff products in 2014 have changed considerably. And as time goes on, individual product categories made corresponding adjustment at regular intervals. Overall, although compared to 2000, China's tariff product categories have changed to some degree in 2014, the trend shows that over a short period of time, China's highest tariff products remain relatively stable.

Further observations of the changes in the characteristics of the highest tariff products are shown in Table 1.7, which lists the HS2 industry codes, average tariff values, product classification by BEC, and import elasticity of substitution of the top ten highest tariff products over the years. For illustrative and explanatory purposes, Table 1.7 only shows the situations in 2000 and 2014 (see Appendix 4 at the end of the book for the complete table).

Similarly, in Table 1.7, the boxed figures in column 2 represent the categories of highest tariff products shared by 2000 and 2014. As can be seen from the results in the table, these two years share five product categories, which are products in Chapters 11, 17, 21, 22, and 24, and all five categories

Table 1.7 Characteristics of China's top ten highest tariff products in 2000 and 2014

Year	*HS code*	*Average tariff (%)*	*Classification by BEC*	*Classification by elasticity of substitution*
2000	4	36.77	Consumer good	High elasticity of substitution
2000	8	30.09	Consumer good	High elasticity of substitution
2000	10	54.38	Intermediate good	Low elasticity of substitution
2000	**11**	44.53	Intermediate good	Low elasticity of substitution
2000	15	40.52	Intermediate good	High elasticity of substitution
2000	**17**	42.88	Intermediate good	High elasticity of substitution
2000	**21**	39.77	Consumer good	Low elasticity of substitution
2000	**22**	56.79	Consumer good	High elasticity of substitution
2000	**24**	56.67	Consumer good	High elasticity of substitution
2000	87	35.00	Intermediate good	High elasticity of substitution
2014	**11**	21.38	Intermediate good	Low elasticity of substitution
2014	**17**	23.00	Intermediate good	High elasticity of substitution
2014	19	18.82	Consumer good	High elasticity of substitution
2014	20	19.59	Consumer good	High elasticity of substitution
2014	**21**	21.48	Consumer good	Low elasticity of substitution
2014	**22**	21.05	Consumer good	High elasticity of substitution
2014	**24**	29.72	Consumer good	High elasticity of substitution
2014	64	19.32	Consumer good	High elasticity of substitution
2014	67	21.45	Intermediate good	Low elasticity of substitution
2014	96	19.34	Consumer good	Low elasticity of substitution

Note
Boxed figures in column 2 indicate products shared by 2000 and 2014.

of products experienced significant tariff reductions, with products in Chapter 22 registering the largest decrease from 56.79% in 2000 to 21.05% in 2014, a reduction of 62.95%. Import tariffs on Chapter 21 products experienced the smallest tariff reduction, and its import tariff also fell by nearly half.

From the perspective of characteristics at the industry level, compared with 2000, the characteristics of China's highest tariff products have changed significantly. Most of the top ten high tariff products in China in 2000 were products with high elasticity of substitution, and proportions of intermediate goods and consumer goods are roughly equal. In contrast, consumer goods accounted for the majority of the top ten highest tariff products in 2014, and the share of products with low elasticity of substitution also registered a minor increase. In other words, compared to 2000, China's highest tariff products showed varying degrees of increase in both consumer goods and products with low elasticity of substitution.

In terms of specific product categories, most of the new product categories added to the highest tariff products in 2014 are cereals, vegetable products, and footwear, headgear and parts thereof; whereas the product categories withdrew in 2000 were mostly live animals, animal and plant products (mainly products in the first three sections of HS), etc. Specifically, most of the categories of highest tariff products withdrew in 2000 are agricultural by-products and their processed products, which are highly dependent on the primary industry, while the new product categories mostly belong to manufacturing and processing industries such as vegetable, footwear, and headgear industries, which tend to be more reliant on the secondary industry. This demonstrates that from the perspective of changes of the highest tariff products, China still has a certain degree of protection on traditional industries with comparative advantages, such as garment making.[16]

1.3.3 Comparison between the highest and lowest tariff products

Figure 1.8 is obtained through further superimposing and comparing the change diagrams in the categories of the highest and lowest tariff products. In the figure, solid blocks represent the highest tariff products while hollow blocks represent the lowest tariff products. Compared with the lowest tariff products, the categories of China's highest tariff products have changed significantly over the years; that is, tariff structures of such products are comparatively unstable. At the same time, there is little overlap between the industries to which the highest and lowest tariff products belong, and products of both categories have very distinctive distribution areas. For example, the lowest tariff products are mainly concentrated in industries of Chapters 25–35, 45–55 and 70–90, while the highest tariff products mainly in industries of Chapters 0–25, 55–70 and 90–100. The two have a certain degree of overlap and similarity in the front part of the HS2 industry classification, but as the industry codes increase, the overlap of the industries to which the two belong decreases, especially when they are subject to larger

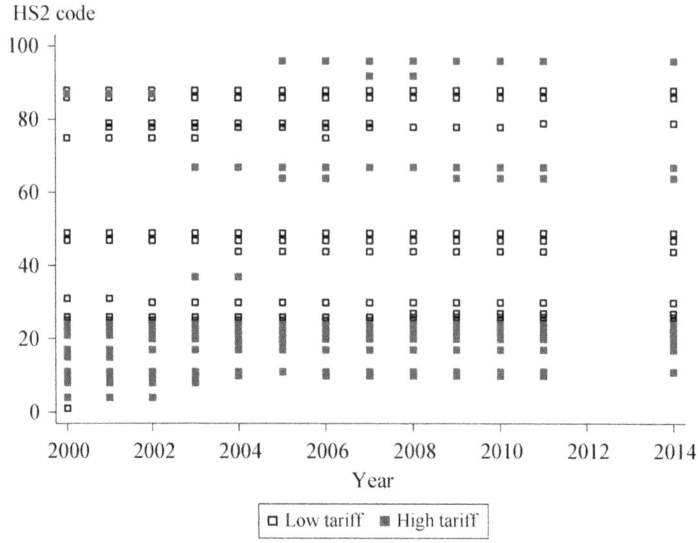

Figure 1.8 Changes and overlaps of China's high and low tariff products during 2000–2014.

industry codes. For example, in HS2 chapters, almost all products in Chapter 18 and above are highest tariff products.

In combination with Appendix 1 at the end of the book, "Name and corresponding codes of HS2 chapter commodities," it can be seen that among the lowest tariff products, products in Chapters 25–35 are mainly mineral, chemical industries, and chemical products, most of which are used in intermediate good production and inputs. Meanwhile, among the highest tariff products, those in Chapters 0–25 are mostly animal and plant products, as well as food, tobacco and alcohol, beverages, etc., the majority of which belong to agricultural products, by-products, and processed products. Most of the above two categories of products are primary products; yet, they belong separately to the highest and lowest tariff products. This means that even for different products in the same category, their import tariffs vary considerably, and the main manifestation is as follows: among primary products, mineral products are subject to lower import tariffs while agricultural products and cash crops to higher.

A study of other product categories finds that products in Chapters 45–55 are mostly wood pulp, silk, and other textile raw materials, while those in Chapters 55–70 include products such as textile articles and plaster, cement, and ceramic products. Relatively speaking, these products undergo a deeper degree of processing and are subject to higher import tariffs in China; a large proportion of products in Chapters 70–90 consists of machinery, mechanical parts, and appliances, as well as vehicles, aircraft, vessels, and associated transport equipment and parts thereof; meanwhile, most of the products in Chapters 90 and above are precision instruments and parts, as well as arms, ammunition, and accessories thereof, and works of art, collectors' pieces, etc. Although products of both categories undergo a deep degree of processing, tariffs levied on the latter are higher. In conjunction with the previous discussion of characteristics at the industry level, though China currently displays a relatively pronounced cascading tariff structure, the levels of tariffs imposed on products with similar degrees of processing still vary significantly.

Summary

Summarizing the above-mentioned studies, the following main findings can be drawn.

1. From an overall perspective, China's imported products and tariff structure have the following characteristics.
   i. The overall tariff level of China shows a trend of a sharp decrease over time. Meanwhile, the overall tariff structure tends to be centralized, and the basic tariff structure has been formed and it remains relatively stable.
   ii. Although China's overall tariff is already at a relatively low level, the number of tariff peak industries remains high and import restrictions still exist extensively in China.
   iii. In general, categories of tariff peak products in China are relatively constant, concentrating mainly on live animals, animal products; vegetable products; animal or vegetable fats and oils and their cleavage products; prepared food stuffs, beverages, tobacco, and manufactured tobacco substitutes; raw hides and skins, leather, fur skins, and article thereof; textiles and textile articles; footwear, headgear, umbrellas, etc. and parts thereof; and articles of stone, plaster, cement, glass, or similar materials and articles. These industries are concentrated in the first 14 of the 22 HS industry sections, and are mainly in Sections 1–4, 8, and 11–12.
2. At the industry level, China's imported products and tariff structure have the following characteristics.
   i. At present, China presents a relatively obvious cascading tariff structure; that is, of imported products, the tax rate on manufactured goods is significantly higher than that on intermediate inputs and primary products. The greater the degree of processing of the imported products, the higher the tariff value.
   ii. Among China's imported products, intermediate goods account for an overwhelming majority, and the import share of consumer goods

remains small. The greater the elasticity of substitution of China's imports, the higher the import tariff charged on that product, and the two display an obvious positive correlation. Meanwhile, tariff levels of products with higher elasticity of substitution are always greater than those of products with lower elasticity of substitution.

iii. In terms of tariff distribution structure, tariff distributions of products with different characteristics in China are different. As time passes by, both of the tariff structures of imported products with high and low elasticity of substitution in China tend to be centralized, but the tariff distribution of products with low elasticity of substitution is more centralized and stable, while that of products with high elasticity of substitution is more decentralized.

3. From the perspective of tariff changes, tariff structures of China's lowest (highest) tariff products show the following characteristics.

   i. In terms of the characteristics of product changes, except for elasticity of substitution, China's lowest tariff products exhibit inconspicuous changeability, and the highest tariff products, on the other hand, show a certain degree of changeability. As for the changes in the highest tariff products, China is relatively competitive in aspects such as garment making, and the protection for industries with comparative advantages is still fairly intense.
   ii. From the perspective of the stability of product structures, on the whole, compared with the lowest tariff products, the tariff structure of the highest tariff products is less stable, but it still exhibits relatively good stability in a certain period of time.
   iii. Though China currently displays a comparatively pronounced cascading tariff structure, there is still huge disparity in the levels of tariffs imposed on products with similar degrees of processing. Moreover, for different products in the same category, their import tariffs vary considerably. The main manifestation is as follows: among primary products, mineral products are subject to lower import tariffs while agricultural products and cash crops to higher.

Notes

1 Krugman, P. (2013). *International economics: Theory and policy* (8th ed.). Beijing, China: Renmin University Press.

2 Statistical analysis studies by other scholars have reached similar conclusions, such as Hecht (1997), Finger and Yeats (1976), Clark (1985), Chen and Feng (2000), and David Tarr (2005).

3 Considering the limitations of the data intervals used in the study, Part 2 only focuses on the period from 2000 to 2014, which basically covers the main

intervals before and after China's accession to the WTO and the outbreak of the Sino–U.S. trade friction.

4 The data of the Most-Favored-Nation Rate of Duty mainly comes from the WITS (World Integrated Trade Solution) database, which was jointly developed by the World Bank and UNCTAD. It is a global trade database universally used at present, from which relatively systematic and complete data of MFN Rate of Duty can be obtained.

5 MFN rate of duty is a type of tariff rates specified by the WTO. In accordance with relevant provisions of the WTO, the MFN rate of duty is granted to countries that have reached MFN agreements. According to the provisions in the MFN treatment principle of WTO, generally, the MFN rates shall be no higher than the tariff rates currently enjoyed or will be enjoyed by similar products from third countries.

6 Bound tariff is a type of tariff rate specified by the WTO. It generally refers to the tariff rate established in WTO member countries through WTO negotiations, which means that it is the ceiling on tariffs that can be levied by a member making tariff concessions. In general, for developed countries, bound tariffs are basically the same as the actual tariffs imposed. For most developing countries, the actual tariffs levied are lower than bound tariffs; that is, developing countries normally treat bound tariffs as the ceiling of tariffs levied by a country. Therefore, a country is not considered to be in breach of its bound tariff obligations if the tariffs it actually collects stay within the limits of the bound tariffs. If a WTO member raises its tariff rates above the bound level, with reference to the relevant WTO provisions, the affected exporting country is entitled to take retaliatory measures against an equivalent value of the importing country's exports or demand and receive compensation.

7 The reason for this is that the higher the import tariff, the lower the import volume of the good is likely to be. When the tariff level for a particular category of goods is raised to a certain level, its import volume will remain at an extremely low level. If the trade weighted average method is applied at this point, the calculated weights will be close to zero. Therefore, the weighted average tariff will extensively mask the true tariff level of the good, resulting in a large bias in the study of tariff structures. However, considering the practical and policy implications of the study, this book also provides a further depiction of tariff structure from the perspective of trade volumes. Also, unless otherwise stated, tariffs throughout this book refer to average tariffs.

8 For industrialized countries, tariff levels of 15% and above can be called tariff peaks, and for the purposes of international comparison, we use the same criteria to define tariff peaks here.

9 See Appendix 2 at the end of this book.

10 The meaning of the numbers in parentheses is explained as follows: the latter number indicates the total number of industry categories included in the broad industry section, and the former number indicates the number of tariff peak industries in that broad industry section.

11 The Chapter 87 industry ranked 92nd in terms of import share. By removing the Chapter 87 industry, tariff peak industries, which account for one-third of the total classification, only make up for nearly 6% of the imports.

12 This finding is also largely supported by the mapping of the import shares of China's tariff peak industries during the years between 2000 and 2014.

13 To be specific, rank all products in the past years according to their elasticity of substitution from high to low, and plot the median value of the elasticity of substitution. Products with elasticity of substitution above the median are

regarded as products with higher elasticity of substitution; otherwise, they are regarded as products with lower elasticity of substitution.

14 Due to missing tariff data for China for some years, HS2 codes for those years are incomplete (specifically 2012 and 2013).

15 Since the indicators of the classification by BEC can be refined to the HS6 level, we adjust such indicators at the HS2 level in Table 1.6 as follows: First, capital goods are also included in the category of intermediate goods; that is, all imported products are classified into intermediate goods and consumer goods. After that, we calculate the proportion of the number of intermediate goods and consumer goods in HS6 subheading classification at the same HS2 level among products imported by China over the years. If the number of intermediate goods accounts for more than 50%, then the HS2 industry is considered as an intermediate good; otherwise, it is classified as a consumer good.

16 This finding is also supported by a study of the change characteristics of the highest tariff products during the period 2000–2014 (see Appendix 4 at the end of the book for details).

2 Characteristics and evolution trends of the U.S. tariff structure and comparisons between China and the U.S.

2.1 Characteristics at the overall level

2.1.1 Average tariff

Table 2.1 presents the average tariff and variance changes of U.S. MFN rate of duty at the HS2 industry level from 2000 to 2014. In terms of average tariff values, in the years between 2000 and 2014, the average U.S. tariff rates had been at a low level, but in general, it still showed a downward trend; the tariff variance remained basically unchanged, showing a slight upward trend compared with that of 2000. In contrast with relevant situations of China's tariff structure in Chapter 1, the tariff variance of the U.S. is significantly larger.

In summary, during the sample period, China's tariff structure underwent a process from decentralization to centralization, while the overall U.S. tariff structure was relatively stable, showing a trend from centralization to slight decentralization. Compared with China, the tariff structure of the U.S. is more decentralized, yet also more stable.

2.1.2 Tariff peaks

Table 2.2 depicts the situation of tariff peaks in the U.S. during the period between 2000 and 2014. In terms of the number of tariff peak sectors, from 2000 to 2014, tariff peak sectors of the U.S. displayed a strong stability. The number of tariff peak sectors remained basically unchanged at a stable level, with its share constantly at around 16%. Tariff levels of the highest tariff products and their industry categories are still extremely stable. During 2000–2014, U.S. tariff peak products are mostly concentrated in Chapter 24 of the HS2 (tobacco and manufactured tobacco substitutes), and the highest tariff levels barely changed.

Taking 2014 as an example, the industry categories to which tariff peak products of the U.S. belong and the import situation are further depicted in Tables 2.3 and 2.4.[1]

According to Table 2.3, in terms of the quantity of tariff peak industries, the product categories of 15 U.S. tariff peak industries in 2014 were mainly

Table 2.1 Changes in average tariffs and variances of the U.S. during 2000–2014

Year	*2000*	*2001*	*2002*	*2003*	*2004*	*2005*	*2006*	*2007*
Average tariff (%)	4.19	4.11	4.07	3.98	3.91	3.91	3.91	3.80
Tariff variance	9.09	9.07	9.13	9.11	9.10	9.10	9.10	9.42
Year	*2008*	*2009*	*2010*	*2011*	*2012*	*2013*	*2014*	
Average tariff (%)	3.99	3.98	3.99	3.79	3.78	3.77	3.77	
Tariff variance	9.35	9.35	9.35	9.37	9.39	9.39	9.39	

Table 2.2 Situation of tariff peaks in the U.S. (2000–2014)

Year	*HS2 code*	*Highest tariff (%)*	*Quantity*	*Share (%)*
2000	24	204.17	15	15.63
2001	24	204.17	16	16.67
2002	24	204.17	15	15.63
2003	24	204.17	15	15.63
2004	24	204.17	16	16.67
2005	24	204.17	16	16.67
2006	24	204.17	16	16.67
2007	24	204.98	16	16.67
2008	24	204.17	15	15.63
2009	24	204.17	15	15.63
2010	24	204.17	15	15.63
2011	24	204.17	16	16.67
2012	24	204.17	16	16.67
2013	24	204.17	16	16.67
2014	24	204.17	16	16.67

Table 2.3 Tariff peak industries in the U.S. in 2014

Year	*HS2 code*	*Starting year*	*Year*	*HS2 code*	*Starting year*
2014	4	2000	2014	54	2000
2014	7	2000	2014	55	2000
2014	12	2000	2014	58	2000
2014	20	2000	2014	60	2000
2014	24	2000	2014	61	2000
2014	42	2000	2014	62	2000
2014	51	2000	2014	63	2000
2014	52	2000	2014	64	2000

Note
Please refer to Appendix 2 at the end of the book for the complete table for 2000–2014.

Table 2.4 Import characteristics of tariff peak industries in the U.S. in 2014

HS2 code	*Import share*	*Ranking*	*HS2 code*	*Import share*	*Ranking*
51	0.01%	5	12	0.16%	40
58	0.04%	10	20	0.32%	59
60	0.05%	13	7	0.39%	64
52	0.05%	14	42	0.54%	70
55	0.09%	22	63	0.57%	72
24	0.09%	24	64	1.10%	80
54	0.10%	28	62	1.73%	84
4	0.12%	31	61	2.01%	87

Note
Please refer to Appendix 2 at the end of the book for the complete table for 2000–2014.

concentrated in Section 11 (textile and textile articles), while other products scattered in Sections 1, 2, and 4, and their industries are generally centralized. Compared to previous years (see Appendix 2 at the end of the book), tariff peak product categories of the U.S. undergo limited change, and most of the new and withdrawn products belong to the same broad product category as before. In other words, overall, as for both new and withdrawn product categories, the U.S. tariff peak product categories show comparatively strong stability. The starting year denotes the year in which the industry first appeared in the rank of tariff peak industries between 2000 and 2014. For example, the corresponding starting year for Chapter 4 industry is 2000, which indicates that it became a member of tariff peak industries in 2000. The 16 tariff peak industries of the U.S. in 2014 had been among the range since 2000, with the majority of them basically concentrated in Section 11, that is textile and textile articles.

Table 2.4 presents the import situation of tariff peak industries of the U.S. in 2014, including HS2 chapter codes, import shares, and import ranks of these industries.

Further observation of the import situation of tariff peak industries in 2014 reveals that 16 tariff peak industries in the U.S. in 2014 only account for 7.37% of the imports. In other words, similar to the situation in China, the U.S. tariff peak industries are indeed subject to considerable import restrictions in 2014.

Summary

Through the aforementioned analysis, we found that the overall tariff structure of the U.S. shows the following characteristics.

1. The overall level of tariff for the U.S. is already relatively low, but as time passes, its tariff level still displays an obvious downward trend.

2. In terms of the stability of the tariff structure, the U.S. has been very stable, but internally, it remains largely decentralized – there are obvious differences in the tariff levels of different products.
3. From the perspective tariff peaks, during the sample period, both the quantity of tariff peak products and the industries to which they belonged were relatively stable, mainly concentrated in the textile and textile articles industry. Both the new and withdrawn product categories are consistent with the categories of tariff peak products in previous years. Moreover, tariff peak products are still subject to significant import restrictions.

2.2 Characteristics at the industry level

From the use of imported products and their elasticity of substitution, this section separately depicts the development and evolution characteristics of the tariff structure of the U.S. at the industry level, and discusses the similarities and differences in the structure characteristics between China and the U.S. at the industry level.

2.2.1 Use of imports

Figure 2.1 depicts the change trend of the import tariffs on three product categories in the U.S. according to the classification by BEC for the period

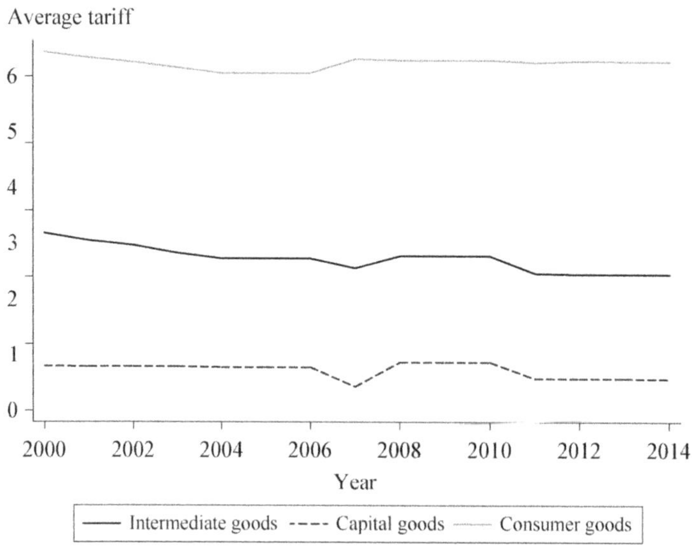

Figure 2.1 Changes in the average tariff of three categories of imports in the U.S. during 2000–2014.

2000–2014. As can be seen in Figure 2.1, in terms of the use of imported products, tariff structure of the U.S. exhibits obvious characteristics of cascading tariff structure; that is, among the imports of the U.S., consumer goods are subject to the highest tariff, followed by intermediate goods, with the tariff levied on capital goods being the lowest:

$$Tariff_{\text{consumer goods}} > Tariff_{\text{intermediate goods}} > Tariff_{\text{capital goods}}$$

In other words, as its processing degree increases, the import tariff levied on the product gradually increases as well.

Combining the change trends of import tariff levels of the three categories of products in China in Figure 1.1, it is easy to see that, compared with China, the overall tariff levels of these imports of the U.S. are lower, which is related to its high degree of openness. It is particularly worth noting that compared to China, the intermediate inputs of the U.S. (including intermediate and capital goods) are subject to lower tariff. In particular, compared with intermediate goods, tariffs on the imported capital goods in the U.S. remain at an extremely low level, while China's tariffs on these two categories of imported intermediate inputs are roughly similar.[2]

Further combining the change characteristics of the total volume of the three categories of imports (as shown in Figure 2.2), it is easy to note that similar to the share of the total import volume of the three categories of products in China, imported intermediate goods still have the highest share among the three. The share of imported capital goods in China is significantly larger than that of imported consumer goods, however, the shares of these two imports in the U.S. are basically equal. On the whole, in

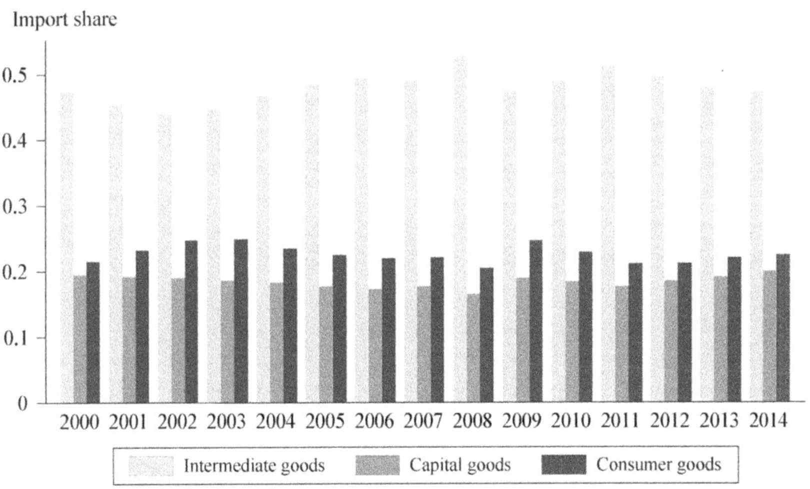

Figure 2.2 Changes in total import shares of three categories of products in the U.S. during 2000–2014.

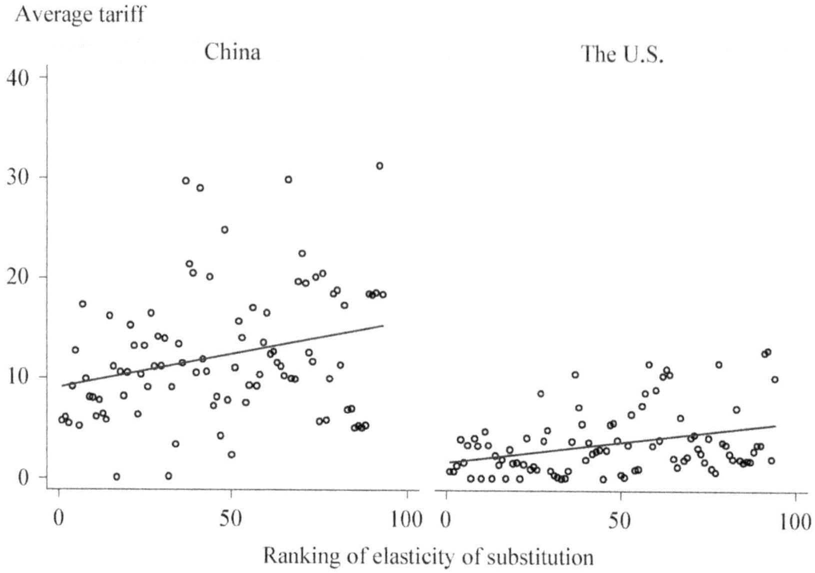

Figure 2.3 Correlation between elasticities of substitution and average tariffs of China and the U.S.

contrast with China, the U.S. tariff structure exhibits more pronounced characteristics of cascading tariff structure, and its import share of final goods is higher than that of China.

2.2.2 Elasticity of substitution of imports

In terms of the elasticity of substitution of imports (as shown in Figure 2.3), similar to the case of China, there is also a clear positive correlation between the average tariffs and the elasticity of substitution of the U.S. imports. Relatively speaking, the greater the elasticity of substitution of the imports, the greater the level of import tariffs levied on them. According to their elasticity of substitution, imported products are divided into two categories, namely, products with high and low elasticity of substitution. Average tariff values and variance changes are plotted, respectively (as shown in Figure 2.4 and Table 2.5). We observed that, similar to the situation in China, the average tariff value of products with higher elasticity of substitution in the U.S. is always greater than that of products with lower elasticity of substitution, and the average tariff values of the two display an obvious paralleled changing trend.

After observing the changes in the tariff variance of the two categories of

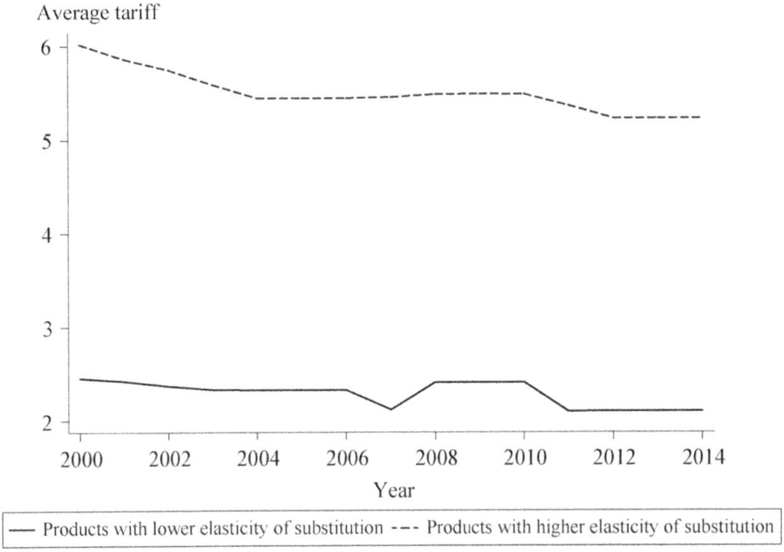

Figure 2.4 Tariff changes over time of products with high and low elasticity of substitution of the U.S.

products (as shown in Table 2.5), we found that (1) the tariff variances of the two categories of products, products with high and low elasticity of substitution, display relatively stable characteristics over time; (2) the tariff variance of products with lower elasticity of substitution is much smaller than that of products with higher elasticity of substitution; moreover, as time passes, the tariff variance of products with lower elasticity of substitution slightly decreases, while that of products with higher elasticity of substitution moderately increases. In other words, tariff values of the various categories of products with lower elasticity of substitution in the U.S. are slightly different, while those of products with higher elasticity of substitution are considerably different.

This means that: (1) on the whole, tariff structures of both products with high and low elasticity of substitution in the U.S. are very stable; and (2) the tariff distribution of products with low elasticity of substitution is more centralized, while that of products with high elasticity of substitution is more decentralized.

The above characteristics are generally similar to those of China's tariff structure for products with different elasticity of substitution, but there are specific differences between the two countries. For example, on the whole, the tariff structure of products with lower elasticity of substitution is more

Table 2.5 Import tariffs and variances of products with high and low elasticity of substitution in the U.S. during 2000–2014

	Year	*2000*	*2001*	*2002*	*2003*	*2004*	*2005*	*2006*	*2007*
Tariff (%)	Low elasticity of substitution	2.45	2.42	2.37	2.33	2.33	2.33	2.33	2.11
	High elasticity of substitution	6.02	5.86	5.74	5.58	5.44	5.44	5.44	5.45
Variance	Low elasticity of substitution	3.34	3.29	3.23	3.18	3.15	3.15	3.15	3.29
	High elasticity of substitution	14.62	14.61	14.44	14.44	14.44	14.44	14.44	14.97
	Year	*2008*	*2009*	*2010*	*2011*	*2012*	*2013*	*2014*	
Tariff (%)	Low elasticity of substitution	2.41	2.41	2.41	2.10	2.10	2.10	2.10	
	High elasticity of substitution	5.48	5.48	5.48	5.36	5.23	5.22	5.22	
Variance	Low elasticity of substitution	3.19	3.19	3.19	3.07	3.09	3.09	3.09	
	High elasticity of substitution	14.68	14.69	14.66	14.68	14.67	14.67	14.68	

centralized, and that of products with higher elasticity of substitution is more decentralized in both countries. However, China has a more fragmented tariff structure for products with lower elasticity of substitution, with greater differences in the tariff values among these products. In contrast, the tariff structure of its products with higher elasticity of substitution is more centralized than that of the U.S., which means that the U.S. has greater differences in average tariff values among products with higher elasticity of substitution.

2.3 Characteristics of tariff change

From the perspective of changes in the highest and lowest tariff products, this section examines the characteristics of change in the tariff structure of the U.S. and the similarities and differences with those of China at the product level.

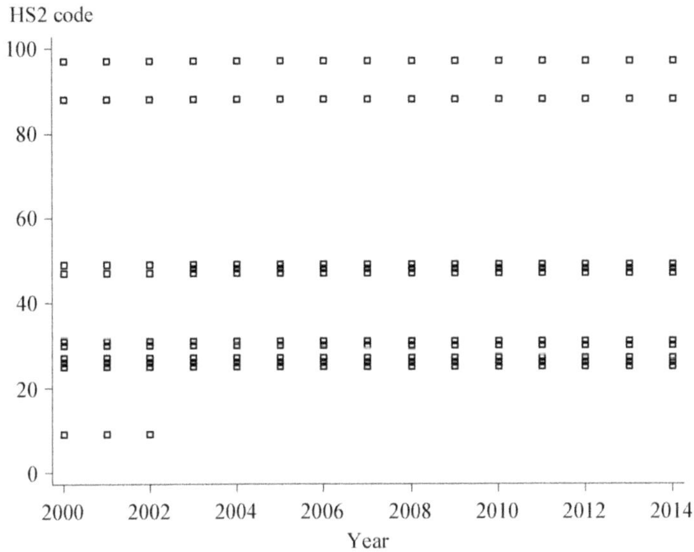

Figure 2.5 Changes in the categories of the lowest tariff products in the U.S. during 2000–2014.

2.3.1 Lowest tariff products

Figure 2.5 reflects changes in the categories of lowest tariff products of the U.S. from 2000 to 2014. The vertical axis represents the HS2 code for each product, and the horizontal axis represents the year. The lowest tariff products are selected in the following way. First, tariffs of the products are averaged at the HS2 level. Then, tariffs of the products at the HS2 level are ranked in ascending order, with the top ten products being those with the lowest tariffs of the year. Figure 2.5 records and depicts the trend of how the categories of lowest tariff products at the HS2 level change over time in the U.S. According to Figure 2.5, the categories of lowest tariff products in the U.S. have remained largely unchanged over the years and are roughly concentrated in two product areas, that is, products in Chapters 20–50 and products in Chapter 80 and above of the HS2, respectively. Products in these two areas are mainly mineral products, products of the chemicals or allied industries, pulp of wood or of other fibrous cellulosic material, paper or paperboard scraps and wastes, paper and paperboard and articles thereof. On the whole, these products are mainly intermediate inputs related to relevant production.

From the further mapping of the lowest tariff products in the U.S. from 2000 to 2014 and their product characteristics (see Appendix 3 at the end of

Table 2.6 Characteristics of the top ten lowest tariff products in the U.S. in 2000 and 2014

Year	*HS code*	*Average tariff*	*Classification by BEC*	*Classification by elasticity of substitution*
2000	9	0.38	Consumer good	High elasticity of substitution
2000	**25**	0.26	Intermediate good	Low elasticity of substitution
2000	**26**	0.00	Intermediate good	High elasticity of substitution
2000	**27**	0.16	Intermediate good	High elasticity of substitution
2000	**30**	0.00	Consumer good	High elasticity of substitution
2000	**31**	0.00	Intermediate good	Low elasticity of substitution
2000	**47**	0.00	Intermediate good	High elasticity of substitution
2000	**49**	0.35	Consumer good	Low elasticity of substitution
2000	**88**	0.20	Intermediate good	High elasticity of substitution
2000	**97**	0.00	Consumer good	Low elasticity of substitution
2014	**25**	0.24	Intermediate good	Low elasticity of substitution
2014	**26**	0.03	Intermediate good	High elasticity of substitution
2014	**27**	0.17	Intermediate good	High elasticity of substitution
2014	**30**	0.00	Consumer good	High elasticity of substitution
2014	**31**	0.00	Intermediate good	Low elasticity of substitution
2014	**47**	0.00	Intermediate good	High elasticity of substitution
2014	48	0.08	Intermediate good	High elasticity of substitution
2014	**49**	0.00	Consumer good	Low elasticity of substitution
2014	**88**	0.21	Intermediate good	High elasticity of substitution
2014	**97**	0.00	Consumer good	Low elasticity of substitution

the book), the results of 2000 and 2014 are illustrated in Table 2.6. The boxed figures in column 2 indicate products shared by 2000 and 2014. It is easy to see that, of the ten categories of the lowest tariff products in the U.S., 9 categories are common to both 2000 and 2014. Meanwhile, in terms of product categories alone, those of lowest tariff imports have not changed much. Although the tariff levels of some products experienced slight increase (e.g., the average tariff level of products in Chapter 88 increased from 0.2 to 0.21) or decrease (e.g., the tariff value of products in Chapter 49 was already at a relatively low level of 0.35 in 2000, and it declined to 0.00 in 2014), overall, the tariff levels of various categories of products have remained largely unchanged and are rather stable.

In terms of specific characteristics at the product level, the characteristics of lowest tariff products of the U.S. has not changed much. For example, in 2000, the majority of the lowest tariff imports of the U.S. were intermediate goods and products with high elasticity of substitution, while such products still constituted the majority of the lowest tariff products in 2014 and no obvious changeability was displayed. An examination of the top ten lowest tariff products for the years between 2000 and 2014 shows that these characteristics still exist.[3]

Summing up the previous studies, during the sample period (1) the categories of lowest tariff products of the U.S. and the tariff levels of each product have shown a strong stability, and most of its lowest tariff imports are intermediate goods and products with high elasticity of substitution; (2) on

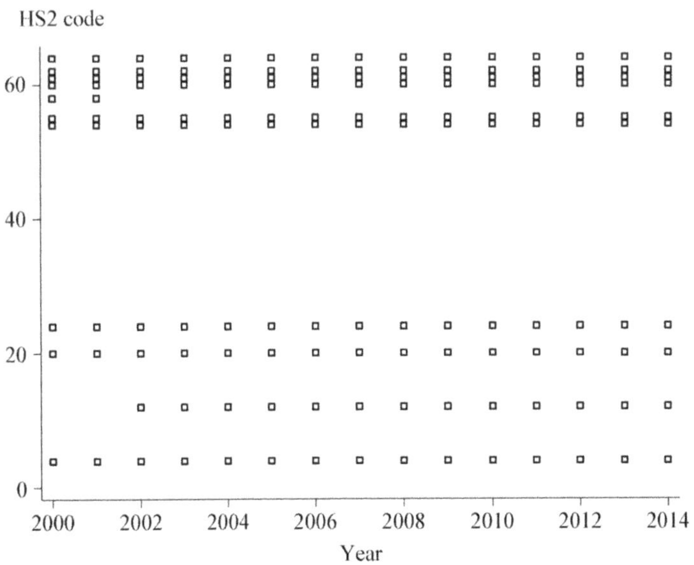

Figure 2.6 Changes in the categories of the highest tariff products in the U.S. during 2000–2014.

the whole, the lowest tariff imports of the U.S. display inconspicuous characteristics of changeability over time.

2.3.2 Highest tariff products

Figure 2.6 describes the changes in the top ten highest tariff products in the U.S. over time, with the numbers on the vertical axis representing the HS2 codes of the products, and horizontal axis the time. During the period, the categories of highest tariff products in the U.S. are also extremely stable, with those categories over the years remaining basically unchanged. In addition, these products are mainly concentrated in two parts of the HS2, namely, Chapters 0–30 and Chapters 50–70. In terms of product categories, these products are mainly textile and textile articles.

Appendix 4 is obtained by mapping the characteristics of all categories of highest tariff products over the years, and listing indicators such as the HS2 industry codes, average tariff values, classification of BEC that they belong to, and the value of elasticity of substitution of the top ten highest tariff products. For the convenience of comparison, Table 2.7 only shows the situation in 2000 and 2014, and the boxed figures in column 2 represent the categories of the highest tariff products shared by 2000 and 2014. In terms of tariff levels, similar to the lowest tariff products, although during the sample period, the average tariff values of the highest tariff products in the U.S. have not changed much and have been relatively stable; on the whole, there has been a slight decline. For example, the average tariff value of products in Chapter 55 in 2000 was 11.88%, while in 2014 it decreased slightly to 10.62%; the tariff level for products in Chapter 62 was 10.75% in 2000, and it dropped to 10.08% in 2014.

At the industry level, the characteristics of the highest tariff products in the U.S. are also quite stable: in 2000, the top ten highest tariff products in the U.S. are predominately consumer goods and products with high elasticity of substitution, while such products still constituted the majority of the highest tariff products in 2014. Meanwhile, product characteristics are extremely similar over time.

2.3.3 Comparison between the highest and lowest tariff products

Figure 2.7 overlays and compares the distribution of categories of the highest and lowest tariff products in the U.S. for the period 2000–2014, with hollow blocks representing the top ten lowest tariff products, and the solid blocks the top ten highest tariff products. According to the graph, both the highest and lowest tariff products are basically concentrated in their respective fixed product categories. The only exception is the overlapping of some products in Chapters 20–30, and most of the overlapping products are

Table 2.7 HS2 codes and characteristics of the top ten highest tariff products in the U.S. in 2000 and 2014

Year	*HS code*	*Average tariff (%)*	*Classification by BEC*	*Classification by elasticity of substitution*
2000	**4**	12.66	Consumer good	High elasticity of substitution
2000	**20**	10.64	Consumer good	High elasticity of substitution
2000	**24**	204.17	Consumer good	High elasticity of substitution
2000	**54**	11.29	Intermediate good	Low elasticity of substitution
2000	**55**	11.88	Intermediate good	High elasticity of substitution
2000	58	10.21	Intermediate good	High elasticity of substitution
2000	**60**	11.97	Intermediate good	High elasticity of substitution
2000	**61**	13.71	Consumer good	High elasticity of substitution
2000	**62**	10.75	Consumer good	High elasticity of substitution
2000	**64**	12.26	Consumer good	High elasticity of substitution
2014	**4**	12.66	Consumer good	High elasticity of substitution
2014	12	10.55	Intermediate good	Low elasticity of substitution
2014	**20**	10.79	Consumer good	High elasticity of substitution
2014	**24**	204.17	Consumer good	High elasticity of substitution
2014	**54**	10.31	Intermediate good	Low elasticity of substitution
2014	**55**	10.62	Intermediate good	High elasticity of substitution
2014	**60**	10.70	Intermediate good	High elasticity of substitution
2014	**61**	12.78	Consumer good	High elasticity of substitution
2014	**62**	10.08	Consumer good	High elasticity of substitution
2014	**64**	10.49	Consumer good	High elasticity of substitution

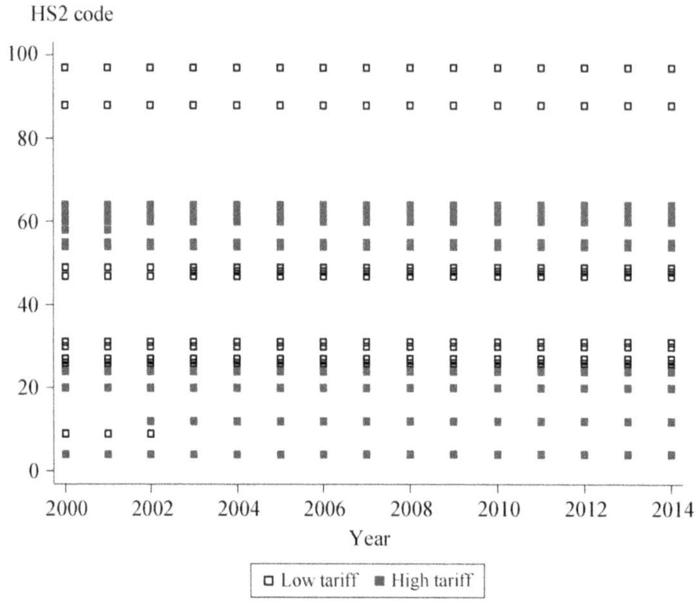

Figure 2.7 Changes and overlaps of the highest and lowest tariff products in the U.S. during 2000–2014.

mineral products, products of the chemicals and articles thereof. In other words, the characteristics of both highest and lowest tariff products in the U.S. are relatively stable and show no obvious changeability over the sample period.

Summing up the aforementioned findings, it can be concluded that (1) with the passage of time, the two product categories in the U.S., the highest and lowest tariff products, exhibit very strong stability, with the highest tariff products concentrated in textiles and textile articles, and the lowest tariff products in mineral products, products of the chemicals or allied industries; (2) although the overall tariff level of the U.S. shows a gradual downward trend, for the highest tariff products, their average tariff values have not changed much; and (3) both categories of imports are dominated by products with higher elasticity of substitution, but the highest tariff products are predominately consumer goods, while the lowest tariff products are mainly intermediate goods. This is consistent with the cascading tariff structure of the U.S.

2.4 Comparison summary of characteristics of tariff structures of China and the U.S.

Taking all the relevant analysis results in this chapter and Chapter 1 into consideration, we found that the characteristics of tariff structures of China and the U.S. have the following similarities and differences.

2.4.1 At the overall level

1. In terms of average tariff values, as time passes, those in both countries have shown an obvious downward trend; as the tariffs of the U.S. have been at a low level sincc the beginning of the sample period, even though China's tariff level has been slashed significantly, it is still higher than that of the U.S. and there is still some room for adjustment.
2. As for tariff variances, during the sample period, the changes of tariff variances over the years in the U.S. are comparatively limited and very stable; however, the large variance value indicates high decentralization on the inside, and there are relatively conspicuous differences in tariff levels across different products. Meanwhile, it shows a slight decentralization trend over the sample period. On the other hand, though the tariff variance of China changes considerably over the years, it gradually decreases over the sample period, showing a general trend of change from decentralization to centralization. In addition, it is relatively stable and has barely changed since 2005.
3. From the perspective of tariff peaks, the categories of tariff peak products in both countries exhibit comparatively strong stability. Apart from a few products, tariff peak products in both countries are subject to prevalent import restrictions. During the sample period, the number of tariff peak sectors in China gradually declined, while that in the U.S. remained basically unchanged. Tariff peak products in the U.S. are mainly concentrated in the textiles and textile articles industries, while those in China are scattered in cereals, beverages, spirits and vinegar; tobacco and manufactured tobacco substitutes.

On the whole, since 2004, in terms of average tariff values, tariff variances, and tariff peaks, tariff structures of the two countries have exhibited comparatively strong stability. In particular, China's tariff structure displays characteristics very similar to those of the U.S. Their tariff structures are relatively stable, and the number of categories of tariff peak products remains at a fairly constant level; though there are certain import restrictions, they have little impact on individual products.

2.4.2 At the industry level

In terms of characteristics at the industry level, tariff structures of China and the U.S. display the following differences and similarities.

1. In terms of the use of imported goods, both countries show very obvious characteristic of cascading tariff structure: the tariffs on imported consumer goods are significantly larger than those on imported intermediate goods. However, comparatively speaking, the cascading tariff structure of the U.S. is more pronounced and more stable. Although the tariff structures of the two countries show fairly similar characteristics, the changes in the import shares of products for different uses display significant differences. To be specific, imports of intermediate goods account for the highest proportion of total imports in both countries, with intermediate goods making up for a larger share in China, a proportion as high as 70%–90%. On the other hand, the import share of intermediate goods in the U.S. is around 60%. As for capital goods and consumer goods, the import shares of products of these two categories in the U.S. are relatively equal, and the imports of consumer goods are slightly higher than those of capital goods. In contrast, China imports more capital goods and less consumer goods.
2. From the perspective of elasticity of substitution of imports, as it increases, the average tariff values of imports in both countries are also on gradual rise, and the two display a relatively obvious positive correlation. In the meantime, as time passes, both of the tariff structures of products with high and low elasticity of substitution in the two countries show a very stable feature: within each of the two countries, the average tariff values of products with lower elasticity of substitution are smaller and more centrally distributed, while those of products with higher elasticity of substitution are larger and more decentralized. Compared to the U.S., China has a more fragmented tariff structure for products with lower elasticity of substitution, with greater differences in the tariff values among these products. In contrast, the tariff structure of its products with higher elasticity of substitution is more centralized than that of the U.S., which means that the U.S. has greater differences in average tariff values among products with higher elasticity of substitution.

2.4.3 At the tariff change level

1. In terms of lowest tariff products, the tariff structures of both countries are highly stable and similar. Over the sample period (2000–2014), the categories of lowest tariff products of the two countries have remained

almost unchanged, with intermediate goods and products with higher elasticity of substitution accounting for a relatively large proportion. Basically, the tariff levels of the lowest tariff products barely change and are relatively stable.

i. Specifically, China's top ten lowest tariff products are concentrated in mineral products, chemical industries, or chemical products; products of pulp, silk, and other textiles; machinery, mechanical parts, and appliances; as well as vehicles, aircraft, vessels, and associated transport equipment and parts thereof. Most of these products belong to intermediate inputs.
ii. In the U.S., the top ten lowest tariff products are concentrated in mineral products, products of the chemicals, or allied industries. The lowest tariff products of the U.S. are more centralized, while those of China are scattered among several categories of products.

2. From the perspective of the highest tariff products, there are differences in the tariff structures of the two countries. During the sample period, China's highest tariff products underwent a certain degree of change, while those of the U.S. showed a fairly stable feature. To be specific:

   i. In terms of average tariff values, those of China's highest tariff products underwent a significant decline, while those of the highest tariff products of the U.S. hardly changed.
   ii. As for product characteristics, compared to 2000, among the highest tariff imports of China in 2014, the number of consumer goods and products with low elasticity of substitution both increased. In contrast, the highest tariff imports of the U.S. have always been mainly consumer goods and products with high elasticity of substitution.
   iii. Judging from specific product categories, during the sample period, most of the categories of highest tariff products that China withdrew from were agricultural by-products and their processed products, and the new product categories mainly belonged to vegetable products, footwear, headgear, and other manufacturing and processing industries. Meanwhile, the categories of highest tariff product in the U.S. were extremely stable as those categories barely changed in the past years and mainly consisted of textiles and textile articles.

3. In terms of the distribution range, in both countries, there is little overlap in the industries to which the categories of highest and lowest tariff products belong. China has certain overlaps and similarities mainly in industries in front HS2 chapters, and the U.S. only has overlaps in a few products such as mineral products, chemical products and articles thereof. The highest and lowest tariff products in both countries are obviously distributed in some fixed product categories. Relatively

speaking, there is a greater overlap in the product category distribution of the highest and lowest categories in China; that is, for different products in the same category, their import tariffs vary considerably. For example, among primary products, mineral products are subject to lower import tariffs while agricultural products and cash crops to higher.[4]

Notes

1 The depiction and analysis of tariff peak sector categories for the years during 2000–2014 remains largely consistent.
2 See Figure 1.2 in Chapter 1 of this book.
3 See Appendix 3 at the end of the book for the complete table.
4 We would like to thank the project of "Tariff Structure Analysis and International Comparison Study" jointly implemented by the Ministry of Finance and universities and hosted by the author in 2016 for its support in the studies in the aforementioned chapter. The original research has been revised and edited for the convenience of the readers.

Part 2

Sino–U.S. trade friction in 2018 and the analysis of the impact

The first part of this book focuses on the characteristics, evolution trends, and comparative differences of tariff structures of China and the U.S. From the analysis in Part 1, we can see that both China and the U.S. have very obvious features of cascading tariff structure, but there are distinctive differences in the changes of import shares of goods for different uses. For example, the imports of consumer and capital goods in the U.S. both account for about 20% of the imports, while China's imported consumer goods account for only around 3%. At the same time, China imported a considerable proportion of intermediate goods. Taking the period 2000–2006 as an example, intermediate goods made up 74% of China's total imports, and if capital goods were also considered as intermediate goods, then the percentage would be as high as 93%. Meanwhile, the share of consumer goods is only 4% for the same time period.[1]

Does this difference in import shares of intermediate goods have a particular impact on the Sino–U.S. trade friction? The answer is obviously yes. In recent years, a series of studies on the liberalization of trade in intermediate goods (e.g., Amiti & Konings, 2007; Bas, 2012) show that such trade occupies a very important position in global trade (e.g., Johnson & Noguera, 2012; Koopman, Wang, & Wei, 2014) and has a very significant impact on the performance of enterprises.[2] Studies of Amiti and Konings (2007), Gopinath and Neiman (2014), and others have found that importing intermediate goods of higher quality is conductive to increasing the total factor productivity of enterprises.[3] Studies of Amiti and Khandelwal (2013); Bas and Strauss-Kahn (2015); and Fan, Li, and Yeaple (2015) show that a decline in tariffs on intermediate inputs helps motivate enterprises to improve the quality of their products. Goldberg et al. (2010); Feng, Li, and Swenson (2012); and Fan, Lai, and Qi (2017), on the other hand, point out that liberalization of trade in intermediate goods plays an imperative role in improving the export performance of enterprises, expanding their range of exported products, and adjusting the cost-plus of multi-product enterprises. These studies have all demonstrated the importance of the liberalization of trade in intermediate goods from different perspectives and have also, from another dimension, revealed the importance of considering the impact of the Sino–U.S. trade friction from the perspective of trade in intermediate goods. Will the differences in imports of intermediate and consumer goods between the two countries have an impact on the Sino–U.S. trade friction? What will be the impact? These are the main questions to be answered in the second part of this book.

Considering that quantitative analysis allows for a more accurate and effective analysis and prediction of the expected effects of the various policies to be implemented, this part will specifically start with the perspective of quantitative analysis and will analyze the relevant impact of Sino–U.S. trade friction. In recent years, the quantitative analysis method has become increasingly popular among international scholars. Caliendo and Parro (2015) have analyzed the impact of exogenous tariff changes on welfare changes after the establishment of the North American Free Trade Agreement (NAFTA). Ossa (2014) and Alvarez and Lucas (2007) have discussed the trade gains under optimal tariffs. Hsieh and Ossa (2016) have examined the impact of China's productivity growth on the welfare levels of 14 major countries and four major international regions in the period 1992–2007. Di Giovanni, Levchenko, and Zhang (2013) apply the Ricardian-Heckscher-Ohlin model to quantify, analyze, and evaluate the impact of China's trade integration and technological progress on the welfare levels of 75 countries.

As a whole, this part contains three chapters: Chapter 3 outlines the development process of Sino–U.S. trade friction, and analyzes the (potential) impact of this trade friction on Chinese and American enterprises as well as possible coping strategies of the two countries based on specific cases. From the perspective of classic trade theories and cost–benefit analysis, Chapter 4 provides a brief introduction and analysis of basic theoretical concepts such as terms of trade, tariffs, and determination of welfare levels. Chapter 5 takes the Sino–U.S. trade friction as a specific research object and combines it with the relevant analysis of tariff structures in Part 1 to conduct a quantitative assessment of the welfare impact of trade frictions.

3 Retrospect on the Sino–U.S. trade friction in 2018

3.1 Retrospect on the Sino–U.S. trade friction

This chapter is divided into two sections. The first section mainly sorts out the development of the Sino–U.S. trade friction in 2018, while the second one illustrates the potential impact of this trade friction on U.S. enterprises, using the semiconductor industry as an example.

3.1.1 Sorting out the major events in the Sino–U.S. trade friction

On April 4, 2018, the U.S. side announced that it would impose a 25% tariff on a number of products with a total value of 50 billion U.S. dollars imported from China, and proposed an additional tariff list; in that day, in response, China decided to impose a 25% import tariff on 50 billion U.S. dollars worth of goods originated from the U.S. A new round of Sino–U.S. trade friction officially started. On April 16 of the same year, the U.S. Department of Commerce announced that U.S. companies were prohibited from selling parts, goods, software, and technology to ZTE, with a time span up to seven years. The Sino–U.S. trade friction escalated again.

In order to enable readers to have a more comprehensive understanding of this trade friction, based on people.com, the announcements from Customs Tariff Commission of the State Council and the Office of the United States Trade Representative (USTR), and other public media materials, the author detailed the Sino–U.S. trade friction in accordance with the timeline as follows. The overall span covers the period from the second half of 2007 to early 2019.[4]

- **2017**

On **August 19, 2017**, President Trump instructed USTR to initiate a Section 301 Investigation against China.[5] This became the trigger for the Sino–U.S. trade friction in 2018.

- **2018**

On **February 16, 2018**, the U.S. Department of Commerce disclosed the results of Section 232 investigation, concluding that steel and aluminum imports may now jeopardize the national security of the U.S.[6]

On **February 27, 2018**, the U.S. Department of Commerce announced the affirmative final determination that aluminum foil imports from China were dumped and subsidized, and issued a statement finalizing that the dumping margin of aluminum foil imported from China to the U.S. was 48.64%–106.09%, and the subsidies range from 17.17% to 80.97%.

From **February 27 to March 3, 2018**, Liu He, a member of the Political Bureau of the CPC Central Committee, Director of the Office of the CPC Central Leading Group for Financial and Economic Affairs, and the chief of the Chinese side of the Sino–U.S. comprehensive economic dialogue, visited the U.S. During the visit, Liu He met with Mnuchin, the Secretary of the Treasury; Cohn, White House National Economic Council Director; and Lighthizer, the Trade Representative, and consultations were held on economic and trade cooperation between China and the U.S. as well as other important issues of mutual interest.

On **March 8, 2018**, President Trump signed a proclamation imposing high tariffs on imported steel and aluminum products. The U.S. would impose a 25% tariff on imported steel and a 10% tariff on imported aluminum products.

On **March 15, 2018**, the U.S. International Trade Commission made a final determination that the U.S. would levy anti-dumping and countervailing ("double reverse") duties on aluminum foil products imported from China.[7]

On **March 19, 2018**, the spokesman of China's Foreign Ministry commented on the U.S. decision to take restrictive measures against imports of steel and aluminum products, saying that in the current situation, beggar-thy-neighbor policies, and letting bullets fly are by no means beneficial and effective ways to solve the problem, and they are not constructive in any way.

On **March 22, 2018**, USTR issued the "Findings of the Investigation into China's Acts, Policies, and Practices Related to Technology Transfer, Intellectual Property, and Innovation Under Section 301 of the Trade Act of 1974." Based on this, Trump imposed massive tariffs on imports from China and restricted Chinese companies' investment and acquisitions in the U.S. Trump told the media before signing in the White House that the size of the Chinese goods involved in the tax could be as large as 60 billion U.S. dollars.

On **March 23, 2018**, China's Ministry of Commerce issued the "Notice on Soliciting Public Comments on U.S. Section 232 Measures for Imported Steel and Aluminum Products and China's Responses," which stated that it intended to terminate the implementation of substantially equal concessions and other obligations to the U.S., that is, additional tariffs would be levied on certain products imported from the U.S.

On **April 2, 2018**, China's Customs Tariff Commission of the State Council announced a tariff list of products in response to the U.S. Section 232 measures, and it terminated tariff concession obligations on

128 items of seven categories of imports originating from the U.S. According to statistics in 2017, the list involved approximately 3 billion U.S. dollars of U.S. exports to China.

On **April 3, 2018**, the United States Trade Representative announced a list of China's goods to be subject to additional tariffs based on the results of the Section 301 investigation. The list named products of 1,300 separate tariff items with a total annual value of roughly 50 billion U.S. dollars. The goods on the list mainly aimed at "Made in China 2025" industrial policy, with a punitive tariff of 25%.

On **April 4, 2018**, China's Ministry of Commerce released an announcement regarding the imposition of additional tariffs on certain imported goods originating from the U.S. In response to the Section 301 investigation announced by the U.S., China decided to impose a 25% additional tariff on imports of soya beans, automobiles, aircraft, and other goods from the U.S., involving about 50 billion U.S. dollars of imports from the U.S. On the same day, China requested a consultation under the WTO dispute settlement mechanism regarding the tax proposals under the U.S. Section 301 investigation, formally initiating the WTO dispute settlement procedure.

On **April 5, 2018**, Trump issued a statement requesting to instruct the United States Trade Representative to consider additional tariffs under Section 301 against the 100 billion in China's imports as a countermeasure against China's tariffs. On the same day, China proposed consultations to the U.S. side on the Section 232 measure on U.S. imports of steel and aluminum products under the WTOs dispute settlement mechanism, officially initiating the dispute settlement procedure.

On **April 6, 2018**, the spokesperson of China's Ministry of Commerce, Gao Feng, said that there had been no talks over economic and trade issues between Chinese and U.S. economic officials recently. China was fully prepared and would not hesitate to strike back fiercely if the U.S. said it was considering levying additional tariffs on 100 billion U.S. dollars of China's exports.

On **April 10, 2018**, President Xi Jinping of China proposed four initiatives at the Boao Forum for Asia regarding further opening-up: (1) substantial liberalization of market access; (2) creation of a more attractive investment climate; (3) further strengthening of protection of intellectual property rights; (4) and further expanding imports and reducing tariffs on imported automobiles.

On **April 11, 2018**, President Trump tweeted on a social media platform that he was very thankful for President Xi and that they would make great progress together.

On **April 16, 2018**, the U.S. Department of Commerce announced that U.S. companies were prohibited from selling parts, goods, software, and technology to ZTE, with a time span up to seven years. The Sino–U.S. trade friction escalated again.

On **April 17, 2018**, the Chinese side declared that it would take temporary antidumping measures against imported sorghum originating from the U.S. with immediate effect.

On **April 18, 2018**, the U.S. announced that it would launch a new investigation to address whether some steel wheels imported from China were dumped in the U.S. and whether they received unfair subsidies.

On **April 19, 2018**, China decided to impose provisional antidumping measures on chlorobutyl rubber imported from the U.S., the E.U., and Singapore. Importers of the product are required to pay deposits.

On **May 1, 2018**, China's Tariff Commission of the State Council adjusted import tariffs to temporary tax rates of zero for a total of 28 tariff items of all general drugs and alkaloid drugs with anti-cancer effects, including Chinese patent medicines with actual imports.

On **May 3 to 4, 2018**, U.S. Secretary of the Treasury, Mnuchin, visited China. Liu He, a member of the Political Bureau of the CPC Central Committee and the Vice Premier of the State Council, met with the U.S. delegation led by the special envoy of the President of the U.S. and the Secretary of the Treasury, Mnuchin. A frank, efficient, and constructive discussion was held regarding the Sino–U.S. economic and trade issues of common concern.

On **May 13, 2018**, President Trump tweeted: President Xi of China, and I, are working together to give massive Chinese phone company ZTE, a way to get back into business, fast. Too many jobs in China lost (due to ZTE's failure to conduct normal businesses). Commerce Department has been instructed to get it done!

On **May 14, 2018**, China's Ministry of Commerce restarted its review of Qualcomm's acquisition of NXP Semiconductors, resuming work on the review that had been at a standstill as a result of the trade dispute between China and the U.S.

On **May 15, 2018**, a Chinese economic and trade delegation led by Liu He, the special envoy of President Xi Jinping, a member of the Political Bureau of the CPC Central Committee, Vice Premier of the State Council, and the chief of the Chinese side of the Sino–U.S. comprehensive economic dialogue, arrived in Washington, D.C.

On **May 19, 2018**, the most significant outcome of the bilateral economic and trade consultations between China and the U.S. in Washington, D.C., on May 19, local time, was that the two sides reached a consensus not to engage in a trade war and to stop imposing additional tariffs on each other.

On **May 20, 2018**, U.S. Secretary of the Treasury Mnuchin said that the Sino–U.S. economic and trade consultations that just finished had made meaningful progress, and the two sides would continue the consultations on economic and trade issues.

On **May 25, 2018**, U.S. President Trump said he would let ZTE reopen with "high level security guarantees, change of management and board, must purchase U.S. parts and pay a 1.3 billion U.S. dollars fine."

On **May 29, 2018**, the White House released a statement saying that by June 15, the U.S. would announce a list of China's industrially significant technology products exported to the U.S. with a total value of approximately 50 billion U.S. dollars, and a 25% tariff would be levied on them. On the same day, China's Ministry of Commerce responded that they were both surprised by and expecting the statement issued by the White House, and that China had the confidence, capability, and experience in safeguarding the interests of the Chinese people and its national interests.

On **May 30, 2018**, China's Foreign Ministry Spokeswoman Hua Chunying responded to the White House statement, noting that when it came to international relations, each and every flip-flop would only lead to further depletion and squandering of a country's credibility and reputation. The U.S.'s statement explicitly ran against the consensus it reached with the Chinese side in Washington, D.C., not long ago.

On **June 2–3, 2018**, U.S. Secretary of Commerce Ross visited China. Liu He, a member of the Political Bureau of the Communist Party of China Central Committee, Vice Premier of the State Council, and chief of the Chinese side of the Sino–U.S. comprehensive economic dialogue, led the Chinese team to meet with the American delegation led by U.S. Secretary of Commerce Ross, and consultations were held in Beijing on economic and trade issues between the two countries. To implement the consensus reached in Washington, D.C., the two sides conducted good communication in various areas such as agriculture and energy, and made positive and concrete progress while relevant details are yet to be confirmed by both sides. The two sides have not issued a joint statement on this negotiation.

On **June 16, 2018**, the U.S. government released a list of goods and would impose a 25% additional tariff on approximately 50 billion U.S. dollar goods imported from China, of which the additional tariffs on 818 items worth about 34 billion U.S. dollars would be implemented from July 6, 2018. The main categories of goods subject to the tariffs are machinery parts, machine tools, generators, transformers, metals, and railroads. USTR would further assess the second set of tariff lines, which cover approximately 16 billion U.S. dollar worth of imports from China.

On **June 16, 2018**, China's Customs Tariff Commission of the State Council decided to impose additional tariffs of 25% on 659 items of U.S. products worth about 50 billion U.S. dollars, of which additional tariffs for 545 items worth about 34 billion U.S. dollars, including agricultural products, vehicles, and aquatic products, would be effective from July 6, 2018. The implementation date for imposing additional tariffs on the remaining 114 items, covering chemical products, medical equipment, and energy products, would be announced later.

On **June 18, 2018**, Trump instructed the USTR to identify 200 billion U.S. dollars worth of Chinese goods, and if China took retaliatory measures and refused to change "unfair" trade practices, a 10% additional tariff would be imposed. Trump then claimed a further escalation to products of 500 billion

U.S. dollars, which essentially achieved full coverage of Chinese exports to the U.S.

On **June 19, 2018**, a spokesman of China's Ministry of Commerce said that after unveiling plans to impose additional tariffs on Chinese goods worth around 50 billion U.S. dollars, the U.S. went even further by threatening to identify 200 billion U.S. dollars worth of Chinese products for additional tariffs. if the U.S. lost its rationality and unveiled another list of Chinese products for additional tariffs, China would have no choice but to take comprehensive measures combining quantitative and qualitative ones to resolutely strike back.

On **June 21, 2018**, the spokesperson of China's Ministry of Commerce, Gao Feng said at a press conference that we had noted the deep concern in the U.S. over unilateral tariff measures by the US. The number of opponents was growing, and the scale was spreading. China would comprehensively take measures, including quantitative and qualitative tools to resolutely strike back against the U.S. side. Sion–U.S. economic and trade consultations were once fruitful, but the U.S. side had been capricious. Regardless of the attitude of the U.S. side, China would face it with an open mind.

On **June 26, 2018**, China cut import tariffs on some Asian countries, reducing tariffs on soya beans and other products to zero.

On **June 26, 2018**, Trump said he would tighten the control of all countries' investment in American technologies through the Committee on Foreign Investment.

On **June 29, 2018**, China released a new negative list for market access of foreign investment, which introduced opening-up measures in 22 fields, almost completely liberalizing investment restrictions in the manufacturing sector, and it announced to remove all the foreign ownership limits in the financial sector in 2021.

On **July 1, 2018**, China began lowering the MFN rate of duty on certain imported consumer goods, covering 1,449 tariff items, with an average tax reduction of 56%.

On **July 1, 2018**, China began reducing import tariffs on automobiles and parts and components, covering those of 218 tariff items.

On **July 2, 2018**, the U.S. National Telecommunications and Information Administration blocked China Mobile from providing services to the U.S. telecommunications market.

On **July 3, 2018**, a Chinese court issued a preliminary injunction stopping Micron from selling chips in the mainland.

On **July 6, 2018**, China filed a complaint at the WTO over the U.S.'s tariff measures on 200 billion U.S. dollars of products from China under the Section 301 investigation.

On **July 6, 2018**, the U.S. imposed 25% additional taxes on 818 categories of Chinese goods worth 34 billion U.S. dollars on the first round of the list. On the same day, USTR announced the Section 301 Chinese tariff exemption procedure. Chinese products involved in the above-mentioned effective 818 items of Chinese goods had a chance of special exemption from the Section 301 tariffs.

On **July 6, 2018**, according to the statement of the relevant head of the General Administration of Customs, China's 25% additional tariff on 34 billion U.S. dollars of imports from the U.S. was officially implemented on July 6, 2018 (Beijing time).

On **July 11, 2018**, the U.S. side announced its intention to impose additional import tariffs of approximately 10% on around 200 billion U.S. dollars of products imported from China. On the same day, China's Ministry of Commerce responded that the U.S. side's announcement of the additional tax list in an accelerated and escalating manner was completely unacceptable. Foreign Ministry Spokeswoman Hua Chunying responded that the U.S. side's behavior was typical of trade bullying.

On **August 2, 2018**, the U.S. side said that it planned to raise the additional tariff rate on the 200 billion U.S. of goods announced on July 11 from 10% to 25%.

On **August 3, 2018**, China responded by imposing additional tariffs of 5%, 10%, 20%, and 25% on 60 billion U.S. dollars of goods from the U.S., with implementation dates depending on the U.S. side. The Sino–U.S. trade escalated again.

On **August 7, 2018**, USTR officially announced a list of 16 billion U.S. dollars of Chinese goods subject to 25% additional tariffs. The newly announced 16 billion U.S. dollars of products included 279 items, five items fewer than the initial 284 items in the proposed list announced on June 15. It included some chemical products (lubricants, plastics, etc.), mechanical products, semiconductors, and semiconductor manufacturing machineries for high-tech manufacturing, which would come into effect on August 23.

On **August 8, 2018**, the Tariff Commission of the State Council decided to impose a 25% additional tariff at 12:01 on August 23, 2018, after making appropriate adjustments on products in the second list of U.S. products subject to additional tariff in the "Notice of the Tariff Commission of the State Council on Additional Tariff on 50 Billion U.S. Dollars of Imports from the U.S. (Taxation Committee Announcement [2018] No. 5)," which covered 333 tariff items, including lignite, diesel, lubricants, petroleum asphalt, large passenger buses, automobiles, and SUVs.

On **August 22–23, 2018**, at the invitation of the U.S. side, China's Vice Minister of Commerce and Deputy Representative on International Trade Negotiations, Wang Shouwen, led a Chinese delegation to Washington, D.C., to communicate with the U.S. delegation led by U.S. Treasury Undersecretary Malpass.

On **August 23, 2018**, China filed a complaint at the WTO against tax measures imposed on 16 billion U.S. dollars of Chinese exports to the U.S. under Section 301 investigation.

On **September 12, 2018**, the U.S. side took the initiative to propose a new round of trade talks with China and stated that the aim was to offer China an opportunity to resolve the Sion–U.S. trade dispute before the U.S. imposed additional tariffs on imports from China. On September 13, the Ministry of Commerce responded by saying, China welcomed the invitation, and an escalation of the trade conflict was not in anyone's interests.

On **Sept. 18, 2018**, the U.S. government announced that it would, starting from September 24, impose additional 10% tariffs on about 200 billion U.S. dollars of products imported from China, and the tariff would rise to 25% on January 1, 2019. It also said that it would pursue additional tariffs on approximately 267 billion U.S. dollars of imports if China took retaliatory action against farmers or other industries in the U.S. China's Ministry of Commerce responded on the same day that, in order to safeguard its legitimate rights and interests and the global free trade order, China would have to carry out countermeasures simultaneously.

On **September 18, 2018**, Customs Tariff Commission of the State Council decided to impose an additional 10% or 5% tariff on approximately 600 billion U.S. dollars of goods of 5,207 tariff items from the U.S., taking effect at 12:01 on September 24, 2018. Details can be found in Appendix 1, Appendix 2, Appendix 3, and Appendix 4. A 10% additional tariff would be levied on 2,493 tariff items listed in Appendix 1, and 1,078 tariff items listed in Appendix 2, 5% on 974 tariff items in Appendix 3, and 662 tariff items in Appendix 4. If the U.S. side insisted on further hiking the tariff rates, China would respond accordingly, and the relevant matters would be announced later.

On **September 18, 2018**, China filed an additional complaint at the WTO against the U.S. on implementing tax measures on 200 billion U.S. dollars of China's exports to the U.S. under the Section 301 investigation.

On **October 17, 2018**, the U.S. Department of the Treasury released its semiannual Report on Exchange Rate Policies, concluding that none of the major trading partners of the U.S., including China, manipulated currency exchange rates.

On **October 29, 2018**, the U.S. Department of Commerce announced to restrict exports to Fujian Jinhua Integrated Circuit Company, Ltd. by adding them to the Entity List.

On **October 30, 2018**, China's Ministry of Commerce spokesperson made a statement opposing the U.S. unilateral sanctions and urged the U.S. government to take measures and immediately stop its wrongful practices.

On **November 1, 2018**, Chinese Premier Li Keqiang met with a delegation of U.S. senators and congressmen led by Senator Alexander in China. Li Keqiang stressed that China would firmly deepen its reform and further open up to the world. The U.S. side stated that both countries needed to resolve issues in the economic and trade fields through fair and equal consultations. The U.S. senators stated that they would play a constructive role in promoting the U.S.–China relations and enhancing understanding and cooperation between the two countries.

On **November 1, 2018**, Chinese President Xi Jinping and U.S. President

Donald Trump held a telephone conversation. The two leaders agreed to meet bilaterally during the upcoming G20 summit in Argentina for in-depth discussions on some major questions.

On **November 1, 2018**, the Customs Tariff Commission of the State Council of China issued a public notice announcing that as of November 1, 2018, it would reduce the MFN rate of duty for selected industrial products of a total 1,585 tax items, including textiles; stone, ceramics, and glass products; selected iron and steel and base metals products; electromechanical equipment and parts, such as metalworking machineries, textile machineries, engineering machineries, power transmission and distribution equipment, electrical apparatus, instruments, and meters, etc.; resource commodities and primary processed goods such as non-metallic minerals, inorganic chemicals, wood and paper products, precious stones, etc. These accounted for about 19% of the total number of tax items in the country, with the average tariff rate dropping from 10.5% to 7.8%, down by 26%. As a result, China's overall tariff level would be reduced from 9.8% in the previous year to 7.5%, with an average reduction of 23%.

On **November 2, 2018**, U.S. Secretary of the Treasury Mnuchin announced that sanctions on Iran would go back into full effect after 23:59 EST on November 4, with Mainland China receiving a temporary waiver to purchase 360,000 barrels per day of Iranian crude oil for 180 days.

On **November 19, 2018**, the U.S. Department of Commerce's Bureau of Industry and Security (BIS) introduced a technology export compliance program proposing to control the technological export of 14 items involving national security and cutting-edge technologies, and sought for public comments on this program. The 14 items of enhanced control by the U.S. Department of Commerce included artificial intelligence, chips, quantum computing, robotics, face-printing, and voice-printing technology.

On **November 20, 2018**, USTR updated its Section 301 investigation report, accusing the Chinese government of continuing to support theft of intellectual property rights and technology. A spokesperson of China's Ministry of Commerce said that the report made new and groundless accusations against China, which was on hearsay evidence and ignored the facts, and that China found it completely intolerable.

On **December 1**, 2018, Chinese President Xi Jinping was invited to attend a dinner and have a meeting with U.S. President Donald Trump in Buenos Aires, Argentina. The two heads of state had an in-depth exchange of views on the Sino–U.S. relations and international issues of common concern, and important consensus was reached. The two sides agreed not to impose new additional tariffs and instructed the economic teams of both sides to step up negotiations toward the removal of all additional tariffs and reach a concrete deal for mutual benefit and win-win results.

On **December 2, 2018**, the U.S. White House issued a statement saying that Trump and Xi Jinping had a "highly successful meeting." Trump agreed to keep the tariff on goods at 10% on January 1, 2019. China would purchase a large number of products from the U.S. and would start buying agricultural products from the U.S. immediately. China and the U.S. agreed on a 90-day window to negotiate on "structural" issues such as technology transfer and intellectual property rights. If China and the U.S. failed to reach an agreement, the tariff rate would rise to 25%.

On **December 11, 2018**, Liu He, a member of the Political Bureau of the Communist Party of China Central Committee, Vice Premier of the State Council, and chief of the Chinese side of the Sino–U.S. comprehensive economic dialogue, held a telephone conversation with the U.S. Secretary of the Treasury Mnuchin and Trade Representative Lighthizer at the request. The two sides exchanged opinions on implementing the consensus of the meeting between the two heads of state and advancing the timetable and roadmap for the next step of the economic and trade consultations.

On **December 14, 2018**, China's Customs Tariff Commission of the State Council issued an announcement, deciding to suspend imposing additional tariffs on automobiles and parts from the U.S. from January 1, 2019 to March 31, 2019. Two hundred eleven tariff items were involved.

On **December 19, 2018**, China and the U.S. held a vice ministerial–level telephone call on economic and trade issues to communicate on issues of mutual interest.

- **2019**

On **January 4, 2019**, China and the U.S. held a vice-ministerial telephone call, confirming that U.S. Deputy Trade Representative Gerrish would lead a U.S. working group to visit China from January 7–8 to hold positive and constructive discussions with the Chinese working group on implementing the important consensus reached by the two heads of state at the meeting in Argentina.

On **January 30–31, 2019**, Liu He, a member of the Political Bureau of the Communist Party of China Central Committee, Vice Premier of the State Council, and chief of the Chinese side of the Sino–U.S. comprehensive economic dialogue, led the Chinese team to have economic and trade consultations in Washington, D.C., with the U.S. team led by U.S. Trade Representative Lighthizer. Guided by the important consensus reached by the two heads of state at the meeting in Argentina, the two sides discussed trade balance, technology transfer, IPR protection, non-tariff barriers, service sectors, agricultures, and enforcement mechanisms, as well as certain issues of particular concern for the Chinese side. In particular, candid, specific, and constructive discussions were held on such topics of common concern as trade balance, technology transfer, IPR protection, and enforcement mechanism, as well as certain issues of particular concern for the Chinese side. Important progress had been made for the current stage, and the two sides also determined the timetable and roadmap for next-step consultations.

On **February 14-15, 2019**, Liu He, a member of the Political Bureau of the Communist Party of China Central Committee, Vice Premier of the State Council, and chief of the Chinese side of the Sino–U.S. comprehensive economic dialogue, held the sixth round of Sino–U.S. high-level trade talks with U.S. Trade Representative Lighthizer and Secretary of the Treasury Mnuchin in Beijing. The two sides earnestly implemented the consensus reached by the two heads of state at the meeting in Argentina, and conducted in-depth discussion on technology transfer, IPR protection, non-tariff barriers, service sector, agriculture and enforcement mechanisms, as well as certain issues of particular concern to China. The two sides reached consensus in principle on major issues, and had specific discussions about a memorandum of understanding on bilateral economic and trade issues. Both parties stated that they would make persistent efforts to reach agreement in accordance with the deadlines for consultations set by the two heads of state.

On **February 21–24, 2019**, Vice Premier Liu He held the seventh round of Sino–U.S. high-level trade talks with U.S. Trade Representative Lighthizer and Secretary of the Treasury Mnuchin in Washington. The two sides further implemented the important consensus reached by the two heads of state at the meeting in Argentina, and negotiations were conducted on the text of the agreement. Substantial progress was made on specific issues such as technology transfer, IPR protection, non-tariff barriers, service sector, agriculture, and exchange rates. On this basis, the two sides would continue the work in accordance with the instructions of the two heads of state.

On the same day, President Trump announced to delay the plan of tariff hikes on Chinese exports to the U.S. on March 1.

As of this writing, there had been three rounds of tariff lists that China and the U.S. had mutually announced against each other, which are as follows.

- The first round (which came into effect on July 6, 2018) where the U.S. levied an additional 25% import tariff on 818 items imported from China valued at approximately 34 billion U.S. dollars; meanwhile, China also imposed an additional 25% tariff on 545 items imported from the U.S., valued at approximately 34 billion U.S. dollars.
- The second round (which came into effect on August 23, 2018), where the U.S. levied additional 25% tariffs on 279 items imported from China valued at approximately 16 billion U.S. dollars, and in response, China also imposed additional 25% tariffs on 333 items imported from the U.S., valued at approximately 16 billion U.S. dollars.
- The third round (which came into effect on September 24, 2018) where the U.S. levied additional 10% import tariffs on 5,745 items imported from China valued at approximately 200 billion U.S. dollars, and China levied additional 5% or 10% import tariffs on 1,636 items imported from the U.S. valued at approximately 60 billion U.S. dollars.

See the appendices at the end of the book for a detailed breakdown of the list of the three rounds of additional tariff.

3.1.2 U.S. enterprises under the Sino–U.S. trade friction – taking semiconductor industry as an example

Undoubtedly, after the U.S. unilaterally initiated the trade friction, Chinese companies are the first to be impacted. Among them, the semiconductor-related industries would bear the brunt. On April 6, 2018, the U.S. Department of Commerce issued an announcement that, since ZTE violated U.S. sanction by selling U.S. technologies to Iran, the U.S. government would ban American companies from selling components, products, software, and technologies to ZTE in the following seven years. As a result of the denial order, in May 2018, ZTE proclaimed that the company's primary business activities could no longer be carried out. In June of the same year, ZTE reached a settlement with the U.S. Department of Commerce. This event ended with ZTE paying cumulative fines of 2.29 billion U.S. dollars to the U.S. (The penalties were paid in two installments totaling 1.892 billion U.S. dollars, with a suspended penalty money of 400 million U.S. dollars. The total payout equals to three times the net profit of ZTE in 2017).[8]

On the other hand, in the context of today's rapid development of global value chains, the product R&D cooperation, sales cooperation, and processing agent relations between multinational enterprises are becoming increasingly closer. As the world's largest market for semiconductor consumption, the impact on the Chinese market will certainly have an effect on the development of American semiconductor companies. In this section, we will look at specific case studies to analyze the impact of the uncertainty in the Sino–U.S. trade environment caused by the Sino–U.S. trade friction on the development of high-tech companies in the U.S. Focusing on the semiconductor industry, the author selects three types of representative U.S. companies that have close cooperation with Chinese companies in manufacturing and R&D, sales cooperation, and agent processing. Using U.S. companies as a starting point, the (potential) impact of this Sino–U.S. trade friction on the U.S. semiconductor industry is discussed.

3.1.2.1 R&D cooperation type – Intel

As the world's largest manufacturer of PC parts and CPUs, Intel is in the midst of a critical transform to a data-driven business – its PC-based business is gradually shifting towards AI, smart cars, and 5G technology. Meanwhile, China's huge potential market is undoubtedly highly attractive.[9] According to Intel's regional revenue in 2015–2017, nearly 80% of its revenue came from regions outside the U.S., among which the Chinese market contributed nearly half of the revenue, providing an ample source of funding for its R&D investment. On the other hand, China's consistent low-tax policy and relevant industrial policies have further encouraged Intel to establish manufacturing centers across China and form cooperation agreements with various Chinese companies to build strategic partnerships. In January 2018, Intel announced new collaborations with a Chinese automotive manufacturer, SAIC Motor, and a digital mapping company, NavInfo, to jointly develop self-driving cars. In May of the same year, Intel Capital announced investments in three tech startups from China at the Intel Capital Global Summit. However, the strong uncertainty brought by the Sino–U.S. trade friction is likely to have a direct impact on the survival of Intel's cooperation plans with Chinese companies. In fact, back in February 2018, Intel and Chinese company Unisoc announced a 5G global strategic partnership, and both companies planned to simultaneously bring 5G mobile networks to market in 2019; however, in February 2019, Intel announced to end the cooperation plan with Unisoc. Although Intel stated that the termination was a purely commercial decision, the worry over that technology transfer would possibly trigger "sanctions" in the U.S. was undoubtedly a major influence on the collapse of the partnership agreement between the two parties.

3.1.2.2 Sales cooperation type – AMD

Unlike the R&D cooperation between Intel and Chinese companies, AMD and Chinese companies tend to have more of a sales cooperation type of relationship. In January 2018, AMD authorized JD.com as the sole distributor in China to collaborate together to promote and sell AMDs high-end processors. Although there has been no news of a breakdown in partnerships between AMD and the Chinese company, the instability of the Sino–U.S. trade relation and the steep increase in the cooperation cost will undoubtedly have an impact on the sustainability of AMDs cooperation with the Chinese market. In addition, looking at the geographic distribution of AMDs workforce, the distribution of its business locations, and the distribution of its revenue, it is easy to see that AMDs development is largely reliant on the support of the Asian market, especially the Chinese market. In 2017, for example, 74% of AMDs revenue came from non-U.S. regions, while China contributed up to 33% of the revenue. Given that a large portion of AMDs' supply chain operates in China and that a significant proportion of its employees are Chinese workers, the rise on infrastructure costs and the impact of more burdensome rules resulting from trade frictions will unquestionably have a further influence on its revenue.

3.1.2.3 Processing agent type – Skyworks

The cooperation between the American semiconductor company Skyworks and Chinese companies is mostly in the form of processing agent. China is an important place of demand for end products and for intermediate products, which makes Skyworks' production and processing highly dependent on the Chinese market. A large number of Skyworks' high-end semiconductor components are manufactured in China and eventually exported to the U.S. and European markets. It can be foreseen that, due to the Sino–U.S. trade friction, if the U.S. imposes high tariffs on the semiconductor products exported from China, it will directly lead to the rise on prices of semiconductor products of Skyworks that are produced in China and exported to the U.S., which in turn will affect the company's market revenue. Data show that in April 2018, after the U.S. issued a ban on ZTE, the stock price of Skyworks plunged by more than 13%.

The outcome of trade friction is indisputably a lose-lose situation, and only open cooperation can lead to a win-win situation. As the global value chain develops and division of labor continues to deepen, economic and trade friction between the two countries shall be maturely and properly solved, and uncertainties in the development of the world economy and trade shall be further eliminated. Only in this way can the well-being of people in these two countries and in the world be truly improved, and stable and healthy development of the world economy be promoted.

3.2 Coping strategies of Chinese enterprises under the Sino–U.S. trade friction

The previous section provides a summary of development history related to the trade friction between China and the U.S. in 2018, and uses the semiconductor industry as an example to illustrate the potential influences of this trade friction on American companies. This section focuses specifically on Chinese companies and provides an overview of the strategies that Chinese companies are likely to adopt from both long- and short-term perspectives, which is supported by relevant case studies.

3.2.1 Short-term strategies of Chinese enterprises – robbing the exports

In the short term, most Chinese companies prefer to export early (rob the exports) to avoid possible impact of tariff increases, so as to minimize losses.

Robbing the exports by companies is directly reflected in China's foreign trade export data. According to the General Administration of Customs, as of mid-November 2018, the total value of China's foreign trade imports and exports had exceeded the value of the entire year of 2017, with a year-on-year growth of nearly 15%. Against the backdrop of escalating trade friction between China and the U.S., foreign trade imports and exports still achieved rapid growth in 2018. In particular, since the second half of 2018, China's exports to the U.S. performed exceptionally: from July to October, China's exports to the U.S. registered a year-on-year growth of 12.9%, higher than the 9.9% growth rate of the same period in 2017. In addition to domestic policy factors such as China's import expansion in 2018, one of the reasons for the increase in the growth rate of foreign trade is that, in order to avoid the additional tariffs caused by the Sino–U.S. trade friction, Chinese foreign trade enterprises "robbed the export" in 2018 ahead of time to fulfill the export target of 2019.

"Robbing the exports" by companies is also indirectly reflected in the freight rates of Chinese containers shipped to the U.S. Fearing that U.S. tariffs and retaliatory measures would be implemented in September, on the one hand, Chinese exporters and U.S. importers were striving to ship the cargo to the U.S. before the additional tariff lists were officially implemented; on the other hand, all Marine Unions were pulling back on shipping routes and voyages to the U.S. This further led to an undersupply of transportation capacity to the U.S., which directly resulted in a significant increase in the freight rates for sea transportation from various major Chinese ports to the U.S. Taking the container freight index of the two major ports, Ningbo and Shanghai, as an example, the author has mapped the line charts for changes in container freight rates for the two major ports of Ningbo and Shanghai to the East U.S., West U.S., and Europe. As shown in Figure 3.1, the graph in the left depicts the change in the container freight rates of Ningbo corresponding to the three routes, and the one in the right describes the change in that of Shanghai corresponding to the three routes. According to the figure, it can be seen that after May 2018, the prices of containers shipped from both of the two major ports to the U.S. increased conspicuously. Especially compared with the European routes, the freight rates of East U.S. and West U.S. routes had risen significantly, and there was an obvious export robbing effect.

In addition, due to the Sino–U.S. trade friction, there is also a clear export robbing effect on the products in the additional tariff lists announced by the U.S. against China. A study from the Institute of Economics and Finance of Industrial Securities shows that despite the fact that as early as April 4, 2018, the U.S. threatened to impose additional tariffs on 50 billion U.S. dollars worth of products imported from China, the "export robbing effect" did not begin to show until July of that year.[10] Figure 3.2 measures the change in export growth rates of products on the three rounds of additional tariff lists announced by the U.S. against China.[11]

From Figure 3.2, it is easy to see that the export robbing effect of products on the first round of lists was not evident, with growth rates of 34 billion U.S. dollars of products on the list plunging starting from July, and the year-on-year growth rate fell from 9.5% in June to −9.7% in July. After that, the rate of decline gradually expanded, falling to −18.9% in September. This may be due to the fact that the products were subject to additional tariffs for so short a time that exporters had no time to react. The second round of the list of 16 billion U.S. dollars of products that came into effect afterwards had an obvious early export effect. In July, the year-on-year export growth rate of these products were only 17.3%, but it soared to 40.0% in July and

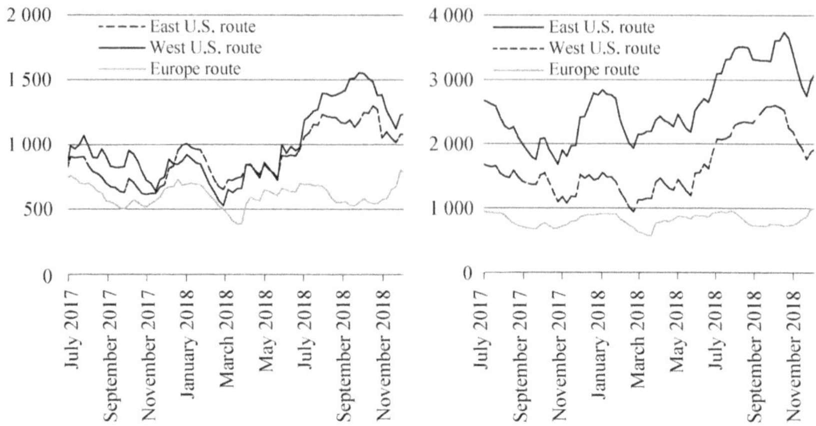

Figure 3.1 Line chart of container freight rates of Ningbo (left) and Shanghai (right) from July 2017 to November 2018.
Source: Wind.

still remained at a high level of 38.1% in August. Likewise, the products on the third round of list were also subject to a relatively significant export robbing effect. The tariff list officially implemented on September 24 had been announced as early as on July 10, 2018, and since then the year-on-year growth rate of the exports of products on the list started to climb rapidly, from 11% in June to 20.7% in September, a marked divergence from its export trend of gradual deceleration since early 2017.

In the short term, robbing the exports before the implementation of additional tariff policies can indeed solve the urgent needs to some extent, but it is difficult to sustain such effect. With the 25% additional tariff coming into effect on August 23, the year-on-year growth rate of exports of products on the second round of tariff list in September rapidly declined to −11.5%. At the end of September 2018, as the third round of additional tariff list involving products valued at 200 billion U.S. dollars officially came into effect, the export growth rate of these products to the U.S. also plummeted from 20.7% in September to 5.3% in October and 1.5% in November. In other words, the data show that the short-term export robbing effect is significantly abated. In January 2019, China's export to the U.S. even registered a negative year-on-year growth rate. Faced with the tremendous pressure brought by the Sino–U.S. trade friction, companies undoubtedly need more long-term initiatives to cope with such severe pressure, as well as the overdraft effect following the short-term export robbing.

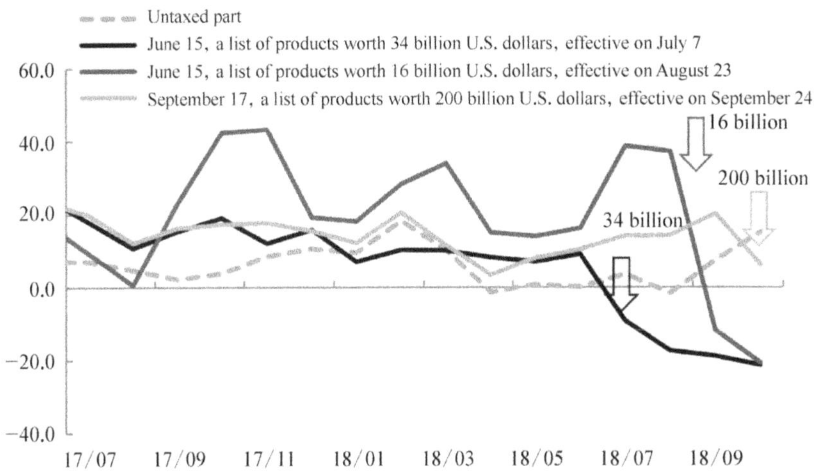

Figure 3.2 Year-on-year percentage of exports to the U.S. under the U.S. additional tariff list, from July 2017 to September 2018.
Source: A study report of Industrial Securities.

3.2.2 Long-term strategies of Chinese enterprises

In the long run, the author believes that Chinese enterprises can cope with the impact of Sino–U.S. trade friction and increasing global economic uncertainty in four ways: industry transfer, export transfer, mastering and improving core competitiveness and reducing dependence on individual trading partners.

3.2.2.1 Industry transfer

Disputes of the Sino–U.S. trade frictions within industries such as the high and new technology sector also reflect another aspect of the development and changes of China's manufacturing sector in recent years. As China's domestic production costs, including labor costs, land costs, and tax burdens, have been on the rise in recent years, the long-term strategy to capture the U.S. market based on price advantages is becoming increasingly difficult. The outbreak of the Sino–U.S. trade friction also further pushes relevant domestic manufacturing companies (industries) in China to move to countries with lower production costs. Taking Vietnam as an example, due to its cheaper labor costs and friendly policies towards foreign investment, a growing number of Chinese enterprises are turning to this country.[12] Sino–U.S. trade friction has also accelerated this transfer process to some extent. In the second half of 2018 alone, the Shenzhen-Vietnam Industrial Park had witnessed a spurt of investment attractions, and most of the related enterprises were concentrated in electronic assembly and other light processing sectors. With China's demographic dividend and cost advantage gradually declining, there is no doubt that industry transfer will become one of the coping strategies for domestic companies to deal with the trade friction and export pressure. It can be foreseen that besides Vietnam, other countries in Asia, Africa, America, and even Europe will also be the destinations for Chinese companies to transfer their industries.

3.2.2.2 Export transfer

A large number of Chinese companies are highly dependent on exports to the U.S., which is also one of the reasons why Chinese companies have been severely affected since the outbreak of the Sino–U.S. trade friction. From the long-term perspective, in order to further offset the impact brought by potential trade frictions and the uncertainties, the development of diversified markets and export transfer are undoubtedly imperative initiatives that Chinese companies can adopt. In fact, many foreign trade enterprises are shifting or have shifted their export destinations to other countries. For example, according to the data from the 124th China Import and Export Fair, Zhejiang Jinhua Jieling Household Products Co. has begun to adjust its market strategy, focusing on developing the European, Southeast Asian, and domestic markets; meanwhile, Kang Mingsheng (Shenzhen) Technology Co., Ltd. focuses on countries along the "the Belt and Road" route. "Do not put all eggs in the same basket." For foreign trade export enterprises, regarding a single country or region as the main exporting market bears extremely great risk. Foreign trade export enterprises should continue to optimize their trade structure, explore diversified international markets, try to minimize the loss of trade friction, and achieve healthy development. To some extent, the Sino–U.S. trade friction is both a challenge and an opportunity, further promoting the awareness and paces of Chinese companies to expand overseas markets.

3.2.2.3 Mastering and improving core competitiveness

From this Sino–U.S. trade friction, those who are most affected are the companies with low profit margins that are solely engaged in processing and have no technological advantage. Meanwhile, companies with advanced technologies and whose products have gradually become rigid-demanded goods for U.S. buyers experience limited impact. Shanghai Zhenhua Heavy Industries Co., Ltd. (hereinafter referred to as ZPMC) is used as an example. Quay-cranes and cranes manufactured by ZPMC were on the third-round additional tariff list against China announced by the U.S. on July 10, 2018, and all their products met the classification of HTS code 84261900 of "overhead traveling cranes, transporter cranes, gantry and bridge cranes." However, on September 24, 2018, when the U.S. officially implemented the additional tariff product list, the above-mentioned products of ZPMC were no longer listed. The reason why ZPMC was "spared from the tariff" was to a large extent due to the hearing held in late August of that year. The American Association of Port Authorities and the port clients of ZPMC in the U.S. complained to the U.S. government. The complaint was filed on the ground that ZPMC's products could meet the demand of the U.S. market in terms of quantities and quality, for which the U.S. had no substitute of its own; giving trade orders to other countries would only lead to higher costs at U.S. ports, which would eventually be detrimental to the interests of the U.S. In the end, in the announced additional tariff list, the U.S. government excluded relevant products of ZPMC.[13] After the outbreak of the trade friction between China and the U.S., only the owners of core technology and competitiveness can occupy the high ground of negotiation. Only by mastering key technologies and continuously improving competitiveness can enterprises stand firm in the ever-changing environment.

3.2.2.4 Reducing dependence on individual trading partners

In addition to more tariffs, the Sino–U.S. trade friction is also reflected on the U.S. frequently citing the so-called intellectual property rights and national security as reasons for sanctioning and cracking down Chinese companies, especially high-tech companies. Since 2018 alone, Chinese companies involved in the various bans and restrictions issued by the U.S. are: China's most powerful electronic technology company, Huawei; the global leader in drones, DJI; once the highest-valued electronics stock in the A-share market, Hikvision; the top four global telecommunication companies and the top three integrated circuit producers in China, ZTE; the leading global nuclear company, China General Nuclear Power Corporation (CGN); China's largest state-owned electronic technology company, China Electronics Technology Group Corporation (CETC); and JHICC, which is responsible for the development of domestically produced storage devices. Without exception, the imports and exports of these companies are heavily relied on the U.S., and one of the ways the U.S. sanctions these companies is to ban on the exports of U.S. companies to them. As mentioned earlier, the ban in the ZTE case alone has brought ZTE to the brink of collapse. This is a further indication that if Chinese companies want to win this enduring war, they should try to reduce their dependence on trade with individual countries and industries. The objective is to diversify risks and improve comprehensive competitiveness in the current volatile trade climate.

Notes

1 This is further supported by the findings of Fan et al. (2017). In addition, the two countries also show relatively significant differences in the import tariff levels on intermediate goods and consumer goods: in the U.S., tariffs on imported consumer goods are significantly higher than those on intermediate inputs and

capital goods, and import tariffs on intermediate inputs are also greater than those on capital goods; In contrast, tariffs on China's imported capital goods and intermediate inputs are roughly similar.

2 For example, according to the studies of Yu (2015) and Halpern, Koren, and Szeidl (2015), a reduction in tariffs on intermediate goods can help enterprises reduce production costs and thus improve their export performance and export product premiums.

3 Some other studies (Feenstra, Markusen, and Zeile, 1992; Kasahara and Rodrigues, 2008; Halpern et al., 2015; Yu, 2010) also further demonstrate this point.

4 The Office of the United States Trade Representative (USTR) was created by Congress under the Trade Expansion Act of 1962 and implemented by President Kennedy in Executive Order 11075 on January 15, 1963. USTR refers to both the United States Trade Representative and the agency responsible for it. The Presidential Executive Order 12188, signed by President Carter on January 4, 1980, authorized USTR to develop and administer all trade policies of the U.S. Meanwhile, USTR is also designated as the chief negotiator of the U.S. and serves as the U.S. representative in major international trade organizations. In terms of specific responsibilities, USTR is responsible for developing and coordinating U.S. international trade, commodities, and direct investment policies; directing or guiding the negotiations with other countries on such matters and providing trade policy guidance and expert opinions on negotiations in the main areas of its responsibilities. In addition, the agency also has administrative responsibility for complaints against foreign unfair trade practices under the Generalized System of Preferences (GSP), Section 301, Section 1377, and Section 337, and for import remedy cases under Section 201.

5 Section 301 investigations are investigations conducted by the U.S. under Section 301. Generally speaking, Section 301 is the legislative authorization clause in the U.S. Trade Act that are related to taking unilateral actions against acts by foreign legislation or administration that breach the agreements and hurt the interests of the U.S. It was originally found under the Trade Expansion Act of 1962, and after a series of amendments, it now commonly refers to all contents of Sections 1301-1310 in the Omnibus Trade and Competitiveness Act of 1988. Its primary meaning is to protect the rights of the U.S. in international trades, and retaliate against countries whose trade practices are considered as "unreasonable" and "unjustified". Under this clause, the U.S. can investigate the trade practices of other countries that it deems "unjustified" and can negotiate with the government of the relevant countries. Ultimately, the President decides on retaliatory measures, such as hiking tariffs, restricting imports, and halting relevant agreements.

6 Section 232 investigation refers to the investigation by the U.S. Department of Commerce, authorized by Section 232 of the Trade Expansion Act of 1962, into whether the import of particular products will jeopardize the national security of the U.S. It is required to submit a report to the President within 270 days after the filing of the investigation, and the President has to make a decision within 90 days on whether to take final action on the import of relevant products.

7 "Double reverse" investigation, a collective term for antidumping and countervailing investigations, refers to simultaneous antidumping and countervailing investigations into the same category of products from a country (or countries) or a region (or regions). If a country's imports enter the domestic market at dumped prices or at low prices while receiving subsidies from the government of the exporting country, and cause material damages or threats to the same industries in that country, WTO allows members to use trade remedies such as antidumping and countervailing measures to protect the legitimate interests of domestic

industries, thus restoring the normal import order and a fair trade environment. According to the relevant provisions of WTO, if a member wants to implement antidumping measures, it must satisfy the following three conditions: First, it must be established that there is dumping. Second, it must be determined that the industry's imports have caused material damage or material threat of damage to the domestic industry. Third, a causal link between dumping and the damage must be determined.

8 Relevant data come from press releases of U.S. Department of Commerce.

9 Citing ongoing AI and automated driving projects as an example, China's vast market and immense scale manufacturing industry provide a huge number of potential users, rich scenarios, and gargantuan market capacity for the application of new technologies of Intel. For instance, China will be a potential future market for pilotless automobiles. Data from the China Association of Automobile Manufacturers (CAAM) show that as the world's largest producer and consumer of automobiles, in 2018, China's production and sales of automobiles were 27.809 million and 28.081 million, respectively, accounting for nearly 1/3 of the shares in the global automotive market.

10 This may be due to the fact that initially, Chinese exporters did not take the threat of additional tariffs imposed by the U.S. very seriously and thus did not react promptly after the first round of tariff list was published.

11 The three rounds of list are: the list of products worth 34 billion U.S. dollars that came into effect on July 6, 2018, the list of products worth 16 billion U.S. dollars that came into effect on August 23, 2018, and the list of products worth 200 billion U.S. dollars came into effect on September 24, 2019. etc. See appendices at the end of the book for specific products related on the three rounds of lists.

12 According to Vietnam tax law, foreign investors can enjoy "two exemptions and four half reductions" for investment projects in many industries, i.e., exemption of corporate income tax for the first two years and half reduction on the tax for the following four years; and for some high-tech industries, Vietnam also offers a more favorable policy of "four exemptions and nine half reductions".

13 In fact, for the U.S. market, the products manufactured by ZPMC have a very high market share (about 75%), and no related enterprise in the U.S. can manufacture bridge cranes by their own. The second largest supplier to ZPMC comes from Europe, whose market share is only 5%, far from meeting the demand of the U.S. market for crane bridges.

4 Tariff, terms of trade and welfare

4.1 Terms of trade and welfare

4.1.1 Influence of terms of trade on welfare

In standard trade theory, the magnitude of and changes in the terms of trade are often used to measure a country's welfare level and changes in trade. By definition, Terms of Trade (TOT) refers to the proportion of foreign imports that a country can exchange for each unit of goods exported over a period of time, and it is often expressed as the ratio of the export price index to the import price index for the period. An improvement in a country's terms of trade implies that it can exchange more foreign imports for each unit of goods exported, which in turn contributes to the improvement in the country's welfare level. In other words, an enhancement in a country's terms of trade improves the welfare level, while a deterioration in the terms of trade decreases the welfare level. Next, this section provides a theoretical analysis of this effect, specifically using the example of a simple economy with two countries and two sectors.

Assuming that the world consists of only the U.S. and China, both of which produce Product A and Product B, the production and trade situation of the two countries are shown in Table 4.1. The output of the two categories of products in the two countries is represented by Q_A and Q_B as well as Q_A^* and Q_B^*, respectively. The U.S. exports Product A, in which it has a comparative advantage, and China exports Product B. Taking the U.S. as an example, as shown in Figure 4.1, when the output of Product A increases and that of Product B decreases, the production point moves from point Q^1 to point Q^2 (*PPF* is the production possibility frontier), and the isovalue line corresponding to the consumption point moves from IL^1 to IL^2. Then, the relative price P_A/P_B rises and the consumption point moves from D^1 to D^2 (the consumption point is the tangent point between the indifference curve and the isovalue line). According to the basic microeconomic principle, the relative magnitude of the consumer's utility level can be used to represent the magnitude of the welfare level, while the indifference curve in turn represents the magnitude of the utility level. It can be found that at this

Table 4.1 Production and trade of China and the U.S.

	Production		*Export*
The U.S.	Q_A	Q_B	Product A
China	Q_A^*	Q_B^*	Product B

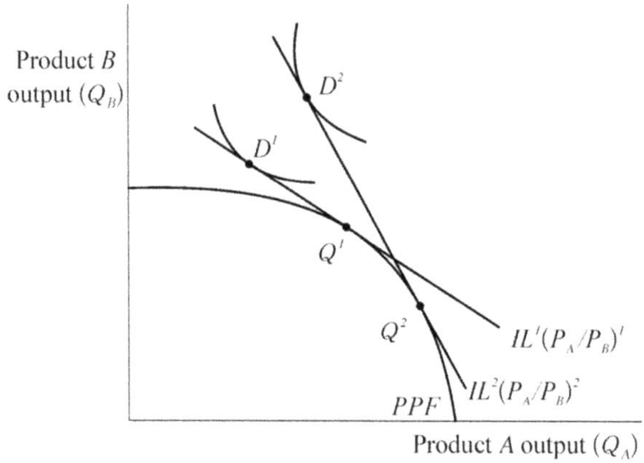

Figure 4.1 Welfare impact of the rise on relative price of Product A.

point, compared to D^1, the consumption point D^2 moves to a higher indifference curve with an improved welfare level.

On the other hand, the relative price of Product A will also rise when product point moves from Q^1 to Q^2. Since it is assumed that the U.S. exports Product A, all else being equal, exporting the same quantity of Product A in this case will be able to exchange for a greater quantity of Product B, which will result in improved terms of trade and welfare.

It is important to note that the movement of the consumption point (D) involves both an income effect and a substitution effect. The income effect leads to an increase in the consumption of both products, while the substitution effect is reflected in a increase in the relative demand for Product B and the reduction in the relative demand for Product A. In general, since the impact of income effect will outweigh the substitution effect, it can be concluded that, in general, when the terms of trade change in a direction that favors an increase in the relative price of Product A, the welfare level of the country producing and exporting Product A will increase; accordingly, when the terms of trade change in a direction that favors an increase in the relative price of Product B, the welfare level of the country producing and exporting Product B will improve.

4.1.2 Determination of terms of trade

So how are the terms of trade (i.e., the relative prices of exported products) determined? In the following part, this section will illustrate and analyze it on the basis of the previous assumptions about national production and trade.

It is still assumed that there are only two countries in the world, the U.S. and China, and that the U.S. exports Product A to and imports Product B from China, while China imports Product A from and exports Product B to the U.S. Terms of trade of the two countries are expressed as the relative prices of the two products of the U.S. (P_A/P_B) and China (P_A/P_B), respectively.

According to basic microeconomic principles, in order to obtain the relative price of Product A, P_A/P_B, it is important to derive the world relative supply curve and the world relative demand curve for Product A from the relative output and price levels of the two categories of products. According to the classical supply and demand theory, when the relative price of Product A rises, both countries produce more of Product A and correspondingly reduce the production input on Product B, meanwhile, the relative demand for Product A to Product B decreases. Therefore, as shown in Figure 4.2, the upward sloping curve RS_A represents the relative supply curve of Product A between China and the U.S., while the downward sloping curve RD_A represents the relative demand curve of Product A. The intersection of the two curves is the resulting relative price $(P_A/P_B)^E$ of Product A at the equilibrium, which is the terms of trade of the U.S.

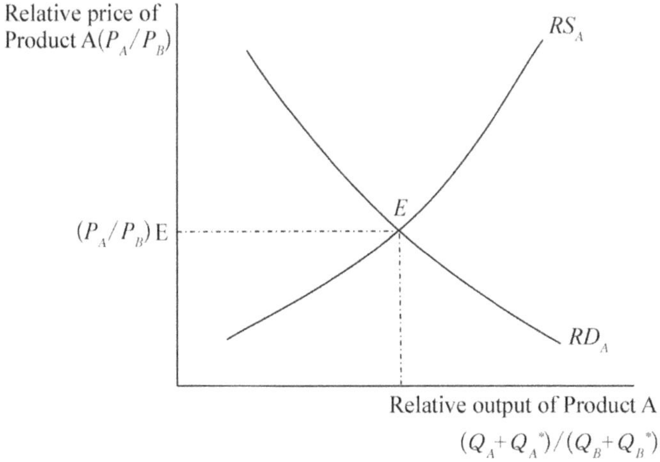

Figure 4.2 The determination of the world relative price.

4.2 Tariff changes, terms of trade, and welfare

In the Sino–U.S. trade friction, tariffs are undoubtedly an important means and measure for both sides to play games with each other. Changes in tariff levels impact the welfare levels in both countries by influencing terms of trade. Based on the standard trade model, this section briefly explains the mechanisms by which tariff changes affect welfare levels at the theoretical level.

Taking the simple economy with two states, China and the U.S., and two sectors. Considering that both countries are large trading nations, a change in their tariff policies will have a large impact on the world relative supply and relative demand, thus changing world relative prices under equilibrium conditions. It needs to be noted in particular that the terms of trade corresponds to the proportion of products exchanged abroad. Therefore, when using relative price to proxy the terms of trade, this price index is an external price index, that is, prices in the world market (external prices) rather than prices in the domestic market (internal price).[1]

When the U.S. unilaterally levies import tariffs on imports from China, Product B, its domestic consumers will face an increase in the relative price (internal price) of the imported Product B, which in turn reduces the demand for it. At the same time, U.S. producers can set higher relative prices for Product B, increasing the relative supply of it. Since the U.S. is a large trading nation, the worldwide demand of Product B will decrease (the RD_A^1 in Figure 4.3 moves to RD_A^2), while the world supply of Product B will increase (RS_A^1 shifts to RS_A^2). Obviously, the world relative price of Product A at the equilibrium rises from $(P_A/P_B)^{E1}$ to $(P_A/P_B)^{E2}$. This also means that the world relative price (external price) of Product B will fall and that of Product A will rise. Thus, when the U.S. unilaterally imposes tariffs on imports from China, it improves its own terms of trade (the relatively prices of its exports increases), while China's terms of trade deteriorate (the relative price of its exports decreases).

4.3 Cost–benefit analysis under the tariff revenue

According to the aforementioned analysis, an increase in the world relative price of exported products implies an improvement in a country's terms of trade, which in turn means that the welfare level in that country has been improved. However, this improvement ignores the impact of tariff revenues, which, in the real world, are undoubtedly one of the imperative and non-negligible factors in trade frictions. In order to better explain the impact of tariffs on a country's overall welfare level in the real world, this section will apply cost–benefit analysis based on the three-sector economy, analyzing the impact of tariff changes on the terms of trade (welfare level) after taking tariff revenues into consideration.

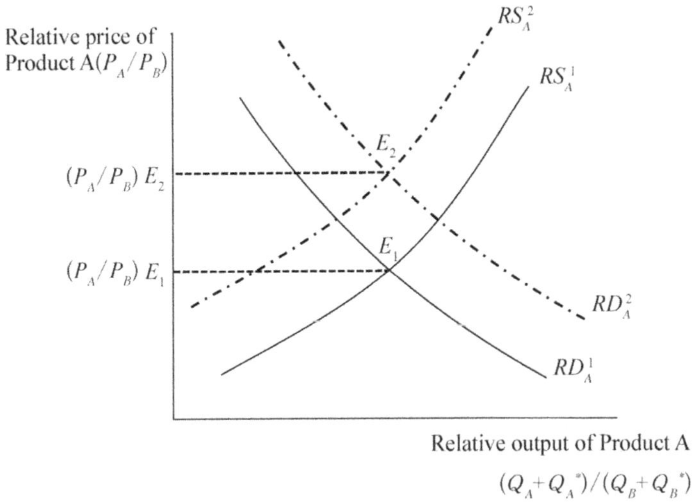

Figure 4.3 Tariffs and terms of trade.

Figure 4.4 specifically depicts the transmission mechanism of the price effect of tariffs across markets. When the U.S. unilaterally levies a tariff on Product B imported from China, the domestic price of the product in the U.S. increases from P_w to P_T. And, domestic producers of the U.S. will be willing to input more resources into the production of Product B, thereby increasing its supply. In the meantime, due to higher relative price of Product B, consumers will reduce their demand for Product B. Given that the U.S. is a large country, this will affect the demand for Product B in the world market through the "large country effect", as reflected in Figure 4.4, that is, the world relative demand will shift from point 1 to point 2 on the curve *MD*. At this point, for Chinese producers, a decline in the market demand for Product B will cause its price to fall to $P_T^* = P_T - t$. Correspondingly, the domestic production level of Product B in China declines, which in turn leads to a reduction in exports (it affects the supply of Product B in the world market, moving from point 1 to point 3 on the *XS* curve). Then, for the U.S., changes in sectoral welfare levels can be measured by changes in producer surplus and consumer surplus.

4.3.1 Producer surplus and consumer surplus

According to basic microeconomics, producer surplus measures the difference between the prices at which producers are willing to sell the products they produce and the actual prices of the goods sold. The larger the difference, the higher the actual selling price of the product produced by the

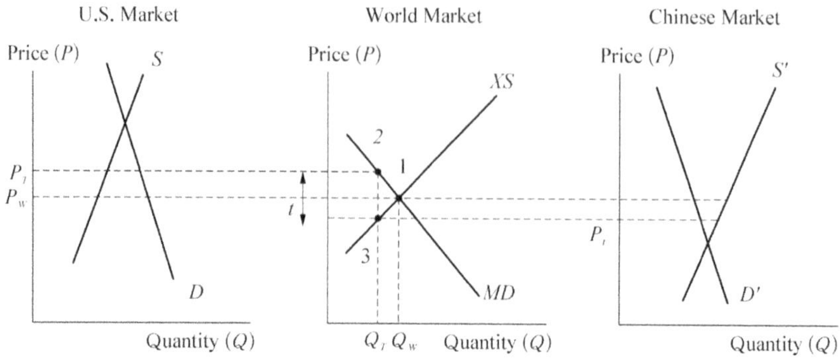

Figure 4.4 Impact of tariffs on terms of trade in different markets.

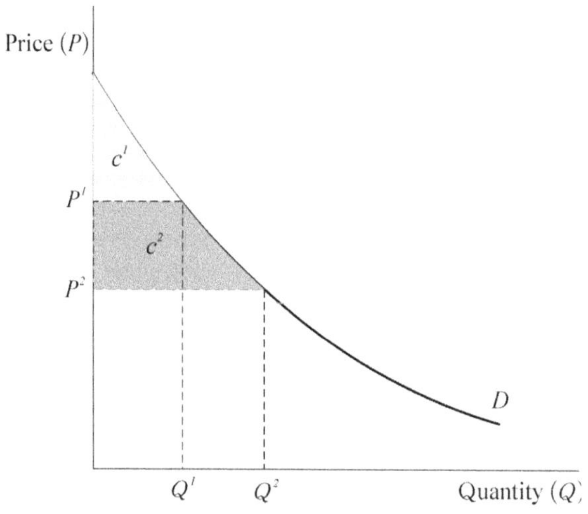

Figure 4.5 Geometric representation of producer surplus.

producer, and the more producer surplus the producer will receive. As shown in Figure 4.5, this is reflected in the expansion in the area above the supply curve and below the price line. It can be seen from Figure 4.5, when the price is P^2, the producer surplus is c^2; and when the price increases to P^1, producer surplus rises to $(c^1 + c^2)$.

Likewise, consumer surplus measures the difference between the price consumers are willing to pay for a product and the price they actually pay. Similar to producer surplus, the larger the difference between prices (the lower the actual price paid), the larger the consumer surplus, which is

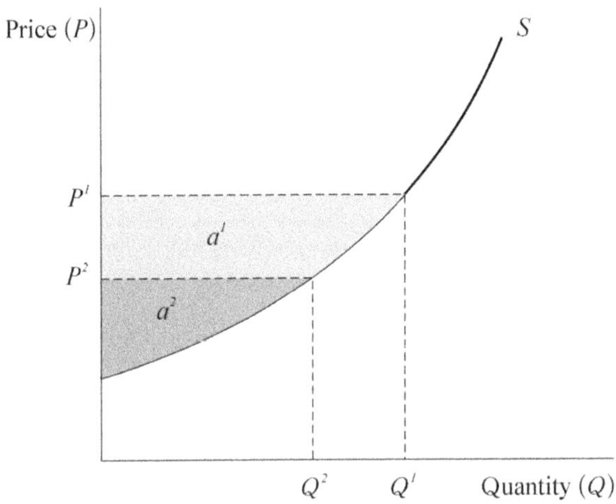

Figure 4.6 Geometric representation of consumer surplus.

reflected in the expansion in the area below the demand curve and above the price line. As shown in Figure 4.6, when the price is at P^1, the consumer surplus is c^1; and when the price falls to P^2, the consumer surplus increases to $(c^1 + c^2)$.

4.3.2 Cost and benefit

Next, combining the aforementioned relevant definitions of producer surplus and consumer surplus, the author uses cost–benefit analysis and specifically takes the example of the unilateral imposition of import tariffs by the U.S. to analyze changes in the welfare level of the importing country after taking into consideration the impact of tariff revenue. As shown in Figure 4.7, when the U.S. unilaterally levies a tariff on Product B, which is imported from China, the world price of the product at this point is denoted as P_W, and its domestic price in the U.S. is raised to P_T. Since the U.S. is a large country, the taxation actions of its government will force a decrease in worldwide demand for products imported from China, which will in turn result in the world price of Product B falling to P_T^*.

First, for the impact of tariff changes on U.S. producers, when the price of Product B is raised to P_T as a result of the imposition of tariff, domestic producers in the U.S. will be more willing to produce Product B, leading to the production quantity rising from S^1 to S^2, and the domestic producer surplus of the U.S. (change in the area above the supply curve and below the price line) increasing by area a.

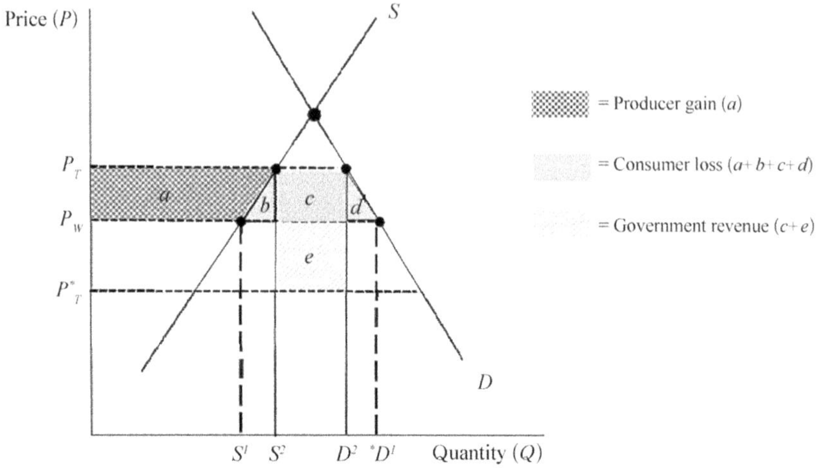

Figure 4.7 Cost and benefit of taxation on China.

Second, for the impact of tariff changes on U.S. consumers, according to the definition of consumer surplus, after the tariff is imposed, the consumer surplus is reduced by $a + b + c + d$ (that is the area between the price change curves and the demand curve).

Since the U.S. is a major trading nation, the imposition of additional tariffs will force a decline in the world price of imported products, so government revenues are equal to the product of tariff rate t $(P_T - P_T^*)$ and the import quantity $(D^2 - S^2)$. This is shown in Figure 4.7 as the area of $(c + e)$.

Combining the profit and loss analysis of the three sectors, it can be concluded that the net effect of tariff changes = government revenue + producer gain − consumer loss. This is expressed in Figure 4.7 as the sum of the following areas:

$$(c + e) + a - (a + b + c + d) = e - (b + d)$$

where the rectangle e measures the trade gains from the change in world price of Product B exported from the U.S. due to the reduction in tariffs. The triangles, b and d, represent the extent to which domestic production and consumption are distorted in the process of tariff imposition, respectively, that is, the efficiency losses in the U.S. consumption and production sectors. In other words, the impact of a country's imposition of tariff on social welfare depends on the magnitude of the trade gains and efficiency losses. Thus, unlike the previous analysis on terms of trade under the standard trade model, the research under cost–benefit analysis shows that even if the U.S. unilaterally levies import tariffs, the welfare effect of its own is not necessarily positive.

Summary

This chapter begins with a study of classic trade theory and analyzes the impact of tariff changes on a country's terms of trade and its welfare level. Specifically, it contains the following main points:

1. Terms of trade refers to the proportion of foreign imports that a country can exchange for each unit of goods exported over a period of time, and it is often expressed as the ratio of the export price index to the import price index for the period.
2. Changes in tariffs can affect the terms of trade and thus the welfare level. For large countries, the imposition of tariffs on imports improve its terms of trade and increase its welfare.
3. After taking into consideration the impact of tariff revenues, a cost–benefit analysis reveals that the impact of the imposition of import tariffs on social welfare depends on the relative magnitude of trade gains and efficiency losses. Analyses based on cost–benefit models implies that in the Sino–U.S. trade friction, even though the unilateral imposition of tariff by the U.S. will improve its terms of trade, the ultimate impact on its welfare may be negative.

Note

1 As can be seen from Figure 4.1, when using the terms of trade to analyze country welfare, we assume that a country's income is always equal to its GDP, where the effect of tariff revenue is neglected.

5 Trade in intermediate goods and Sino–U.S. trade friction

5.1 Stylized facts

According to the relevant research in Chapter 1, it can be learned that under the classification by BEC, a country's imports can be divided into four categories: intermediate goods, capital goods, final goods and other goods.

Figure 5.1 plots the share of various imports of the total imports of the country in China and the U.S. according to the classification by BEC during 2011–2014. Consistent with the relevant studies in Chapters 1 and 2, among various imports of the two countries, intermediate goods account for a relatively high share of approximately 50% or more in each country. If capital goods are also considered as intermediate goods, then the imported intermediate goods of each country make up about 70% of its total imports.[1]

In China, the share is as high as 90%. A further comparison of the composition of imports between the two countries shows that the import share of final products in the U.S. is larger than that in China's, while the import share of intermediate goods in China is far larger than that in the U.S. Based on this, typical fact 1 can be obtained.

5.1.1 Stylized fact 1

Trade in intermediate goods occupies an important position in the trade of both China and the U.S., with the vast majority of products imported by both countries being intermediate goods; however, in relative terms, the import share of intermediate goods in China is much larger than that in the U.S., while the import share of final goods in the U.S. exceeds that of China.

Next, looking at the trade between China and the U.S., Figure 5.2 depicts the share of various categories of imports of the total imports from each other in the period 2011–2014. As can be seen from the graph, among all categories of products the U.S. imported from China, consumer goods, capital goods and final goods account for an equal share; while among the products China imported from the U.S., nearly 60% of the products being intermediate goods, and the import share of final goods being smaller. In other words, a comparison of the composition of imports between the two

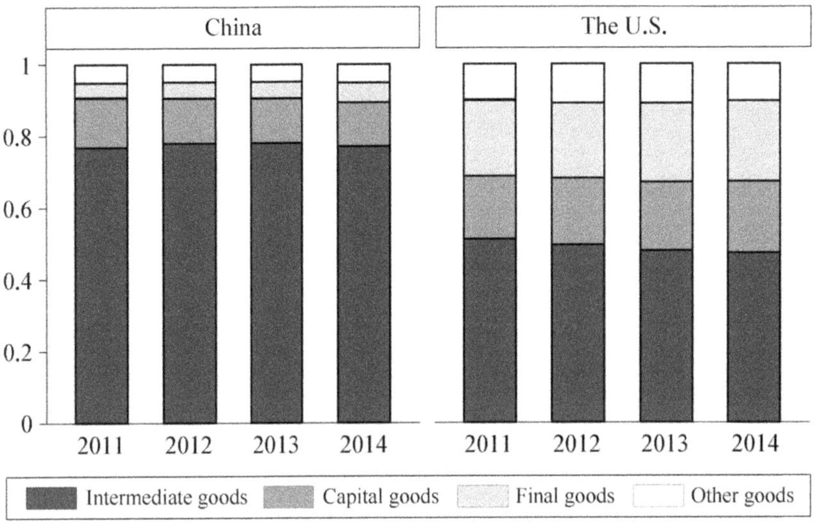

Figure 5.1 The share of various imports of the total imports in China and the U.S. during 2011–2014.
Source: it is depicted by the author according to the CEPII trade data and classification by BEC.

countries shows that most of China's imports from the U.S. are intermediate goods; in contrast, the U.S. imports a higher proportion of final goods from China. According to this, typical fact 2 can be obtained.[2]

5.1.2 Stylized fact 2

In the Sino–U.S. trade, intermediate goods account for the vast majority of China's imports from the U.S. and is significantly higher proportion than the share of intermediate goods imported by the U.S. from China; Meanwhile, the share of final goods imported by the U.S. from China is significantly higher than that of final products imported by China from the U.S.

According to the additional tariff product lists imposed by the two countries against each other during this Sino–U.S. trade friction,[3] it is easy to find that on the lists, with the exception of some final consumer goods, most of the products involved are intermediate goods, such as automobile parts, oxides, etc. So, what will be the result if the impact of the Sino–U.S. trade friction on the welfare levels of the two countries is examined from the perspective of trade in intermediate goods? This issue will be explored more specifically from both theoretical and quantitative analysis perspectives in the following Sections 5.2–5.4.

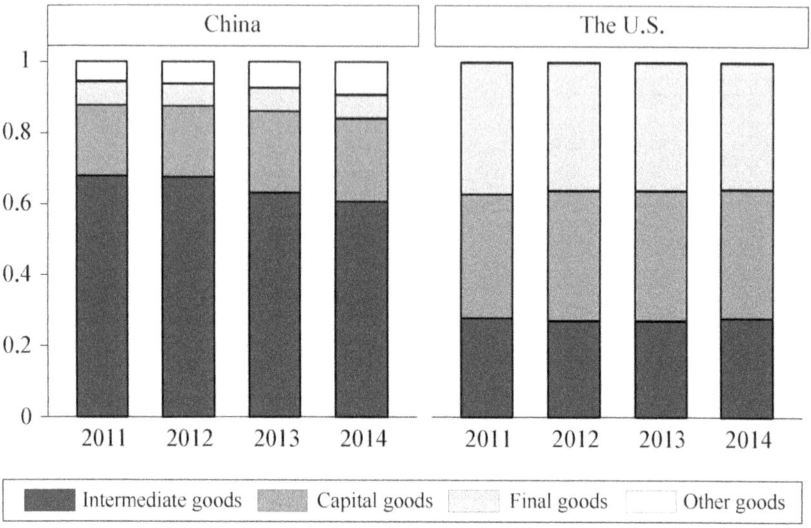

Figure 5.2 The share of various imports of the total imports from each other in China and the U.S. during 2011–2014.
Source: it is depicted by the author according to the CEPII trade data and classification by BEC.

5.2 Theoretical models and parameter estimations

Based on the study of Melitz and Ottaviano (2008), this section constructs a heterogeneous firm model with variable profit markup.[4] This model assumes that the world consists of two countries, a home country (H) and a foreign country (F), and that consumers in each country are denoted as L_H and L_F, respectively. In the meantime, each consumer is also a producer, and each consumer has a unit of labor endowment. The basic framework of the model is as follows.

5.2.1 Demand side model

The utility function of a representative consumer of country $l(l = H, F)$ is as follows:

$$U_l = q_{l,o}^c + \alpha \int_{i\in\Omega_l} q_{l,i}^c di - \frac{1}{2}\gamma \int_{i\in\Omega_l} (q_{l,i}^c)^2 di - \frac{1}{2}\left(\int_{i\in\Omega_l} q_{l,i}^c di\right)^2. \qquad (1)$$

Using homogeneous goods as valuation goods, in the equation, $q_{l,o}^c$ and $q_{l,i}^c$ represent the consumption of a single consumer on homogeneous and heterogeneous goods in Country l; Ω_l is the set of heterogeneous goods sold in Country l; all of the parameters α, γ, and η are positive and γ represents the degree of difference between two goods in any product category; if $\gamma = 0$, then this product is considered to be perfect substitute. And the consumer only needs to maximize the consumption level of all categories of products $Q_l^c = \int_{i\in\Omega_l} q_{l,i}^c di$.

Assuming that the income level of consumers in both countries is sufficiently high, the demand for the valuation goods is positive in both countries, i.e., $q_{l,o}^c > 0$. For Country l, the price level at which the profit of any of its product category i is maximized shall satisfy

$$p_{l,i} = \alpha - \gamma q_{l,i}^c - \eta Q_l^c. \tag{2}$$

Since $q_{l,i}^c > 0$, $M_l \bar{p}_l = \alpha M_l - (\eta M_l + \gamma) Q_l^c$. In the equation, M_l measures the products consumed among the set of heterogeneous goods Ω_l, and $\bar{p}_l = (\frac{1}{M_l}) \int_{i\in\Omega_l} p_{l,i} di$ represents the average price of the products of domestic trade enterprises and export enterprises in Country l.

Replacing Q_l^c in the Equation (2) using the above equation, Equation (3) can be obtained

$$q_{l,i} \equiv L_l q_{l,i}^c = \frac{\alpha L_l}{\eta M_l + \gamma} - \frac{L_l}{\gamma} p_{l,i} + \frac{\eta M_l}{\eta M_l + \gamma} \frac{L_l}{\gamma} \bar{p}_l, \ \forall\ i \in \Omega_l, \tag{3}$$

where $p_{l,\,i}$ satisfies $p_{l,i} \le \frac{\alpha\gamma + \eta M_l \bar{p}_l}{\eta M_l + \gamma} \equiv p_l^{max}$. In the equation, the price in the right side of the equation satisfies $p_l^{max} \le \alpha$: If and only if it is at this price level, consumer demand for the good approaches zero, and the equality holds.

5.2.2 Supply side model

5.2.2.1 Technology level

This section defines technology level as the unit of labor required to produce a unit of homogeneous good. It is assumed that homogeneous external goods are produced jointly by both countries and are freely traded between them, so the wage in both countries can be normalized as 1. Since the production of heterogeneous final goods requires a package of intermediate inputs, and all firms need to pay additional costs when undertaking the production and development of a new product, firms need higher production costs to produce heterogeneous final goods; meanwhile, it is assumed here that their subsequent production will generate incremental returns to scale.

Although a firm may produce multiple heterogeneous products, each of them can produce only one core product. The production of the core product corresponds to the core competitiveness of the company and is related to the core productivity ϕ of the company. To obtain this core productivity, a firm must first pay a cost f_e to enter the market. The model assumes that each firm's core productivity is randomly drawn from its known productivity distribution $G(\phi)$, and the range of ϕ is $[\phi_{min}, \infty)$.

5.2.2.2 *Source of intermediate inputs and marginal costs*

$a_j(v, \phi)$ represents the units of labor needed by country $j(j \in [H, F])$ to produce a unit of intermediate good $v(v \in [0, 1])$

$$c_l(\{h(v)\}_{v=0}^{1}, \phi) = \frac{1}{\phi}\left(\int_0^1 [\tau^g_{h(v)l} a_{h(v)}(v, \phi)]^{1-p} dv\right)^{\frac{1}{1-p}}, \quad (4)$$

where τ^g_{hl} represents the trade cost of Country l importing intermediate goods from the country of origin $h(v)$. When $h(v) \neq l$, $\tau^g_{ll} = 1$, and $\tau^g_{h(v)l} > 1$.[5]

Referring to the study by Eaton and Kortum (2002), it is assumed that the efficiency distribution in the production of intermediate goods in a country follows the following Frechet distribution.

$$\Pr(a_h(v, \phi) \leq a) = e^{-T_h a^{-\theta}},$$

where $T_h > 0$, and this parameter determines the technology level of Country h. θ determines the variation in the selected productivity level. Thus, marginal cost ϕ of the final good produced by Country l is required to satisfy

$$c_l(\phi) = \frac{1}{\phi}[\xi\Theta_l]^{-1/\theta}, \quad (5)$$

where $\Theta_l = T_l + T_h(\tau^g_{hl})^{-\theta}$ represents the ability of enterprises in Country l to obtain intermediate goods, $\xi = [\Gamma(\frac{\theta+1-\rho}{\theta})]^{\theta/(1-\rho)}$, and Γ represents Gamma function.

5.2.2.3 *Corporate behavior*

Given the average price level $\bar{p}_l$ and the number of product M_l, when the profit is maximized, the quantity $q_{lh}(\phi)$ of product ϕ produced by Country l to export to Country h can be expressed as[6]

$$q_{lh}(\phi) = \frac{L_h}{\gamma}[p_h^{max} - p_{lh}(\phi).$$

In the domestic market, under profit maximization conditions, the price of each type of product ϕ to be produced must be lower than p_l^{max}. Denote ϕ_{ll} as the productivity threshold for producing that product when the firm's profit is exactly zero. When its core productivity meets $\phi < \phi_{ll}$, the firm cannot make profit from producing any of its products, including its core product. Then, the firm will withdraw from the production of that product. And $\phi = \phi_{ll}$ represents the exact critical value of productivity at which the firm is able to survive in the market. At this point, it is easy to obtain the critical marginal cost of production in the domestic market

$$c_{ll} = p_{ll}(\phi_{ll}) = p_l^{max}. \tag{6}$$

Solving the profit maximization problem $\max_{pll(\phi)} \pi_{ll}(\phi) = [p_{ll}(\phi) - c_l(\phi) q_{ll}(\phi)]$, the firm's sales price in the domestic market can be calculated as follows:

$$p_{ll}(\phi) = \frac{1}{2}[c_{ll} + c_l(\phi)] = \frac{[\xi\Theta_l]^{-1/\theta}}{2}\left[\frac{1}{\phi_{ll}} + \frac{1}{\phi}\right]. \tag{7}$$

Accordingly, other firm performance indicators related to the firm's domestic sales, including the firm's absolute cost plus $\mu_{ll}(\phi)$, domestic sales volume $q_{ll}(\phi)$, domestic sales revenue $r_{ll}(\phi)$ and domestic sales profit $\pi_{ll}(\phi)$ can be expressed as

$$\mu_{ll}(\phi) = \frac{1}{2}[c_{ll} - c_l(\phi)] = \frac{[\xi\Theta_l]^{-1/\theta}}{2}\left[\frac{1}{\phi_{ll}} - \frac{1}{\phi}\right], \tag{8}$$

$$q_{ll}(\phi) = \frac{L_l}{2\gamma}[c_{ll} - c_l(\phi)] = \frac{L_l[\xi\Theta_l]^{-1/\theta}}{2\gamma}\left[\frac{1}{\phi_{ll}} - \frac{1}{\phi}\right], \tag{9}$$

$$r_{ll}(\phi) = \frac{L_l}{4\gamma}[c_{ll}^2 - c_l(\phi)^2] = \frac{L_l[\xi\Theta_l]^{-2/\theta}}{4\gamma}\left[\frac{1}{\phi_{ll}^2} - \frac{1}{\phi^2}\right], \tag{10}$$

$$\pi_{ll}(\phi) = \frac{L_l}{4\gamma}[c_{ll} - c_l(\phi)]^2 = \frac{L_l[\xi\Theta_l]^{-2/\theta}}{4\gamma}\left[\frac{1}{\phi_{ll}} - \frac{1}{\phi}\right]^2 \tag{11}$$

In addition, when the goods produced by a firm in a country are sold on the domestic market, as long as the firm is able to earn a non-negative profit, it will engage in export trade at the same time. Assuming that transport costs are zero, the trade cost per unit of final goods obeys $\tau_{lh}^{f} > 1$, so that the unit cost of the product ϕ produced by Country l, trade cost included, can be denoted as $\tau_{lh}^{f} c_l(\phi)$. Similar to the previous analysis, in foreign market h, there is a critical marginal cost c_{hh} that corresponds to the critical productivity of a particular product category ϕ_{hh}.

Similarly, maximizing the following export profit level of the firms:

$$\pi_{lh}(\phi) = (p_{lh}(\phi) - \tau_{lh}^{f} c_l(\phi) q_{lh}(\phi),$$

we will have

$$p_{lh}(\phi) = \frac{1}{2}[c_{hh} + \tau_{lh}^{f} c_l(\phi)] = \frac{\tau_{lh}^{f}[\xi\Theta_l]^{-1/\theta}}{2}\left[\frac{1}{\phi_{lh}} + \frac{1}{\phi}\right] \tag{12}$$

$$\mu_{lh}(\phi) = \frac{1}{2}[c_{hh} - \tau_{lh}^{f} c_l(\phi)] = \frac{\tau_{lh}^{f}[\xi\Theta_l]^{-1/\theta}}{2}\left[\frac{1}{\phi_{lh}} - \frac{1}{\phi}\right] \tag{13}$$

$$q_{lh}(\phi) = \frac{L_h}{2\gamma}[c_{hh} - \tau_{lh}^{f} c_l(\phi)] = \frac{L_h \tau_{lh}^{f}[\xi\Theta_1]^{-1/\theta}}{2\gamma} \tag{14}$$

$$r_{lh}(\phi) = \frac{L_h}{4\gamma}[c_{hh}^{2} - \tau_{lh}^{f} c_l(\phi)^2] = \frac{L_h(\tau_{lh}^{f}[\xi\Theta_1]^{-1/\theta})^2}{4\gamma} \tag{15}$$

$$\pi_{lh}(\phi) = \frac{L_h}{4\gamma}[c_{hh} - \tau_{lh}^{f} c_l(\phi)]^2 = \frac{L_h(\tau_{lh}^{f}[\xi\Theta_l]^{-1/\theta})^2}{4\gamma}\left[\frac{1}{\phi_{lh}} - \frac{1}{\phi}\right]^2 \tag{16}$$

In the above equations, ϕ_{lh} represents the productivity of a particular product exported from Country l to Country h, which corresponds to the marginal cost after the deduction of trade cost $\tau_{lh}^{f} c_{lh} = \frac{\tau_{lh}^{f}[\xi\Theta_l]^{-1/\theta}}{\phi_{lh}}$, and this marginal cost should be equal to the maximum price at which the product is sold in the foreign market, i.e.:

$$\tau_{lh}^{f} c_{lh} = p_h^{max} = c_{hh} = \frac{[\xi\Theta_h]^{-1/\theta}}{\phi_{hh}}.$$

Thus, the critical productivity for a particular product satisfies:

$$\phi_{lh} = \frac{\tau_{lh}^{f}[\xi\Theta_l]^{-1/\theta}}{[\xi\Theta_h]^{-1/\theta}}\phi_{hh} \tag{17}$$

5.2.3 General equilibrium analysis

So far, all the results discussed above hold under any core productivity distributions $G(\phi)$. To simplify the analysis, it is assumed that the core productivity ϕ follows the Pareto distribution, which has a scale factor of ϕ_{min}, and a shape parameter $k \geq 1$. The specific distribution equation satisfies: $G(\phi) = (\frac{\phi}{\phi_{min}})^{-k}$, $\phi \in [\phi, \infty)$. From the relevant properties of the Pareto distribution, it can be learned that the parameter k determines the shape of the distribution, depicting the degree of dispersion of the productivity distribution; meanwhile, the productivity distribution of surviving firms still obeys the Pareto distribution, and the shape parameter continues to be k. Therefore, the truncated distribution of productivity of domestic trade and exporting firms in Country l can be expressed as follows:

$$G_{ll}(\phi) = \left(\frac{\phi}{\phi_{ll}}\right)^{-k}; \; G_{lh}(\phi) = \left(\frac{\phi}{\phi_{lh}}\right)^{-k}.$$

The free market entry condition implies that the sunk cost is equal to the expected profit of each potential market entrant, which means:

$$f_e = \int_{\phi_{ll}}^{\infty} \pi_{ll}(\phi)dG(\phi) + \int_{\phi_{lh}}^{\infty} \pi_{lh}(\phi)dG(\phi) = \frac{\phi_{min}^k}{2\gamma(k+1)(k+2)}[L_l[\xi\Theta_l]^{-\frac{2}{\theta}}\phi_{ll}^{-k-2}$$
$$+ L_h(\tau_{lh}^f)^2[\xi\Theta_l]^{-\frac{2}{\theta}}\phi_{lh}^{-k-2}] = \frac{\phi_{min}^k}{2\gamma(k+1)(k+2)}\left\{L_l[\xi\Theta_l]^{-\frac{2}{\theta}}\phi_{ll}^{-k-2}\right.$$
$$\left. + L_h[\xi\Theta_h]^{-\frac{2}{\theta}}\left[\frac{\tau_{lh}^f[\xi\Theta_l]^{-\frac{1}{\theta}}}{[\xi\Theta_h]^{-\frac{1}{\theta}}}\right]^{-k}\phi_{hh}^{-k-2}\right\}.$$

Thus, the free market access conditions for these two countries mentioned above constitute a 2×2 system, which can be solved to obtain the domestic critical productivity of the two countries, that is:

$$\phi_{ll}^{-k-2} = \frac{2\gamma(k+1)(k+2)\phi_{min}^{-k}f_e}{L_l[\xi\Theta_l]^{-\frac{2}{\theta}}} \frac{1 - \left[\frac{\tau_{lh}^f[\xi\Theta_l]^{-\frac{1}{\theta}}}{[\xi\Theta_h]^{-\frac{1}{\theta}}}\right]^{-k}}{1 - (\tau_{lh}^f\tau_{hl}^f)^{-k}} \tag{18}$$

$$\phi_{hh}^{-k-2} = \frac{2\gamma(k+1)(k+2)\phi_{min}^{-k}f_e}{L_h[\xi\Theta_h]^{-\frac{2}{\theta}}} \frac{1 - \left[\frac{\tau_{hl}^f[\xi\Theta_h]^{-\frac{1}{\theta}}}{[\xi\Theta_l]^{-\frac{1}{\theta}}}\right]^{-k}}{1 - (\tau_{lh}^f\tau_{hl}^f)^{-k}} \tag{19}$$

For the domestic critical productivity level, its lower limit is ϕ_{min}. In addition, to ensure that both ϕ_{ll} and ϕ_{hh} are above the minimum productivity level, it must be satisfied that $(\tau_{lh}^f \tau_{hl}^f)^{-k} < [\frac{\tau_{lh}^f [\xi\Theta_l]^{-\frac{1}{\theta}}}{[\xi\Theta_h]^{-\frac{1}{\theta}}}]^{-k} < 1.$[7]

5.2.4 Welfare effect measurement

Similar to the study of Melitz and Ottaviano (2008), we use the real wage level $\frac{W}{P}$ to depict the consumer welfare level. Based on the utility function of Equation (1), the consumer welfare under the Pareto distribution can be represented by the following equation:

$$W_l = 1 + \frac{1}{2\eta}\left(\alpha - \frac{[\xi\Theta_l]^{-\frac{1}{\theta}}}{\phi_{ll}}\right)\left(\alpha - \frac{k+1}{k+2}\frac{[\xi\Theta_l]^{-\frac{1}{\theta}}}{\phi_{ll}}\right) \tag{20}$$

From Equation (20), it can be seen that as $[\xi\Theta_l]^{-\frac{1}{\theta}}/\phi_{ll}$ decreases, the consumer welfare gradually increases. Further combining it with the Equation (18), we will have:

$$(\frac{[\xi\Theta_l]^{-\frac{1}{\theta}}}{\phi_{ll}})^{-k-2} = \frac{L_l}{2\gamma(k+1)(k+2)\phi_{min}^{-k} f_e} \frac{1-(\tau_{lh}^f \tau_{hl}^f)^{-k}}{1-[\frac{\tau_{lh}^f [\xi\Theta_l]^{-\frac{1}{\theta}}}{[\xi\Theta_h]^{-\frac{1}{\theta}}}]^{-k}} [\xi\Theta_l]^{\frac{k}{\theta}}.$$

Therefore, we can depict the impact of changes in tariff levels of both imported intermediate input τ_{hl}^g and final product τ_{hl}^f on the consumer welfare by describing the impact of changes in tariffs of the two categories of goods on $[\xi\Theta_l]^{-\frac{1}{\theta}}/\phi_{ll}$,

Taking the logarithm of the above equation on both sides and deriving the tariffs of imported intermediate input τ_{hl}^g and of final product τ_{hl}^f, the following can be obtained:

$$\Delta\log(\frac{[\xi\Theta_l]^{-\frac{1}{\theta}}}{\phi_{ll}}) = \frac{k}{k+2} \frac{1}{1-[\frac{\tau_{lh}^f [\xi\Theta_l]^{-\frac{1}{\theta}}}{[\xi\Theta_h]^{-\frac{1}{\theta}}}]^{-k}} \frac{1}{\frac{T_l}{T_h}(\tau_{hl}^g)^{\theta}+1} \Delta\log\tau_{hl}^g - \frac{k}{k+2}\frac{(\tau_{lh}^f \tau_{hl}^f)^{-k}}{1-(\tau_{lh}^f \tau_{hl}^f)^{-k}} \Delta\log\tau_{hl}^f \tag{21}$$

Unsurprisingly, in the above equation, the coefficient of $\Delta \log \tau_{hl}^g$ is positive and that of $\Delta \log \tau_{hl}^f$ is negative. It means that, as the tariff on intermediate goods decreases, $[\xi\Theta_l]^{-\frac{1}{\theta}}/\phi_{ll}$ decreases slightly and the consumer welfare shows some improvement, while as the tariff on final goods decreases, $[\xi\Theta_l]^{-\frac{1}{\theta}}/\phi_{ll}$ increases moderately and the consumer welfare level deteriorates. The underlying mechanism is that a decline in tariffs on a country's final goods increases competition among firms and reduces their quantity, which in turn reduces the consumer welfare; a reduction in tariffs on imports of intermediate inputs by a country increases the productivity of firms and thus improves the consumer welfare. Under perfect competition, the profit of the firm is zero. In this situation, the consumer welfare in a country represents the total welfare in that country. That means, a reduction in tariffs on final goods degenerates the total welfare in a country, while a decrease in tariffs on intermediate goods improves the total welfare in that country. This leads to the following proposition that:

A decrease in tariffs on intermediate goods imported into a country increases consumer welfare, while a decrease in tariffs on imported final goods decreases the consumer welfare level.

5.3 Data source and parameter estimation

5.3.1 Data source

According to the theoretical model, in the quantitative analysis, values for several core parameters still need to be estimated and obtained, including the following:

1 The physical trading distance τ between China and the U.S.
2 The import tariffs on intermediate inputs and final goods in the two countries τ_{lh}^{g}, τ_{hl}^{g}, τ_{lh}^{f}, τ_{hl}^{f}.
3 The relative technology level between the two countries T_1/T_2.
4 Relative ability of access to intermediate goods of the two countries Θ_l/Θ_h.
5 Parameters θ, k, etc.

Based on the aforementioned theoretical models and the parameters required to be estimated, it can be seen that the overall data used are mainly:

1 Tariff data for China and the U.S., mainly from the WTO tariff database and the WITS–TRAINS database;
2 Data on trade between China and the U.S., mainly from the CEPII–BACI database.
3 World input-output tables data, mainly from the World Input-Output Database (WIOT).[8]

The detailed estimation process for each parameter is described below.

5.3.2 Core parameter estimation

Following the study of Anderson and Wincoop (2004), we set the parameter that reflects the change in the productivity distribution when goods are produced as $\theta = 3$.[9] The definition of Pareto distribution shows that shape parameter k of the firm's productivity distribution satisfies the following equation:

$$\frac{Median}{Mean} = 2^{\frac{1}{k}}\frac{k-1}{k}, \tag{22}$$

where Median and Mean represent the median and mean values of the estimated productivity of firms, respectively. Specifically, we use the following method to estimate firm productivity using the data for China.

It is assumed that firms' production follows Cobb–Douglas production function $Y = \phi K^a L^b X^c$. In the equation, ϕ represents firm productivity, K denotes cost inputs, L stands for the quantity of labor force, and X represents intermediate inputs. Considering that there are two types of errors, simultaneity bias and selection bias, in traditional OLS estimation of firm productivity, this chapter mainly applies the method of Olley and Pakes (1996) to estimate firm productivity.[10] Based on the input price deflators and final good price deflators provided by Brandt, Van Biesebroeck, and Zhang (2012), the actual labor and capital used by the firm can be calculated.

Specifically, the price deflator is derived from Brandt et al. (2012), while the deflator for final goods is calculated according to the reference prices in the China Statistical Yearbook and the input price deflator is based on the price deflator of final goods and the Input–Output Tables of China (2002).[11] Then, using the perpetual inventory method, we can calculate the actual input of the firm. In the meantime, we use the actual depreciation rate of the firm provided by the firm database to represent its depreciation rate. Finally, in a specific regression process, similar to Amiti and Konings (2007), we also control the dummy variables reflecting the firm's export status (if it equals 1, it means that the firm is engaged in export and otherwise it equals zero) and import status (if it equals 1, it means that the firm is engaged in import and otherwise it equals zero), as well as the WTO dummy variable (if it equals 0, it means the current year is a year before 2002 and if it equals 1, it means that the current year is 2002 or later).[12] Based on this, we obtain the shape parameter of the productivity distribution, $k = 2.28$. For data availability, we assume that China and the U.S. shares the same value for parameter k.[13]

Using l for the U.S. and h for China, it can be learned from the model that the ability of firms in Country l to acquire intermediate goods can be expressed as $\Theta_l = T_l + T_h(\tau_{hl}^g)^{-\theta}$, so that the shares of intermediate inputs imported from the other country and domestically sourced intermediate inputs used in production in each country of the total intermediate inputs used can be denoted as follows:

$$\Pi_{ll} = \frac{T_l}{T_l + T_h(\tau_{hl}^g)^{-\theta}}; \Pi_{hl} = \frac{T_h(\tau_{hl}^g)^{-\theta}}{T_l + T_h(\tau_{hl}^g)^{-\theta}}, \tag{23}$$

$$\Pi_{hh} = \frac{T_h}{T_h + T_l(\tau^g_{hl})^{-\theta}}; \Pi_{lh} = \frac{T_l(\tau^g_{hl})^{-\theta}}{T_h + T_l(\tau^g_{hl})^{-\theta}}. \tag{24}$$

In the equations, Π_{ll} and Π_{hh} represent the shares of domestically sourced intermediate inputs used by the U.S. and China of the total intermediate inputs they use, respectively; Π_{hl} and Π_{lh} represent the share of intermediate inputs imported by the U.S. from China of the total intermediate inputs the U.S. uses and the share of intermediate inputs imported by China from the U.S. of the total intermediate inputs China uses, respectively.[14]

A further transformation of the preceding formula gives:

$$\tau^g_{lh}\tau^g_{hl} = (\frac{\Pi_{lh}\Pi_{hl}}{\Pi_{hh}\Pi_{ll}})^{-\frac{1}{\theta}}. \tag{25}$$

Similar to the setting of Caliendo and Parro (2015), it is assumed that the differences in the tariff levels (τ^g_{hl} and τ^g_{lh}) of intermediate goods imported by China and the U.S. from each other mainly stem from the differences between their actual tariff levels (t^g_{hl} and t^g_{lh}), and the other conditions are similar and symmetric for both countries.

The difference between the two countries other than the actual tariff level is expressed as physical distance τ. Since this value can be considered the same between the two countries, the tariffs of imported intermediate goods of the two countries can be expressed separately as follows:

$$\tau t^g_{lh} = \tau^g_{lh}; \tau t^g_{hl} = \tau^g_{hl}. \tag{26}$$

In the equation, τ represents the physical distance between the two countries, while t^g_{lh} and t^g_{hl} represent the actual tariff levels of intermediate goods imported by China and the U.S. from the other country, respectively.

At this point, Equation (25) can be rewritten as

$$\tau^g_{lh}\tau^g_{hl} = (\frac{\Pi_{lh}\Pi_{hl}}{\Pi_{hh}\Pi_{ll}})^{-\frac{1}{\theta}} = \tau^2 t^g_{lh} t^g_{hl}. \tag{27}$$

In the equation, the share of intermediate inputs can be calculated from the world input-output tables, and the actual tariffs of China and the U.S. can be obtained from the WTO tariff database and the WITS–TRAINS database. After substituting the relevant data, we can estimate the physical distance τ between China and the U.S.[15]

Correspondingly, the tariffs on imported final goods of the two countries satisfy:

$$\tau t_{lh}^{f} = \tau_{lh}^{f};\ \tau t_{hl}^{f} = \tau_{hl}^{f}. \tag{28}$$

Therefore, the tariff levels of intermediate inputs and final goods imported by China and the U.S. from each other can be obtained in turn: $\tau_{lh}^{g}, \tau_{hl}^{g}, \tau_{lh}^{f}, \tau_{hl}^{f}$.

In addition, as a result of $\frac{\Pi_{ll}}{\Pi_{hl}} = \frac{T_l}{T_h(\tau_{hl}^{g})^{-\theta}}$, the relative technology level of production between China and the U.S. can be estimated as $\frac{T_l}{T_h}$. According to the theoretical model, the ability of China and the U.S. to acquire intermediate goods satisfies the following condition:

$$\Theta_l = T_l + T_h(\tau_{hl}^{g})^{-\theta};\ \Theta_h = T_h + T_l(\tau_{lh}^{g})^{-\theta} \tag{29}$$

Therefore, relative ability of the U.S. and China to acquire intermediate goods can be estimated as follows:

$$\frac{\Theta_l}{\Theta_h} = \frac{T_l + T_h(\tau_{hl}^{g})^{-\theta}}{T_h + T_l(\tau_{lh}^{g})^{-\theta}} = \frac{1 + \frac{T_h}{T_l}(\tau_{hl}^{g})^{-\theta}}{\frac{T_h}{T_l} + (\tau_{lh}^{g})^{-\theta}}.$$

So far, basically all the parameters required for the subsequent quantitative analysis are obtained, as shown in Table 5.1.

Table 5.1 Estimated values of relevant parameters

Parameter	*Meaning*	*Estimated value*	*Parameter*	*Meaning*	*Estimated value*
k	Location parameter of Pareto distribution	2.2800	T_l/T_h	Relative technology level when intermediate goods are produced in the two countries	1.3544
τ	Physical distance between the two countries	2.4845	Θ_l/Θ_h	Capability of firms in the two countries to acquire intermediate goods	1.3210

Note: l represents the U.S. while h represents China.

5.4 Basic results and robustness tests

5.4.1 Analysis of basic results

According to the theoretical model, as $[\xi\Theta_l]^{-\frac{1}{\theta}}/\phi_{ll}$ decreases, a country's welfare will increase. Thus, the impact of tariff changes of both categories of products on a country's welfare can be assessed by depicting the impact of the tariff changes in imported intermediate inputs and final goods on $\Delta\log[\xi\Theta_l]^{-\frac{1}{\theta}}/\phi_{ll}$. Considering that tariff changes in imported intermediate and final goods of the two countries involve four aspects τ_{hl}^{g}, τ_{lh}^{g}, τ_{hl}^{f} and τ_{lh}^{f}, after taking the logarithm and taking the total differential of Equation (21), Equation (30) is obtained. Combined with the results related to the theoretical model, if the value of Equation (30) is positive, it indicates that a country's welfare has deteriorated; and if the value is negative, it means that the welfare has improved.

$$\begin{aligned}\Delta\log\left(\frac{[\xi\Theta_l]^{-\frac{1}{\theta}}}{\phi_{ll}}\right) = {} & \frac{k}{k+2}\frac{1}{1-\left[\frac{\tau_{lh}^{f}[\xi\Theta_l]^{-\frac{1}{\theta}}}{[\xi\Theta_h]^{-\frac{1}{\theta}}}\right]^{-k}}\frac{1}{\frac{T_l}{T_h}(\tau_{hl}^{g})^{\theta}+1}\Delta\log\tau_{hl}^{g} \\ & -\frac{k}{k+2}\frac{(\tau_{lh}^{f}\tau_{hl}^{f})^{-k}}{1-(\tau_{lh}^{f}\tau_{hl}^{f})^{-k}}\Delta\log\tau_{hl}^{f} \\ & -\frac{k}{k+2}\frac{(\tau_{lh}^{f}\tau_{hl}^{f})^{-k}}{1-(\tau_{lh}^{f}\tau_{hl}^{f})^{-k}}\Delta\log\tau_{lh}^{f} \\ & +\frac{k}{k+2}\frac{\left[\frac{\tau_{lh}^{f}[\xi\Theta_l]^{-\frac{1}{\theta}}}{[\xi\Theta_h]^{-\frac{1}{\theta}}}\right]^{-k}}{1-\left[\frac{\tau_{lh}^{f}[\xi\Theta_l]^{-\frac{1}{\theta}}}{[\xi\Theta_h]^{-\frac{1}{\theta}}}\right]^{-k}}\Delta\log\tau_{lh}^{f} \\ & -\frac{k}{k+2}\frac{\left[\frac{\tau_{lh}^{f}[\xi\Theta_l]^{-\frac{1}{\theta}}}{[\xi\Theta_h]^{-\frac{1}{\theta}}}\right]^{-k}}{1-\left[\frac{\tau_{lh}^{f}[\xi\Theta_l]^{-\frac{1}{\theta}}}{[\xi\Theta_h]^{-\frac{1}{\theta}}}\right]^{-k}}\frac{1}{\frac{T_h}{T_l}(\tau_{lh}^{g})^{\theta}+1}\Delta\log\tau_{lh}^{g}\end{aligned} \tag{30}$$

Further analysis of Equation (30) reveals that, in addition to tariff changes, changes in a country's welfare depend primarily on the value of and changes in the following items:

1. $\left[\frac{\tau_{lh}^{f}[\xi\Theta_l]^{-\frac{1}{\theta}}}{[\xi\Theta_h]^{-\frac{1}{\theta}}}\right]^{-k}$, the value and changes of which depend on the relative ability of the two countries to acquire intermediate goods $\frac{\Theta_l}{\Theta_h}$, and the initial tariff level of imported final goods of the other country τ_{lh}^{f}.
2. $\frac{1}{\frac{T_l}{T_h}(\tau_{hl}^{g})^{\theta}+1} = \frac{T_h(\tau_{hl}^{g})^{-\theta}}{T_l+T_h(\tau_{hl}^{g})^{-\theta}}$, i.e. the import share of intermediate goods of a country. Its value and changes depend on the relative technology level

of the two countries $\frac{T_l}{T_h}$ and the initial tariff of imported intermediate inputs of the home country τ_{hl}^{g}.

3. $(\tau_{lh}^{f}\tau_{hl}^{f})^{-k}$, that is the product of the initial tariff levels of the final goods imported by the two countries.

Given the initial import tariff levels of intermediate inputs and final goods imported by the two countries, in Equation (30), the values of the second and third terms of the two countries are the same and can be considered constant; therefore, the value and changes of Equation (30) depend mainly on those of the values of the first, third and fifth terms of the equation, and the values of all the three terms are related to the imports of intermediate goods in both countries.

According to the aforementioned theoretical model and parameter estimation, it can be learned that compared with China, the U.S. has a higher technology level (i.e., $T_l/T_h>1$), so the value of $1/(\frac{T_l}{T_h}\left(\tau_{hl}^{g}\right)^{\theta}+1)$ is smaller. Therefore, in Equation (30), the absolute value of the first term of China is greater than that of the U.S., and the absolute value of the fifth term of the U.S. is greater than that of China. Unlike the discussion of standard trade theory in Chapter 4[16], the author expects that, after the outbreak of Sino–U.S. trade frictions, influenced by the trade in intermediate goods, welfare levels will deteriorate in both China and the U.S.

In addition, a series of literatures have shown that most of Chinese firms engaged in export and having comparative advantage and competitiveness are manufacturing firms (Chen et al., 2012; Lv, Luo, & Liu, 2015); Meanwhile, the rapid development of China's manufacturing sector has also, to a large extent, benefited from China's deep integration into the international division of labor of the global value chain (Gereffi and Lee, 2012; Liu, Li, & Liu, 2014). Therefore, in this research, we focus on the manufacturing sector.[17] Based on the industry classification codes of the world input-output tables and the ISIC 2 industry codes, we estimate the changes in welfare in China and the U.S. under two scenarios. The results are shown in Table 5.2.

It is clear from standard trade theory that an increase in U.S. import tariffs will lead to a decrease in U.S. imports. Since the U.S. is a large country, the changes in the price of its imports and volume will further affect the price of the product on the world market, thereby reducing its world price. The price of the U.S. imports declines and the overall terms of trade in the U.S. improve.[18] In theory, therefore, a unilateral imposition of additional import tariff by the U.S. will result in an improvement in the country's terms of trade. However, as shown in Table 5.2, the quantitative estimation in this book suggests that after the U.S. unilaterally imposes additional import tariffs, its welfare experiences a minor deterioration; and,

Table 5.2 Estimation of welfare changes in China and the U.S. in manufacturing sectors

		Welfare change	*1st term*	*2nd term*	*3rd term*	*4th term*	*5th term*
Unilateral	U.S.	0.0045	0.0056	−0.0011	0.0000	0.0000	0.0000
scenario	China	0.0090	0.0000	0.0000	−0.0011	0.0106	−0.0005
Bilateral	U.S.	0.0158	0.0056	−0.0011	−0.0010	0.0133	−0.0009
scenario	China	0.0161	0.0081	−0.0010	−0.0011	0.0106	−0.0005

Note: The unilateral scenario in the table refers to the U.S. unilaterally imposing a 25% additional import tariff on final and intermediate goods imported from China, while the bilateral scenario refers to the full-blown trade friction between China and the U.S., with both countries imposing a 25% additional import tariff on their imports of intermediate and final goods from the other country; the same hereinafter.

according to above analysis, the deterioration in their welfare is mainly due to the first term of Equation (30) (fourth column of Table 5.2), that is, due to an increase in tariffs on intermediate goods.

In the light of the aforementioned theoretical analysis in Section 5.2, an increase in tariffs on the imported intermediate goods of a country reduces its welfare level, while a rise in tariffs on the imported final goods improves its welfare, which is consistent with the expectations of the theoretical model (as shown in the first row of Table 5.2). When the U.S. unilaterally hikes its tariffs on imported intermediate goods, it worsens its welfare level; in contrast, an increase in tariffs on imported final goods improves its welfare level. The U.S. imports a larger share of intermediate goods than final goods. Therefore, when tariffs on both imported intermediate and final goods are raised, an increase in tariffs on intermediate goods has a greater impact on welfare levels. For this reason, unlike the standard trade theory, influenced by trade in intermediate goods, when the U.S. unilaterally imposes additional tariffs on imports from China, its welfare level deteriorates.

5.4.2 Robustness tests

5.4.2.1 Considering agricultural products

According to the additional tariff product lists against the other country announced by the two countries in this Sino-China trade friction, it can be found that, in addition to the aforementioned manufacturing industry, a particularly prominent item on the list announced by China against the U.S. is the agricultural products, such as soya beans. For this reason, in this section, we include agricultural products in our model, using the method mentioned earlier to re-evaluate the relevant parameters and the changes in welfare (see Table 5.3).

Table 5.3 Robustness test 1: considering industries such as agricultural products

		Welfare change	*1st term*	*2nd term*	*3rd term*	*4th term*	*5th term*
Unilateral scenario	U.S.	0.0040	0.0051	−0.0010	0.0000	0.0000	0.0000
	China	0.0086	0.0000	0.0000	−0.0010	0.0100	−0.0004
Bilateral scenario	U.S.	0.0154	0.0051	−0.0010	−0.0010	0.0133	−0.0009
	China	0.0155	0.0079	−0.0010	−0.0010	0.0100	−0.0004

Combined with the aforementioned study, when we take into account the agriculture, forestry, fishing and livestock industries, agricultural products included, the aforementioned conclusion still holds:

1 Consistent with the expectations of the theoretical model (as shown in the first row of Table 5.3), an increase in tariffs on the imported intermediate goods of the U.S. decreases its welfare level, while an increase in tariffs on imported final goods improves its welfare level.
2 Overall, due to the impact of trade in intermediate goods, after the outbreak of the trade friction between China and the U.S., the welfare levels in both countries will further deteriorate.

5.4.2.2 Considering different parameter values

From the relevant studies in Section 5.3, it is clear that all parameter values are estimated from the data, except for the value of the parameter θ, which is derived from the literature. Therefore, different values of θ may have an impact on the conclusions obtained in the previous part. So, in this part, we report different estimation results for different θ values to further test the robustness of the conclusion of the study.

From Eaton and Kortum (2002), Anderson and Wincoop (2004), Fan, Lai, and Qi (2017) and other studies, we report the estimates of welfare changes for two different scenarios of $\theta = 3.6$, and $\theta = 5$, respectively (see Table 5.4).[19] As shown in Table 5.4, the previous conclusion still holds when different values are assigned to the parameter θ. Consistent with the expectations of the model, an increase in tariffs on the imported intermediate goods of the U.S. decreases its welfare level, while an increase in tariffs on imported final goods improves its welfare level. After the outbreak of the trade friction between China and the U.S., the welfare levels in both countries will further deteriorate.[20]

5.4.3 Subsequent analysis

Since export price and export cost plus of the product also affect the consumer welfare, we make similar measurements and estimations for the

Table 5.4 Robustness test 2: considering different values of parameter θ

		Welfare change	*1st term*	*2nd term*	*3rd term*	*4th term*	*5th term*
$\theta = 5$							
Unilateral scenario	U.S.	0.0000	0.0067	−0.0066	0.0000	0.0000	0.0000
	China	0.0237	0.0000	0.0000	−0.0066	0.0317	−0.0014
Bilateral scenario	U.S.	0.0268	0.0067	−0.0066	−0.0062	0.0355	−0.0025
	China	0.0270	0.0095	−0.0062	−0.0066	0.0317	−0.0014
$\theta = 3.6$							
Unilateral scenario	U.S.	0.0036	0.0059	−0.0023	0.0000	0.0000	0.0000
	China	0.0134	0.0000	0.0000	−0.0023	0.0164	−0.0007
Bilateral scenario	U.S.	0.0197	0.0059	−0.0023	−0.0022	0.0196	−0.0014
	China	0.0197	0.0085	−0.0022	−0.0023	0.0164	−0.0007

Note: The results reported in the table keep four decimal places. In fact, when $\theta = 3.6$, in bilateral scenario, the change in the welfare level is 0.01968487 for the U.S. and 0.01969199 for China; when $\theta = 5$, in unilateral scenario, the change in the welfare level for the U.S. is 0.0000448.

average export price and average export cost plus of the two countries to further support the basic conclusions reached in the previous study.

According to the theoretical model, the average export price and the average export cost plus from Country l to Country h can be expressed as

$$\bar{p}_{lh} = \frac{2k+1}{2(k+1)}\frac{\tau_{lh}^{f}[\xi\Theta_l]^{-\frac{1}{\theta}}}{\phi_{lh}} = \frac{2k+1}{2(k+1)} \times \tau_{lh}^{f} \times \frac{[\xi\Theta_l]^{-\frac{1}{\theta}}}{\phi_{ll}} \times \frac{\phi_{ll}}{\phi_{lh}}, \tag{31}$$

$$\bar{\mu}_{lh} = \frac{1}{2(k+1)}\frac{\tau_{lh}^{f}[\xi\Theta_l]^{-\frac{1}{\theta}}}{\phi_{lh}} = \frac{1}{2(k+1)} \times \tau_{lh}^{f} \times \frac{[\xi\Theta_l]^{-\frac{1}{\theta}}}{\phi_{ll}} \times \frac{\phi_{ll}}{\phi_{lh}}. \tag{32}$$

Taking the logarithm of both sides of Equation (31) and then taking the total differential, we will have

$$\begin{aligned}\Delta\log\bar{p}_{lh} = & -\frac{k}{k+2}\frac{(\tau_{hl}^{g})^{-\theta}}{\frac{T_l}{T_h}+(\tau_{hl}^{g})^{-\theta}}\left(1+\frac{(\tau_{lh}^{f})^{-k}\left(\frac{\Theta_l}{\Theta_h}\right)^{\frac{k}{\Theta}}}{1-(\tau_{lh}^{f})^{-k}\left(\frac{\Theta_l}{\Theta_h}\right)^{\frac{k}{\Theta}}}\right.\\ & \left.+\frac{(\tau_{hl}^{f})^{-k}\left(\frac{\Theta_h}{\Theta_l}\right)^{\frac{k}{\Theta}}}{1-(\tau_{hl}^{f})^{-k}\left(\frac{\Theta_h}{\Theta_l}\right)^{\frac{k}{\Theta}}}\right)\log\tau_{hl}^{g} + \frac{k}{k+2}\frac{(\tau_{lh}^{g})^{-\theta}}{\frac{T_h}{T_l}+(\tau_{lh}^{g})^{-\theta}}\\ & \left(1+\frac{(\tau_{lh}^{f})^{-k}\left(\frac{\Theta_l}{\Theta_h}\right)^{\frac{k}{\Theta}}}{1-(\tau_{lh}^{f})^{-k}\left(\frac{\Theta_l}{\Theta_h}\right)^{\frac{k}{\Theta}}}+\frac{(\tau_{hl}^{f})^{-k}\left(\frac{\Theta_h}{\Theta_l}\right)^{\frac{k}{\Theta}}}{1-(\tau_{hl}^{f})^{-k}\left(\frac{\Theta_h}{\Theta_l}\right)^{\frac{k}{\Theta}}}\right)\log\tau_{lh}^{g}\\ & -\frac{k}{k+2}\frac{(\tau_{lh}^{f})^{-k}\left(\frac{\Theta_l}{\Theta_h}\right)^{\frac{k}{\Theta}}}{1-(\tau_{lh}^{f})^{-k}\left(\frac{\Theta_l}{\Theta_h}\right)^{\frac{k}{\Theta}}}\Delta\log\tau_{lh}^{f} + \frac{k}{k+2}\frac{(\tau_{hl}^{f})^{-k}\left(\frac{\Theta_h}{\Theta_l}\right)^{\frac{k}{\Theta}}}{1-(\tau_{hl}^{f})^{-k}\left(\frac{\Theta_h}{\Theta_l}\right)^{\frac{k}{\Theta}}}\\ & +\Delta\log\tau_{hl}^{f}+\Delta\log[\xi\Theta_l]^{-\frac{1}{\theta}}/\phi_{ll}\end{aligned} \tag{33}$$

Unsurprisingly, similar to Equation (30), in addition to the initial tariff levels of the intermediate and final goods of the two countries, changes in the average export price of a firm's products are mainly related to the share of intermediate goods imported from the other country $\frac{T_h(\tau_{hl}^{g})^{-\theta}}{T_l+T_h(\tau_{hl}^{g})^{-\theta}}$ and the relative ability of the two countries to acquire intermediate goods $\frac{\Theta_l}{\Theta_h}$.[21]

As shown in Table 5.5, whether the U.S. unilaterally imposes additional import tariffs on products imported from China in the unilateral scenario,

Table 5.5 Changes in average export prices of the two countries

		Welfare change	1st term	2nd term	3rd term	4th term	5th term
Unilateral scenario	U.S.	0.0090	−0.0061	0.0000	0.0000	0.0106	0.0045
	China	0.0045	0.0000	0.0061	−0.0106	0.0000	0.0090
Bilateral scenario	U.S.	0.0161	−0.0061	0.0090	−0.0133	0.0106	0.0158
	China	0.0158	−0.0090	0.0061	−0.0106	0.0133	0.0161

or both countries impose additional import tariffs on their imports from the other country in the bilateral scenario, the average export prices of firms in both countries increase.

There are two main reasons for this.

1 Imported intermediate goods are often used in firms' production, and an increase in tariffs on them will further increase the production costs of firms in the importing country, which is reflected in the increase in the export prices. At the same time, the typical facts in Section 5.1 also indicate that intermediate goods account for a larger share of imports in both China and the U.S. Therefore, under the Sino–U.S. trade friction, although import tariffs on final goods of both countries also increase, the cost effect caused by the hikes in import tariffs on intermediate good prevails, so the average export prices of both countries have increased.[22]
2 In the U.S., for example, when the U.S. unilaterally imposes additional tariffs on products imported from China, Chinese firms exporting to the U.S. need to pay higher export costs to sell their products to the U.S. markets. According to Melitz (2003), among those Chinese firms formerly engaged in the export business to the U.S., some less productive ones will exit the export market, which in turn results in an increase in average export price of China's goods. Similarly, the escalation of Sino–U.S. trade friction, with both countries imposing additional import tariffs of 25% on products from the other country, will lead to an increase in the average price of their exports.[23]

Summary

By incorporating the behavior of firms importing intermediate goods into the study of De Loecker and Goldberg (2014), this chapter discusses the impact of tariff changes in imported intermediate goods and final goods on a country's welfare level at the theoretical level. Based on the study of the theoretical model, we conduct quantitative analysis in the context of the 2018 Sino–U.S. trade friction and explore the impact of this trade friction on the welfare levels of the two countries. The study shows that, consistent with theoretical expectations, when the U.S. unilaterally increases its tariffs on the imported intermediate goods, its welfare level decreases, and when it increases tariffs on imported final goods, its welfare level improves; meanwhile, influenced by the trade in intermediate goods, when the trade friction between China and the U.S. outbreaks, the welfare levels in both countries will further deteriorate.

This study provides a new perspective on the study of Sino–U.S. trade friction from the liberalization of trade in intermediate goods and quantitative analysis. The positive impact of trade liberalization is also further argued. Based on the findings, we propose the following recommendations.

1 China should continue to reduce the tariff levels of intermediate inputs (including capital goods and intermediate goods) to promote the productivity of domestic firms. Meanwhile, in order to reduce the competition faced by domestic firms of the same type, it is necessary to impose certain tariff restrictions on final goods, so as to improve the overall welfare level in China. The theoretical models and quantitative analyses in this book show that a reduction in tariffs on imported intermediate inputs of a country will improve its welfare, while a decrease in tariffs on imported final goods will deteriorate its welfare. In other words, as China is promoting its opening-up as well as tariff reductions and exemptions, it should pay attention to implementing a differentiated tariff strategy, and implement different reduction and exemption policies, with particular emphasis on decreasing the tariffs of intermediate products.
2 China should continue to insist on trade liberalization, promote the construction of a new pattern of comprehensive opening-up, and improve the overall welfare level. According to the theoretical models and quantitative analyses in this book, the implementation of trade liberalization can improve the welfare level of a country, while trade protection can degenerate its overall welfare level. This result further proves the correctness of China's insistence on the strategy of reform and opening-up for more than 40 years. Similar to the spirit highlighted in the report to the Nineteenth National Congress of the Communist Party of China (CPC), opening-up brings progress, while locking the door unavoidably leads to backwardness. It is foreseeable that globalization is always and inevitably the ultimate direction for the common prosperity, progress and development of mankind in the future; China shall continue to promote opening-up so as to truly enjoy the fruitful results of trade liberalization.
3 All parties should conduct consultation and negotiation, rather than disregard the WTO rules and the long-term development of the global economy to resolve bilateral and multilateral trade issues through unilateralism and trade protectionism. There is no doubt that the U.S. unilaterally provoking trade frictions not only violates the WTO bilateral and multilateral trade rules and agreements, but also further exacerbates the reverse-globalization trend. The quantitative analyses in

this book show that whether the U.S. unilaterally initiates the trade friction and hikes the tariffs on products imported from China or a full-blown trade friction outbreaks between the two countries, welfare levels in both countries will deteriorate. Trade closure and trade protectionism will result in a lose-lose situation for both countries, and liberalization is the right way to improve the welfare level of all countries. Countries should continue to insist on trade liberalization and the settlement of trade disputes through equal consultation, so as to achieve mutual benefit and win-win situation, as well as promote the establishment of a community with a shared future for mankind.[24]

Notes

1 One possible explanation lies in the fact that the tariff structures of both China and the U.S. are characterized by cascading tariff structure; that is, tariffs on imported intermediate goods of both countries are lower than those on their imported final goods (see Figures 1.2 and 2.1), so the share of the imported intermediate goods by both countries is higher than that of final goods. Studies on the cascading tariff structure can be broadly divided into two categories: one is statistical research (e.g. Balassa, 1965; Clark, 1985; Corden, 1966; Finger and Yeats, 1976), while the other category focuses on the role of the cascading tariff structure and the rationale for its setting (e.g., Caves, 1976; McKinnon, 1991, etc.).

2 If World Input–Output Database (WIOT) is used to depict the relevant characteristics of trade in intermediate goods of China and the U.S., the results also further support the two typical facts obtained in the text.

3 See Appendix 2 at the end of the book for details.

4 Based on the model of Melitz (2003), Fan et al. (2017) construct a heterogeneous firm model with two countries and multiple sectors, which also considers the different impact of trade liberalization on final goods and intermediate inputs. However, its theoretical model and empirical analysis place more emphasis on the impact of trade liberalization on the exports of firms, and the differences of this impact on different industries; we, on the other hand, integrate the importing behaviors of firms into the study of Melitz and Ottaviano (2008), and what we examine is the impact of the tariff changes of imported intermediate and final goods on the level of consumer welfare. At the same time, Fan et al. (2017) adopt more of an empirical analysis approach, while more of a quantitative analysis approach is applied here.

5 In all subscripts in this chapter, the first letter indicates the country of origin of the product, and the second one indicates the country to which the product is sold.

6 Since the entry costs of a firm can be considered as sunk costs, the firm only needs to balance the marginal costs of its production related to its core competencies.

7 This condition guarantees that ϕ_{ll} and ϕ_{hh} are at least greater than zero. At the same time, this condition is equivalent to $(\tau_{lh}^{f})^{-1} < \frac{[\zeta\Theta_l]^{-1/\theta}}{[\zeta\Theta_h]^{-1/\theta}} < \tau_{hl}^{f}$.

8 Since the most recent year of world input-output data reported by WIOD as of the time of writing is 2014, we use the relevant data in 2014 to represent the data of initial level prior to the outbreak of the Sino-U.S. trade friction.

9 The conclusions in previous studies still hold when we set different values to the parameter θ (see subsequent 5.4 on robustness test for details).
10 Some studies (Amit & Konings, 2007; Fan, Li, & Yeaple, 2015; Feenstra, Li, & Yu, 2017) also use a similar approach to estimate firm productivity.
11 Deflators come from: http://www.econ.kuleuven.be/public/N07057/CHINA/appendix/.
12 Fan et al. (2015) also controls this WTO dummy variable.
13 Many scholars have made the same assumption in specific studies. For example, in their study of the impact of productivity growth in China on welfare levels in the rest of the world, Hsieh and Ossa (2016) assumed that the shape parameter values (i.e., k) of the productivity distribution are the same across countries.
14 In order to be more consistent with the model, given that our main concern is the impact of the Sino–U.S. trade friction on China, we consider countries other than China as the U.S. with reference to the relevant assumptions in Fan et al. (2017).
15 By using corresponding codes of HS6 and classification by BEC, it is easy to calculate the actual import tariff of intermediate inputs and final goods of China and the U.S. It is worth noting that according to some studies (e.g., Fan et al., 2015; Liu et al., 2016; Manova and Yu, 2016; Zhu, Chen, & Yang, 2013), processing trade is the main trade pattern in China, and compared to other countries, the relatively high market share of processing trade is a distinctive feature of China's foreign trade, and the import tariffs of firms engaged in processing trade are generally exempted or reduced to some extent. Therefore, if changes in import tariffs of processing trade are taken into account, it will have some impact on the estimation. However, since in the analysis, we use world input-output tables data, which does not differentiate between general trade and processing trade, we do not consider the impact brought by changes in tariffs of products of processing trade on the welfare in this study.
16 According to standard trade theory, when the U.S. unilaterally initiates trade friction, its welfare level will improve while that of China will deteriorate.
17 As mentioned earlier, for data reasons, this book cannot and does not consider the impact of tariff changes in products of processing trade on welfare levels in this study.
18 See Paul R. Krugman, Maurice Obstfeld, Marc Meliz, *International Economics: Theory and Policy, 9th Edition,* terms of trade refer to the ratio of a country's export price index to its import price index. However, it is worth noting that this price index is an external price index, i.e., one that excludes tariff prices.
19 In previous studies, Eaton and Kortum (2002) uses θ values of 3.6, 8.28, and 12.86; Anderson and Wincoop (2004) uses θ values of 3, 5, and 8. Here, we report the results for three different assignments of $\theta = 3.6$, $\theta = 5$ and $\theta = 8$, respectively, basically encompassing the range of θ values used in previous studies. Given the length of this book and the aesthetics of the presentation, only the results for the first two cases are introduced here. The aforementioned conclusion still holds; that is, the welfare levels in both countries deteriorate.
20 As shown in the note to Table 5.4, since the data in the table maintain only four decimal places, in Table 5.4, when $\theta = 5$, the change in the welfare level of the U.S. is actually 0.0000, despite the fact that in the unilateral scenario, the change in the welfare of the U.S. is 0.0000448, i.e., in the unilateral scenario, when the U.S. unilaterally imposes import tariffs, its total welfare worsens.
21 A comparison between Equation (31) and Equation (32) reveals that the decomposition of the change in the average export cost plus of a firm is consistent with that of the change in its average export price, so this book only reports the estimates of the change in the average export price of the firm.

22 The study of De Loecker and Goldberg (2014) shows that there are large differences in the impact of tariff decreases in intermediate goods and final goods on the export performance of firms. When the tariff on intermediate goods falls, the decrease in the price of raw materials used for production will further reduce the production cost of the firm, and thus reduce the prices of the firm's exports; whereas a reduction in tariffs on final goods will, through competitive effects, lead to an increase in the prices of the firm's exports.

23 In addition, it is worth noting that in both scenarios, the average export price of U.S. exports to China is greater than that of China's exports to the U.S. In other words, China's imports from the U.S. are more expensive, and therefore the deterioration in welfare levels of Chinese consumers is more prominent. This result is consistent with the conclusions reached earlier.

24 This chapter is adapted from the paper *Trade in Intermediate Goods and the Welfare effect of the Sino–U.S. Trade Friction: A Study Based on Theories and Quantitative Analyses* published in cooperation with Zhang Lina in Issue 9 of China Industrial Economics in 2018. Slight modifications have been made to the original text to make the article easier to read.

Conclusion

Sino–U.S. Trade Friction was unquestionably one of the hottest events in international trade in 2018. Although trade liberalization is still the main trend in the course of world development, it is undeniable that global trade uncertainty is increasing. In this context, the study on Sino–U.S. trade friction in this book becomes very instructive.

This book is compiled on the basis of the author's previous research. The book begins with the analysis of tariff structure in China and the U.S., and summarizes the similarities and differences between the two countries. Then, on the basis of the differences in tariff structures of both countries, the author quantifies the role that trade in intermediate goods plays and its impact on the Sino–U.S. trade friction. The book also provides a brief analysis of the development of the Sino–U.S. trade friction, the potential impact on Chinese and American firms, and their coping strategies. In sum, the book details the evolution of the tariff structures and the trade friction between China and the U.S.

Due to time constraints, practical issues such as tariff revenues, market structures, and labor markets are not included in the scope of research of this book. The author will provide further study and present these issues in the subsequent editions. With the development of modern trade, trade between countries has long gone beyond the exchange of commodities between countries. The production factors embedded in the exchange of commodities and the production global chain have gradually received more attention. In particular, research on shocks on the labor market have been most prominent, which has also, to some extent, become an academic focus on the trade friction between China and the U.S. For example, Autor, Dorn, and Hanson (2013) argue that trade shocks brought by China's low-cost manufacturing goods have led to significant declines in the labor employment in the U.S. manufacturing sector, and its welfare level deteriorated immensely; therefore, the U.S. government should hike tariffs on Chinese products, which in turn will promote employment and welfare in the U.S. However, considering the existence of supply chain, some Chinese scholars (Wang et al., 2018) find that China's burgeoning trade will lead to a significant increase in total employment in the U.S. In other words, it is unlikely that an increase in U.S. tariffs on Chinese products will benefit the U.S. job market. Instead, it may result in a larger scale negative impact on the job market due to the existence of downstream and upstream production and value chain transmission. Combined with higher prices caused by increased tariffs, this will further jeopardize consumers' benefits and reduce the welfare level in the U.S.

Of course, research on these issues needs to be supported by theoretical models with more realistic assumptions as well as richer research data, and implications of the results will also be more practical and policy oriented. These are left for future studies.

References

Alvarez, F., & Lucas, R. (2007). General equilibrium analysis of the Eaton-Kortum model of international trade. *Journal of Monetary Economic*, *54*(6), 1726–1768.

Amiti, M., & Khandelwal, A. (2013). Import competition and quality upgrading. *Review of Economics and Statistics*, *95*(2), 476–490.

Amiti, M., & Konings, J. (2007). Trade liberalization, intermediate inputs, and productivity: Evidence from Indonesia. *American Economic Review*, *97*(5), 1611–1638.

Anderson, J., & Neary, P. (2007). Welfare versus market access: The implications of tariff structure for tariff reform. *Journal of International Economics*, *71*, 187–205.

Anderson, J., & Wincoop, E. (2004). Trade costs. *Journal of Economic Literature*, *42*(3), 691–751.

Antras, P. (2003). Firms, contracts, and trade structures. *Quarterly Journal of Economics*, *118*, 1375–1418.

Antras, P., & Chor, D. (2012). Organizing the globally harmonized system. *Econometrica*, *81*(6), 2127–2204.

Antras, P., Chor, D., Fally, T., & Hillberry, R. (2012). Measuring the upstreamness of production and trade flows. *American Economic Review: Papers & Proceedings*, *102*(3), 412–416.

Antrás, P., Fort, T., & Tintelnot, F. (2017). The meaning of global sourcing: Theory and evidence from U.S. firms. *American Economic Review*, *10*(9), 2514–2564.

Armington, P. (1969). A theory of demand for products distinguished by place of production. *IMF Staff Papers*, *16*, 159–176.

Autor, D., Dorn, D., & Hanson, G. (2013). The China syndrome: Local labor market effects of import competition in the United States. *American Economic Review*, *103*(6), 2121–2168.

Balassa, B. (1965). Tariff protection in industrial countries: An evaluation. *Journal of Political Economy*, *73*(6), 575–594.

Bas, M. (2012). Input-trade liberalization and firm export destinations: Evidence from Argentina. *Journal of Development Economics*, *97*(2), 481–493.

Bas, M., & Strauss-Kahn, V. (2015). Input trade liberalization, export prices and quality upgrading. *Journal of International Economics*, *95*(2), 250–262.

Brainard, S. (1997). An empirical assessment of the proximity-concentration trade-off between multination al sales and trade. *American Economic Review*, *87*, 520–544.

Brandt, L., Van Biesebroeck, J., & Zhang, Y. (2012). Creative accounting or creative destruction? Firm-level productivity growth in Chinese manufacturing. *Journal of Development Economics, 97*(2), 339–351.

Broda, C., & Weinstein, D. E. (2006). Globalization and the gains from variety. *The Quarterly Journal of Economics*, *121*(2), 541–585.

Caliendo, L., & Parro, F. (2015). Estimates of the trade and welfare effects of NAFTA. *The Review of Economic Studies*, *82*(1), 1–44.

Caves, R. (1976). Models of political choice: Canada's tariff structure. *The Canadian Journal of Economics*, *9*(2), 278–300.

Chen, B., & Feng, Y. (2000). Openness and trade policy in China: An industrial analysis. *China Economic Review*, *11*, 323–341.

Chen, X., Cheng, L., Fung, K., Lau, L., Sung, Y., Zhu, K., Yang, C., Pei, J., & Duan, Y. (2012). Domestic value added and employment generated by chinese exports: a quantitative estimation. *China Economic Review*, *3*(4), 850–864.

Clark, D. (1985). Protection and developing country export: The case of vegetable oils. *Journal of Economic Studies*, *12*(5), 3–18.

Cohen, W., & Klepper, S. (1992). The anatomy of industry R&D intensity distributions. *American Economic Review*, *82*, 773–799.

Corden, W. (1966). The structure of a tariff system and the effective protection rate. *Journal of Political Economy*, *74*(3), 221–238.

De Loecker, J., & Goldberg, P. (2014). Firm performance in a global market. *Annual Review of Economics*, *6*(1), 201–227.

DiGiovanni, J., Levchenko, A., & Zhang, J. (2014). The global welfare impact of China: Trade integration and technological change. *American Economic Journal: Macroeconomics*, *6*(3), 153–183.

Eaton, J., & Kortum, S. (2002). Technology, geography, and trade. *Econometrica*, *70*(5), 1741–1779.

Fally, T. (2001). *On the fragmentation of production in the U.S. working paper*. University of Colorado-Boulder, mimeo

Fan, H., Gao, X., Li, Y., & Luong, T. (2017). Trade liberalization and markups: Micro evidence from China. *Journal of Comparative Economics*, *5*(50), 1–28.

Fan, H., Lai, E., & Qi, S. (2017). *Trade liberalization and firm's export performance in China: Theory and evidence*. *Cesifo Working Paper*. CESifo Group Munich.

Fan, H., Li, Y., & Yeaple, S. (2015). Trade liberalization quality and export prices. *Review of Economics and Statistics*, *97*(5), 1033–1051.

Fan, H., & Zhang, L. (2018). Trade in intermediate goods and the welfare effect of the Sino-U.S. trade friction: A study based on theories and quantitative analyses. *China Industrial Economics*, *9*, 41–59.

Feenstra, R. (1994). New product varieties and the measurement of international prices. *The American Economic Review*, *84*, 157–177.

Feenstra, R. (2010). *Product variety and the gains from international trade*. Cambridge, MA: Cambridge MIT Press.

Feenstra, R., Li, Z., & Yu, M. (2017). Exports and credit constraints under incomplete information: Theory and evidence from China. *Journal of Finance and Economics*, *96*(4), 729–744.

Feenstra, R., Markusen, J., & Zeile, W. (1992). Accounting for growth with new inputs: Theory and evidence. *American Economic Review*, *82*(2), 418–421.

Feng, L., Li, Z., & Swenson, D. (2012). The connection between imported intermediate inputs and exports: Evidence from Chinese firms. *Journal of International Economics*, *101*, 86–101.

Finger, J., & Yeats, A. (1976). Effective protection by transportation costs and tariffs: A comparison of magnitudes. *Quarterly Journal of Economics, 90*(1), 169–176.

Fukushima, T. (1979). Tariff structure, nontraded good sand theory of piecemeal policy recommendations. *International Economic Review, 20*(2), 427–435.

Gereffi, G., & Lee, J. (2012). Why the world suddenly cares about global supply chain. *Journal of Supply Chain Management, 48*(1), 24–32.

Goldberg, P., Khandelwal, A., Pavcnik, N., & Topalova, P. (2010). Imported intermediate inputs and domestic product growth: Evidence from India. *The Quarterly Journal of Economics, 125*(4), 1727–1767.

Gopinath, G., & Neiman, B. (2014). Trade adjustment and productivity in large crises. *American Economic Review, 104*(3), 793–831.

Halpern, L., Koren, M., & Szeidl, A. (2015). Imported inputs and productivity. *American Economic Review, 105*(12), 3660–3703.

Hatta, T. (1977). Theory of piecemeal policy recommendations. *Review of Economic Studies, 44*, 1–22.

Hecht, J. (1997). Impacts of tariff escalation on the environment: Literature review and synthesis. *World Development, 25*(10), 1701–1716.

Hsieh, C., & Ossa, R. (2016). A global view of productivity growth in China. *Journal of International Economics, 102*, 209–224.

Johnson, R., & Noguera, G. (2012). *Fragmentation and trade in value added over four decades. NBER Working Paper*. Cambridge, MA: National Bureau of Economic Research.

Ju, J., & Yu, X. (2015). Productivity, profitability, production and export structures along the value chain in China. *Journal of Comparative Economics, 43*, 33–54.

Kasahara, H., & Rodrigues, J. (2008). Does the use of imported intermediates increase productivity? Plant-level evidence. *Journal of Development Economics, 87*(1), 106–118.

Koopman, R., Wang, Z., & Wei, S. (2014). Tracing value added and double counting in gross exports. *American Economic Review, 104*(2), 459–494.

Krugman, P. (2013). *International economics: Theory and policy (8th edn.)*. Beijing: China Renmin University Press.

Krugman, P., Obstfeld, M., & Melitz, M. (2012). *International economics: Theory and policy (9th edn.)*. Boston: Pearson Pearson Education Inc.

Kugler, M., & Verhoogen, E. (2012). Prices, plant size, and product quality. *Review of Economic Studies, 79*, 307–339.

Leonard, W. (1971). Research and development in industrial growth. *Journal of Political Economy, 79*(2), 232–256.

Liu, B., Wei, Q., Lv, Y., & Zhu, K. (2016). Servitization of the manufacturing industry and upgrading of the value Chain. *Economic Research Journal, 3*, 151–162.

Liu, H., & Wu, R. (2007). Political economy explanation of tariff structure—A game analysis based on the "protection for sale model". *Economic Quarterly, 1*, 345–358.

Liu, W., Li, L., & Liu, Y. (2014). The impact of global value chain integration on the export technological complexity of China. *China Industrial Economics, 6*, 83–95.

Lv, Y., Luo, W., & Liu, B. (2015). Heterogeneous firms and global value chain integration: A perspective based on efficiency and finance. *The Journal of World Economy, 8*, 29–55.

Manova, K., & Yu, Z. (2016). How firms export: Processing vs. ordinary trade with financial frictions. *Journal of International Economics, 100*, 120–137.

McKinnon, R. (1991). *The order of economic liberalization: Financial control in the transition to a market economy*. Baltimore: The Johns Hopkins University Press.

Melitz, M. (2003). The impact of trade on intra-industry reallocations and aggregate industry productivity. *Econometrica, 71*(6), 1695–1725.

Melitz, M., & Ottaviano, G. (2008). Market size. trade, and productivity. *Review of Economic Studies, 75*, 295–316.

Nunn, Nathan, & Trefler, D. (2010), *The structure of tariffs and long term growth. American Economic Journal: Macroeconomics, 2,* 158–194.

Olley, S., & Pakes, A. (1996). The dynamics of productivity in the telecommunications equipment industry. *Ecomometrica, 64*, 1263–1298.

Ossa, R. (2014). Trade wars and trade talks with data. *American Economic Review, 104*(12), 4104–4146.

Rodriguez, P. (1998). *Essays in international trade and political-economy*. Princenton, NJ: Princenton University.

Sutton, J. (1998). *Technology and market structure: Theory and history*. Cambridge: MIT Press.

Tarr, D., Shepotylo, O., & Koudoyarov, T. (2005). *The structure of import tariffs in Russia: 2001–2003*. The World Bank Policy Research Working Paper Series.

Wang, Z., Wei, S., Yu, X., & Zhu, K. (2018). *Re-examining the effects of trading with China on local labor markets: A supply chain perspective*. NBER Working Papers 24886.

Yu, M. (2010). Trade liberalization and productivity of manufacturing firms in China: An empirical analysis from the corporate level. *Economic Research Journal, 12*, 97–110.

Yu, M. (2015). Processing trade, firms productivity, and tariff reductions: Evidence from Chinese products. *Economic Journal, 125*(585), 943–988.

Zhen, Y., Zhou, B., Xie, X., & Wang, Z. (2018). Participation in the reconstruction of the GVCs and Sino-U.S. trade frictions. *China Industrial Economics, 7*, 24–42.

Zhou, H., Li, F., Zhao, X., & Li, P. (2016). The design and application of measuring non-equidistant industry upstreamness and trade upstreamness. *The Journal of Quantitative & Technical Economics, 6*, 128–143.

Zhu, K., Chen, X., & Yang, C. (2013). Analysis of the domestic value added of China's exports and the influencing factors. *International Economic Review, 4*, 116–127.

Appendix

Appendix 1 Name and corresponding codes of HS2 chapter commodities

HS2 code	*HS classification*	*Classification details*
Section 1		Live Animals; Animal Products
1	Chapter 1	Live Animals
2	Chapter 2	Meat and Edible Meat Offal
3	Chapter 3	Fish and Crustaceans, Mollusks, and Other Aquatic Invertebrates
4	Chapter 4	Dairy Products; Birds' Eggs; Natural Honey; Edible Products of Animal Origin, Not Elsewhere Specified or Included
E	Chapter 5	Products of Animal Origin, Not Elsewhere Specified or Included
Section 2		Vegetable Products
6	Chapter 6	Live Trees and Other Plants; Bulb, Roots and the Like; Cut Flowers and Ornamental Foliage
7	Chapter 7	Vegetable Seeds; Edible Vegetables and Certain Roots and Tubers
8	Chapter 8	Edible Fruit and Nuts; Peel of Citrus Fruit or Melons
9	Chapter 9	Coffee, Tea, Mate, and Spices
10	Chapter 10	Cereals
11	Chapter 11	Products of the Milling Industry; Malt; Starches; Inulin Wheat Gluten
12	Chapter 12	Oil Seeds and Oleaginous Fruits; Miscellaneous Grains, Seeds, and Fruit; Industrial or Medicine Plante; Straw and Fodder
13	Chapter 13	Lac; Gums; Resins and Other Vegetable Saps and Extracts
14	Chapter 14	Vegetable Plaiting Material; Vegetable Products Not Elsewhere Specified or Included
Section 3		Animal or Vegetable Fats and Oils and their Cleavage Products, Prepared Animal Fats, Animal or Vegetable Waxes
15	Chapter 15	Animal or Vegetable Fats and Oils and their Cleavage Products, Prepared Animal Fats, Animal or Vegetable Waxes

HS2 code	*HS classification*	*Classification details*
Section 4		Prepared Foodstuffs; Beverages, Spirits, and Vinegar; Tobacco and Manufactured Tobacco Substitutes
16	Chapter 16	Preparations of Meat, of Fish, or of Crustaceans, Mollusks, or Other Aquatic Invertebrates
17	Chapter 17	Sugars and Sugar Confectionery
18	Chapter 18	Cocoa and Cocoa Preparations
19	Chapter 19	Preparations of Cereals, Flour, Starch, or Milk; Pastrycooks' Products
20	Chapter 20	Preparations of Vegetables, Fruit, Nuts, or Other Parts of Plants
21	Chapter 21	Miscellaneous Edible Preparations
22	Chapter 22	Beverages, Spirits, and Vinegar
23	Chapter 23	Residues and Waste from the Food Industries; Prepared Animal Fodder
24	Chapter 24	Tobacco and Manufactures; Tobacco Substitutes
Section 5		Mineral Products
25	Chapter 25	Salt; Sulphur; Earths and Stone; Plastering Materials, Lime, and Cement
26	Chapter 26	Ores, Slag, and Ash
27	Chapter 27	Mineral Fuels, Mineral Oils, and Products of Their Distillation; Bituminous Substances, Mineral Waxes
Section 6		Products of the Chemicals or Allied Industries
28	Chapter 28	Inorganic Chemicals; Organic or Inorganic Compounds of Precious Metals, of Rare-Earth Metals, of Radioactive Elements of Isotopes
29	Chapter 29	Organic Chemicals
30	Chapter 30	Pharmaceutical Products
31	Chapter 31	Fertilizers
32	Chapter 32	Dyeing Extracts; Tannins and Their Derivatives; Dyes, Pigments, and Other Coloring Matter; Paints and Varnishes; Putty and Other Mastics; Inks
33	Chapter 33	Essential Oils and Resinoids; Perfumery Cosmetic or Toilet Preparations
34	Chapter 34	Soap, Organic Surface-Active Agents, Washing Preparations, Lubricating Preparations, Artificial Waxes, Prepared Waxes, Polishing or Sourcing Preparations, Candles and Similar Articles, Modelling Pastes, "Dental Waxes" and Dental Preparations
35	Chapter 35	Albuminoidal Substances; Modified Starches; Glues; Enzymes
36	Chapter 36	Explosives; Pyrotechnic Products; Matches; Pyrophoric Alloys; Certain Combustible Preparations
37	Chapter 37	Photographic or Cinematographic Goods
38	Chapter 38	Miscellaneous Chemical Products
Section 7		Plastics and Articles Thereof; Rubber and Articles Thereof
39	Chapter 39	Plastics and Articles Thereof
40	Chapter 40	Rubber and Articles Thereof

(*Continued*)

Appendix 1 (Continued)

HS2 code	*HS classification*	*Classification details*
Section 8		Raw Hides and Skins, Leather, Furskins, and Articles Thereof; Saddlery and Harness; Travel Goods, Handbags, and Similar Containers; Articles of Animal Gut (Other Than Silk-Worm Gut)
41	Chapter 41	Raw Hides and Skins (Other Than Furskins) and Leather
42	Chapter 42	Articles of Leather; Saddlery and Harness; Travel Goods, Handbags, and Similar Containers; Articles of Animal Gut (Other Than Silk-Worm Gut)
43	Chapter 43	Furskins and Artificial Fur; Manufactures Thereof
Section 9		Wood and Articles of Wood; Wood Charcoal; Cork and Articles or Cork; Manufactures of Straw, of Esparto, or of Other Plaiting Materials; Basketware and Wickerwork
44	Chapter 44	Wood and Articles of Wood; Wood Charcoal
45	Chapter 45	Cork and Articles or Cork
46	Chapter 46	Manufactures of Straw, of Esparto, or of Other Plaiting Materials; Basketware and Wickerwork
Section 10		Pulp of Wood or of Other Fibrous Cellulosic Material; Recovered (Waste and Scrap) Paper or Paperboard; Paper and Paperboard and Articles Thereof
47	Chapter 47	Pulp of Wood or of Other Fibrous Cellulosic Material; Recovered (Waste and Scrap) Paper or Paperboard
48	Chapter 48	Paper and Paperboard; Article of Paper Pulp, of Paper or of Paperboard Currency Paper (Water-Mark Bank Note Paper)
49	Chapter 49	Printed Books, Newspapers, Pictures, and Other Products of the Printing Industry; Manuscripts, Typescripts, and Plans
Section 11		Textile and Textile Articles
50	Chapter 50	Silk
51	Chapter 51	Wool, Fine or Coarse Animal Hair, Hose Hair Yarn, and Woven Fabric
52	Chapter 52	Cotton
53	Chapter 53	Other Vegetable Textile Fibers; Paper Yarn and Woven Fabrics of Paper Yarn
54	Chapter 54	Man-made Filaments
55	Chapter 55	Man-made Staple Fibers
56	Chapter 56	Wadding, Felt, and Nonwovens; Special Yarns, Twine, Cordage, Ropes, and Cables and Articles Thereof
57	Chapter 57	Carpets and Other Textile Floor Coverings
58	Chapter 58	Special Woven Fabrics; Tufted Textile Fabrics; Lace; Tapestries; Trimmings; Embroidery
59	Chapter 59	Impregnated, Coated, Covered or Laminated Textile Fabrics; Textile Articles of a Kind Suitable for Industrial Use
60	Chapter 60	Knitted or Crocheted Fabrics
61	Chapter 61	Articles of Apparel and Clothing Accessories, Kitted or Crocheted
62	Chapter 62	Articles of Apparel and Clothing Accessories Not Knitted or Crocheted
63	Chapter 63	

HS2 code	HS classification	Classification details
		Other Made-Up Textile Articles; Sets; Worn Clothing and Worn Textile Articles; Rags
Section 12		Footwear, Headgear, Umbrellas, Sun Umbrellas, Walking-Sticks, Seat-Sticks, Whips, Riding-Crops, and Parts Thereof; Prepared Feathers and Articles Made Therewith; Artificial Flowers; Articles of Human Hair
64	Chapter 64	Footwear, Gaiters, and the Like; Parts of Such Articles
65	Chapter 65	Headgear and Parts Thereof
66	Chapter 66	Umbrellas, Sun Umbrellas, Walking-Sticks, Scat-Sticks, Whips, Riding-Crops, and Parts Thereof
67	Chapter 67	Prepared Feathers and Down and Articles Made of Feathers or of Down; Artificial Flowers; Articles of Human Hair
Section 13		Articles of Stone, Plaster, Cement, Asbestos, Mica, or Similar Materials; Ceramic Products; Glass and Glassware
68	Chapter 68	Articles of Stone, Plaster, Cement, Asbestos, Mica, or Similar Materials
69	Chapter 69	Ceramic Products
70	Chapter 70	Glass and Glassware
Section 14		Natural or Cultured Pearls, Precious or Semi-Precious Stones, Precious Metals, Metals Clad with Precious Metal, and Articles Thereof; Imitation Jewelry; Coin
71	Chapter 71	Natural or Cultured Pearls, Precious or Semi-Precious Stones, Precious Metals, Metals Clad with Precious Metal, and Articles Thereof; Imitation Jewelry; Coin
Section 15		Base Metals and Articles of Base Metal
72	Chapter 72	Iron and Steel
73	Chapter 73	Articles of Iron or Steel
74	Chapter 74	Copper and Articles Thereof
75	Chapter 75	Nickel and Articles Thereof
76	Chapter 76	Aluminium and Articles Thereof
77	Chapter 77	(Reversed for Possible Future Use in the Tariff)
78	Chapter 78	Lead and Articles Thereof
79	Chapter 79	Zinc and Articles Thereof
80	Chapter 80	Tin and Articles Thereof
81	Chapter 81	Other Base Metals; Cements Articles and Thereof
82	Chapter 82	Tools, Implements, Cutlery, Spoons and Forks, of Base Metal, Parts Thereof Base Metal
83	Chapter 83	Miscellaneous Articles of Base Metal
Section 16		Machinery and Mechanical Appliances; Electrical Equipment; Parts Thereof; Sound Recorders and Reproducers, Television Image and Sound Recorders and Reproducers, and Parts and Accessories of Such Article
84	Chapter 84	Nuclear Reactors, Boilers, Machinery and Mechanical Appliances, Parts Thereof
85	Chapter 85	Electrical Machinery and Equipment and Parts Thereof; Sound Recorders and Reproducers, Television Image and

(*Continued*)

Appendix 1 (Continued)

HS2 code	*HS classification*	*Classification details*
		Sound Recorders and Reproducers, and Parts and Accessories of Such Article
Section 17		Vehicles, Aircraft, Vessels, and Associated Transport Equipment
86	Chapter 86	Railway or Tramway Locomotives, Rolling-Stock, and Parts Thereof; Railway or Tramway Track Fixtures and Fittings and Parts Thereof; Mechanical (Including Electronic Mechanical) Traffic Signaling Equipment of All Kinds
87	Chapter 87	Vehicles Other Than Railway or Tramway Rolling-Stock, and Parts and Accessories Thereof
88	Chapter 88	Aircraft, Spacecraft, and Parts Thereof
89	Chapter 89	Ships, Boats, and Floating Structures
Section 18		Optical, Photographic, Cinematographic, Measuring, Checking, Precision, Medical, or Surgical Instruments and Apparatus; Clocks and Watches; Musical Instruments; Part and Accessories Thereof
90	Chapter 90	Optical, Photographic, Cinematographic, Measuring, Checking, Precision, Medical, or Surgical Instruments and Apparatus; Parts and Accessories Thereof
91	Chapter 91	Clocks and Watches and Part Thereof
92	Chapter 92	Musical Instruments Parts and Accessories of Such Articles
Section 19		Arms and Ammunition; Parts and Accessories Thereof
93	Chapter 93	Arms and Ammunition; Parts and Accessories Thereof
Section 20		Miscellaneous Manufactured Articles
94	Chapter 94	Furniture; Bedding, Mattresses, Mattresses Supports, Cushions, and Similar Stuffed Furnishings; Lamps and Lighting Fittings, Not Elsewhere Specified or Included; Illuminated Signs, Illuminated Name-Plates and the Like; Prefabricated Building
95	Chapter 95	Toys, Games, and Sports Requisites; Parts and Accessories Thereof
96	Chapter 96	Miscellaneous Manufactured Articles
Section 21		Works of Art, Collectors' Pieces, and Antiques
97	Chapter 97	Works of Art, Collectors' Pieces, and Antiques
Section 22		Trading Products Special and Not Otherwise Classified
98	Chapter 98	Trading Products Special and Not Otherwise Classified

Note: HS code list is obtained from the World Customs Organization (WCO). Over 5,000 commodity groups in HS 6-digit code are broken down into 22 HS sections, with 98 HS chapters in total. Please see more description from the WCO website.

Appendix 2 Tariff peaks in China and the U.S. in 2000–2014

Country	*Year*	*HS2 code*	*Proportion*	*Ranking*	*Quantity of tariff peak sectors*	*Proportion of tariff peak sectors*
China	2000	2	0.34%	59	35	36.46%
China	2000	3	0.65%	67	35	36.46%
China	2000	4	0.10%	38	35	36.46%
China	2000	8	0.30%	55	35	36.46%
China	2000	10	0.30%	57	35	36.46%
China	2000	11	0.03%	19	35	36.46%
China	2000	15	0.48%	64	35	36.46%
China	2000	16	0.01%	9	35	36.46%
China	2000	17	0.08%	31	35	36.46%
China	2000	19	0.04%	22	35	36.46%
China	2000	20	0.03%	17	35	36.46%
China	2000	21	0.08%	29	35	36.46%
China	2000	22	0.07%	28	35	36.46%
China	2000	24	0.10%	34	35	36.46%
China	2000	33	0.10%	35	35	36.46%
China	2000	37	0.23%	52	35	36.46%
China	2000	42	0.03%	16	35	36.46%
China	2000	43	0.04%	25	35	36.46%
China	2000	54	1.69%	86	35	36.46%
China	2000	55	1.34%	79	35	36.46%
China	2000	56	0.19%	47	35	36.46%
China	2000	57	0.02%	10	35	36.46%
China	2000	58	0.32%	58	35	36.46%
China	2000	60	0.81%	72	35	36.46%
China	2000	61	0.20%	49	35	36.46%
China	2000	62	0.36%	61	35	36.46%
China	2000	63	0.03%	15	35	36.46%
China	2000	64	0.18%	44	35	36.46%
China	2000	65	0.01%	3	35	36.46%
China	2000	67	0.03%	13	35	36.46%
China	2000	69	0.08%	30	35	36.46%
China	2000	87	1.90%	89	35	36.46%
China	2000	92	0.03%	18	35	36.46%
China	2000	94	0.17%	43	35	36.46%
China	2000	96	0.24%	53	35	36.46%
China	2001	2	0.32%	61	34	35.42%
China	2001	4	0.11%	34	34	35.42%
China	2001	8	0.26%	57	34	35.42%
China	2001	10	0.29%	58	34	35.42%
China	2001	11	0.04%	23	34	35.42%
China	2001	15	0.37%	63	34	35.42%
China	2001	16	0.02%	14	34	35.42%
China	2001	17	0.18%	43	34	35.42%
China	2001	19	0.05%	25	34	35.42%
China	2001	20	0.04%	22	34	35.42%
China	2001	21	0.08%	26	34	35.42%

(*Continued*)

Appendix 2 (Continued)

Country	*Year*	*HS2 code*	*Proportion*	*Ranking*	*Quantity of tariff peak sectors*	*Proportion of tariff peak sectors*
China	2001	22	0.10%	31	34	35.42%
China	2001	24	0.11%	36	34	35.42%
China	2001	33	0.10%	33	34	35.42%
China	2001	37	0.23%	52	34	35.42%
China	2001	42	0.03%	18	34	35.42%
China	2001	43	0.18%	45	34	35.42%
China	2001	54	1.45%	84	34	35.42%
China	2001	55	1.14%	80	34	35.42%
China	2001	56	0.18%	46	34	35.42%
China	2001	57	0.02%	11	34	35.42%
China	2001	58	0.29%	60	34	35.42%
China	2001	60	0.72%	70	34	35.42%
China	2001	61	0.24%	55	34	35.42%
China	2001	62	0.34%	62	34	35.42%
China	2001	63	0.03%	17	34	35.42%
China	2001	64	0.18%	42	34	35.42%
China	2001	65	0.01%	4	34	35.42%
China	2001	67	0.03%	16	34	35.42%
China	2001	69	0.08%	27	34	35.42%
China	2001	87	2.17%	88	34	35.42%
China	2001	92	0.03%	19	34	35.42%
China	2001	94	0.19%	44	34	35.42%
China	2001	96	0.19%	48	34	35.42%
China	2002	2	0.44%	64	35	36.46%
China	2002	4	0.15%	45	35	36.46%
China	2002	8	0.27%	59	35	36.46%
China	2002	10	0.20%	51	35	36.46%
China	2002	11	0.05%	24	35	36.46%
China	2002	15	0.62%	69	35	36.46%
China	2002	16	0.02%	15	35	36.46%
China	2002	17	0.09%	34	35	36.46%
China	2002	19	0.06%	25	35	36.46%
China	2002	20	0.04%	23	35	36.46%
China	2002	21	0.07%	31	35	36.46%
China	2002	22	0.07%	26	35	36.46%
China	2002	24	0.11%	38	35	36.46%
China	2002	33	0.10%	36	35	36.46%
China	2002	37	0.21%	54	35	36.46%
China	2002	42	0.03%	19	35	36.46%
China	2002	43	0.07%	30	35	36.46%
China	2002	51	0.65%	70	35	36.46%
China	2002	54	1.10%	82	35	36.46%
China	2002	55	0.98%	76	35	36.46%
China	2002	56	0.17%	47	35	36.46%
China	2002	57	0.02%	10	35	36.46%
China	2002	58	0.25%	57	35	36.46%
China	2002	60	0.54%	66	35	36.46%

Country	*Year*	*HS2 code*	*Proportion*	*Ranking*	*Quantity of tariff peak sectors*	*Proportion of tariff peak sectors*
China	2002	61	0.20%	52	35	36.46%
China	2002	62	0.30%	61	35	36.46%
China	2002	63	0.03%	17	35	36.46%
China	2002	64	0.13%	44	35	36.46%
China	2002	65	0.00%	4	35	36.46%
China	2002	67	0.02%	16	35	36.46%
China	2002	69	0.07%	28	35	36.46%
China	2002	87	2.95%	89	35	36.46%
China	2002	91	0.20%	53	35	36.46%
China	2002	92	0.03%	22	35	36.46%
China	2002	96	0.16%	46	35	36.46%
China	2003	2	0.21%	59	32	33.33%
China	2003	4	0.12%	42	32	33.33%
China	2003	8	0.19%	55	32	33.33%
China	2003	10	0.12%	43	32	33.33%
China	2003	11	0.05%	25	32	33.33%
China	2003	15	0.82%	75	32	33.33%
China	2003	17	0.06%	26	32	33.33%
China	2003	19	0.05%	24	32	33.33%
China	2003	20	0.04%	23	32	33.33%
China	2003	21	0.09%	36	32	33.33%
China	2003	22	0.07%	29	32	33.33%
China	2003	24	0.08%	33	32	33.33%
China	2003	33	0.09%	35	32	33.33%
China	2003	37	0.18%	53	32	33.33%
China	2003	42	0.03%	19	32	33.33%
China	2003	43	0.16%	50	32	33.33%
China	2003	51	0.42%	66	32	33.33%
China	2003	55	0.76%	73	32	33.33%
China	2003	57	0.02%	9	32	33.33%
China	2003	58	0.17%	52	32	33.33%
China	2003	60	0.42%	67	32	33.33%
China	2003	61	0.14%	46	32	33.33%
China	2003	62	0.22%	60	32	33.33%
China	2003	63	0.02%	15	32	33.33%
China	2003	64	0.11%	41	32	33.33%
China	2003	65	0.00%	4	32	33.33%
China	2003	67	0.02%	14	32	33.33%
China	2003	69	0.06%	28	32	33.33%
China	2003	87	3.52%	89	32	33.33%
China	2003	91	0.18%	54	32	33.33%
China	2003	92	0.03%	21	32	33.33%
China	2003	96	0.13%	44	32	33.33%
China	2004	2	0.10%	40	30	31.25%
China	2004	4	0.11%	43	30	31.25%
China	2004	8	0.16%	51	30	31.25%
China	2004	10	0.38%	66	30	31.25%

(*Continued*)

Appendix 2 (Continued)

Country	*Year*	*HS2 code*	*Proportion*	*Ranking*	*Quantity of tariff peak sectors*	*Proportion of tariff peak sectors*
China	2004	11	0.04%	22	30	31.25%
China	2004	15	0.81%	76	30	31.25%
China	2004	17	0.06%	26	30	31.25%
China	2004	19	0.04%	25	30	31.25%
China	2004	20	0.03%	21	30	31.25%
China	2004	21	0.09%	38	30	31.25%
China	2004	22	0.07%	29	30	31.25%
China	2004	24	0.07%	32	30	31.25%
China	2004	33	0.10%	41	30	31.25%
China	2004	37	0.18%	55	30	31.25%
China	2004	42	0.03%	18	30	31.25%
China	2004	43	0.07%	28	30	31.25%
China	2004	51	0.40%	68	30	31.25%
China	2004	57	0.01%	10	30	31.25%
China	2004	61	0.13%	47	30	31.25%
China	2004	62	0.17%	54	30	31.25%
China	2004	63	0.02%	15	30	31.25%
China	2004	64	0.09%	37	30	31.25%
China	2004	65	0.00%	5	30	31.25%
China	2004	67	0.02%	13	30	31.25%
China	2004	69	0.07%	31	30	31.25%
China	2004	70	0.44%	69	30	31.25%
China	2004	87	2.88%	89	30	31.25%
China	2004	91	0.16%	52	30	31.25%
China	2004	92	0.03%	17	30	31.25%
China	2004	96	0.12%	44	30	31.25%
China	2005	2	0.13%	47	31	32.29%
China	2005	4	0.09%	36	31	32.29%
China	2005	8	0.16%	53	31	32.29%
China	2005	9	0.01%	8	31	32.29%
China	2005	10	0.24%	59	31	32.29%
China	2005	11	0.04%	23	31	32.29%
China	2005	15	0.57%	73	31	32.29%
China	2005	17	0.07%	30	31	32.29%
China	2005	19	0.05%	24	31	32.29%
China	2005	20	0.03%	21	31	32.29%
China	2005	21	0.06%	26	31	32.29%
China	2005	22	0.09%	35	31	32.29%
China	2005	24	0.08%	33	31	32.29%
China	2005	33	0.10%	40	31	32.29%
China	2005	42	0.03%	20	31	32.29%
China	2005	43	0.13%	48	31	32.29%
China	2005	57	0.01%	11	31	32.29%
China	2005	61	0.12%	44	31	32.29%
China	2005	62	0.16%	52	31	32.29%
China	2005	63	0.02%	17	31	32.29%
China	2005	64	0.09%	37	31	32.29%

Country	Year	HS2 code	Proportion	Ranking	Quantity of tariff peak sectors	Proportion of tariff peak sectors
China	2005	65	0.00%	5	31	32.29%
China	2005	67	0.02%	14	31	32.29%
China	2005	68	0.10%	41	31	32.29%
China	2005	69	0.05%	25	31	32.29%
China	2005	70	0.36%	66	31	32.29%
China	2005	87	2.60%	88	31	32.29%
China	2005	91	0.14%	50	31	32.29%
China	2005	92	0.02%	19	31	32.29%
China	2005	93	0.00%	4	31	32.29%
China	2005	96	0.11%	43	31	32.29%
China	2006	2	0.13%	50	32	33.33%
China	2006	4	0.09%	36	32	33.33%
China	2006	8	0.15%	53	32	33.33%
China	2006	9	0.01%	8	32	33.33%
China	2006	10	0.11%	45	32	33.33%
China	2006	11	0.04%	23	32	33.33%
China	2006	15	0.60%	76	32	33.33%
China	2006	17	0.09%	35	32	33.33%
China	2006	19	0.06%	30	32	33.33%
China	2006	20	0.03%	22	32	33.33%
China	2006	21	0.05%	26	32	33.33%
China	2006	22	0.09%	38	32	33.33%
China	2006	24	0.05%	28	32	33.33%
China	2006	33	0.10%	39	32	33.33%
China	2006	37	0.15%	52	32	33.33%
China	2006	42	0.03%	20	32	33.33%
China	2006	43	0.04%	24	32	33.33%
China	2006	51	0.32%	64	32	33.33%
China	2006	57	0.01%	9	32	33.33%
China	2006	61	0.10%	42	32	33.33%
China	2006	62	0.13%	51	32	33.33%
China	2006	63	0.02%	18	32	33.33%
China	2006	64	0.09%	34	32	33.33%
China	2006	65	0.00%	5	32	33.33%
China	2006	67	0.02%	17	32	33.33%
China	2006	69	0.06%	29	32	33.33%
China	2006	70	0.33%	65	32	33.33%
China	2006	87	2.77%	88	32	33.33%
China	2006	91	0.11%	47	32	33.33%
China	2006	92	0.02%	16	32	33.33%
China	2006	93	0.00%	2	32	33.33%
China	2006	96	0.10%	41	32	33.33%
China	2007	2	0.21%	58	31	32.29%
China	2007	4	0.12%	42	31	32.29%
China	2007	8	0.17%	55	31	32.29%
China	2007	9	0.01%	11	31	32.29%
China	2007	10	0.07%	29	31	32.29%

(*Continued*)

Appendix 2 (Continued)

Country	*Year*	*HS2 code*	*Proportion*	*Ranking*	*Quantity of tariff peak sectors*	*Proportion of tariff peak sectors*
China	2007	11	0.04%	23	31	32.29%
China	2007	17	0.07%	30	31	32.29%
China	2007	19	0.07%	31	31	32.29%
China	2007	20	0.04%	22	31	32.29%
China	2007	21	0.05%	26	31	32.29%
China	2007	22	0.16%	51	31	32.29%
China	2007	24	0.08%	35	31	32.29%
China	2007	33	0.12%	43	31	32.29%
China	2007	37	0.16%	53	31	32.29%
China	2007	42	0.03%	21	31	32.29%
China	2007	43	0.11%	39	31	32.29%
China	2007	51	0.38%	67	31	32.29%
China	2007	57	0.01%	12	31	32.29%
China	2007	61	0.10%	37	31	32.29%
China	2007	62	0.13%	46	31	32.29%
China	2007	63	0.02%	18	31	32.29%
China	2007	64	0.09%	36	31	32.29%
China	2007	65	0.00%	4	31	32.29%
China	2007	67	0.02%	15	31	32.29%
China	2007	69	0.06%	27	31	32.29%
China	2007	70	0.34%	63	31	32.29%
China	2007	87	3.29%	87	31	32.29%
China	2007	91	0.14%	48	31	32.29%
China	2007	92	0.02%	17	31	32.29%
China	2007	93	0.00%	3	31	32.29%
China	2007	96	0.10%	38	31	32.29%
China	2008	2	0.22%	62	29	30.21%
China	2008	4	0.10%	43	29	30.21%
China	2008	8	0.18%	57	29	30.21%
China	2008	9	0.01%	12	29	30.21%
China	2008	10	0.07%	33	29	30.21%
China	2008	11	0.03%	20	29	30.21%
China	2008	17	0.05%	28	29	30.21%
China	2008	19	0.08%	36	29	30.21%
China	2008	20	0.03%	22	29	30.21%
China	2008	21	0.05%	30	29	30.21%
China	2008	22	0.15%	52	29	30.21%
China	2008	24	0.09%	39	29	30.21%
China	2008	42	0.04%	23	29	30.21%
China	2008	43	0.04%	26	29	30.21%
China	2008	51	0.27%	64	29	30.21%
China	2008	57	0.01%	9	29	30.21%
China	2008	61	0.08%	35	29	30.21%
China	2008	62	0.12%	48	29	30.21%
China	2008	63	0.03%	19	29	30.21%
China	2008	64	0.09%	38	29	30.21%
China	2008	65	0.00%	4	29	30.21%

Country	Year	HS2 code	Proportion	Ranking	Quantity of tariff peak sectors	Proportion of tariff peak sectors
China	2008	67	0.02%	16	29	30.21%
China	2008	68	0.10%	41	29	30.21%
China	2008	70	0.30%	65	29	30.21%
China	2008	87	3.04%	89	29	30.21%
China	2008	91	0.14%	51	29	30.21%
China	2008	92	0.02%	18	29	30.21%
China	2008	93	0.00%	3	29	30.21%
China	2008	96	0.08%	34	29	30.21%
China	2009	2	0.24%	63	29	30.21%
China	2009	4	0.14%	47	29	30.21%
China	2009	8	0.24%	62	29	30.21%
China	2009	9	0.01%	10	29	30.21%
China	2009	10	0.11%	40	29	30.21%
China	2009	11	0.05%	25	29	30.21%
China	2009	17	0.06%	29	29	30.21%
China	2009	19	0.13%	44	29	30.21%
China	2009	20	0.04%	22	29	30.21%
China	2009	21	0.06%	30	29	30.21%
China	2009	22	0.17%	53	29	30.21%
China	2009	24	0.11%	39	29	30.21%
China	2009	42	0.04%	21	29	30.21%
China	2009	43	0.11%	41	29	30.21%
China	2009	51	0.27%	64	29	30.21%
China	2009	57	0.01%	9	29	30.21%
China	2009	61	0.07%	31	29	30.21%
China	2009	62	0.12%	42	29	30.21%
China	2009	63	0.03%	18	29	30.21%
China	2009	64	0.08%	35	29	30.21%
China	2009	65	0.00%	3	29	30.21%
China	2009	67	0.02%	16	29	30.21%
China	2009	68	0.09%	36	29	30.21%
China	2009	70	0.32%	67	29	30.21%
China	2009	87	3.68%	89	29	30.21%
China	2009	91	0.14%	48	29	30.21%
China	2009	92	0.02%	17	29	30.21%
China	2009	93	0.00%	4	29	30.21%
China	2009	96	0.08%	33	29	30.21%
China	2010	2	0.17%	54	29	30.21%
China	2010	4	0.18%	57	29	30.21%
China	2010	8	0.22%	61	29	30.21%
China	2010	9	0.02%	14	29	30.21%
China	2010	10	0.12%	44	29	30.21%
China	2010	11	0.04%	22	29	30.21%
China	2010	17	0.09%	36	29	30.21%
China	2010	19	0.11%	41	29	30.21%
China	2010	20	0.04%	23	29	30.21%
China	2010	21	0.06%	30	29	30.21%

(Continued)

Appendix 2 (Continued)

Country	*Year*	*HS2 code*	*Proportion*	*Ranking*	*Quantity of tariff peak sectors*	*Proportion of tariff peak sectors*
China	2010	22	0.18%	55	29	30.21%
China	2010	24	0.08%	34	29	30.21%
China	2010	42	0.04%	27	29	30.21%
China	2010	43	0.11%	42	29	30.21%
China	2010	51	0.24%	63	29	30.21%
China	2010	57	0.01%	10	29	30.21%
China	2010	61	0.06%	29	29	30.21%
China	2010	62	0.11%	40	29	30.21%
China	2010	63	0.02%	19	29	30.21%
China	2010	64	0.07%	32	29	30.21%
China	2010	65	0.00%	3	29	30.21%
China	2010	67	0.02%	15	29	30.21%
China	2010	68	0.10%	39	29	30.21%
China	2010	70	0.36%	68	29	30.21%
China	2010	87	4.54%	90	29	30.21%
China	2010	91	0.15%	52	29	30.21%
China	2010	92	0.02%	17	29	30.21%
China	2010	93	0.00%	4	29	30.21%
China	2010	96	0.07%	31	29	30.21%
China	2011	2	0.24%	63	29	30.21%
China	2011	4	0.19%	57	29	30.21%
China	2011	8	0.23%	62	29	30.21%
China	2011	9	0.02%	14	29	30.21%
China	2011	10	0.16%	52	29	30.21%
China	2011	11	0.05%	25	29	30.21%
China	2011	17	0.15%	51	29	30.21%
China	2011	19	0.11%	39	29	30.21%
China	2011	20	0.04%	23	29	30.21%
China	2011	21	0.06%	30	29	30.21%
China	2011	22	0.20%	58	29	30.21%
China	2011	24	0.08%	32	29	30.21%
China	2011	42	0.06%	29	29	30.21%
China	2011	43	0.11%	40	29	30.21%
China	2011	51	0.26%	64	29	30.21%
China	2011	57	0.01%	9	29	30.21%
China	2011	61	0.07%	31	29	30.21%
China	2011	62	0.14%	48	29	30.21%
China	2011	63	0.03%	19	29	30.21%
China	2011	64	0.08%	34	29	30.21%
China	2011	65	0.00%	4	29	30.21%
China	2011	67	0.02%	12	29	30.21%
China	2011	68	0.09%	36	29	30.21%
China	2011	70	0.33%	68	29	30.21%
China	2011	87	4.69%	92	29	30.21%
China	2011	91	0.18%	55	29	30.21%
China	2011	92	0.02%	16	29	30.21%
China	2011	93	0.00%	3	29	30.21%

Country	Year	HS2 code	Proportion	Ranking	Quantity of tariff peak sectors	Proportion of tariff peak sectors
China	2011	96	0.06%	28	29	30.21%
China	2014	2	0.37%	69	29	30.21%
China	2014	4	0.39%	70	29	30.21%
China	2014	8	0.31%	66	29	30.21%
China	2014	9	0.02%	16	29	30.21%
China	2014	10	0.34%	67	29	30.21%
China	2014	11	0.08%	33	29	30.21%
China	2014	15	0.52%	75	29	30.21%
China	2014	17	0.12%	46	29	30.21%
China	2014	19	0.17%	51	29	30.21%
China	2014	20	0.05%	22	29	30.21%
China	2014	21	0.09%	36	29	30.21%
China	2014	22	0.20%	57	29	30.21%
China	2014	24	0.07%	29	29	30.21%
China	2014	42	0.08%	31	29	30.21%
China	2014	43	0.12%	44	29	30.21%
China	2014	57	0.01%	10	29	30.21%
China	2014	61	0.10%	40	29	30.21%
China	2014	62	0.20%	55	29	30.21%
China	2014	63	0.03%	20	29	30.21%
China	2014	64	0.11%	43	29	30.21%
China	2014	65	0.00%	4	29	30.21%
China	2014	67	0.02%	12	29	30.21%
China	2014	68	0.10%	37	29	30.21%
China	2014	70	0.40%	71	29	30.21%
China	2014	87	5.61%	92	29	30.21%
China	2014	91	0.14%	49	29	30.21%
China	2014	92	0.02%	14	29	30.21%
China	2014	93	0.00%	2	29	30.21%
China	2014	96	0.05%	26	29	30.21%
U.S.	2000	4	0.07%	24	15	15.63%
U.S.	2000	7	0.26%	56	15	15.63%
U.S.	2000	12	0.07%	18	15	15.63%
U.S.	2000	20	0.25%	54	15	15.63%
U.S.	2000	24	0.10%	25	15	15.63%
U.S.	2000	42	0.57%	72	15	15.63%
U.S.	2000	52	0.20%	48	15	15.63%
U.S.	2000	54	0.19%	46	15	15.63%
U.S.	2000	55	0.11%	28	15	15.63%
U.S.	2000	58	0.06%	16	15	15.63%
U.S.	2000	60	0.09%	23	15	15.63%
U.S.	2000	61	2.26%	89	15	15.63%
U.S.	2000	62	2.87%	91	15	15.63%
U.S.	2000	63	0.41%	70	15	15.63%
U.S.	2000	64	1.19%	79	15	15.63%
U.S.	2001	4	0.11%	25	16	16.67%
U.S.	2001	7	0.30%	59	16	16.67%

(Continued)

Appendix 2 (Continued)

Country	*Year*	*HS2 code*	*Proportion*	*Ranking*	*Quantity of tariff peak sectors*	*Proportion of tariff peak sectors*
U.S.	2001	12	0.07%	17	16	16.67%
U.S.	2001	20	0.26%	55	16	16.67%
U.S.	2001	24	0.11%	31	16	16.67%
U.S.	2001	42	0.61%	72	16	16.67%
U.S.	2001	51	0.04%	12	16	16.67%
U.S.	2001	52	0.18%	44	16	16.67%
U.S.	2001	54	0.18%	43	16	16.67%
U.S.	2001	55	0.11%	26	16	16.67%
U.S.	2001	58	0.06%	15	16	16.67%
U.S.	2001	60	0.10%	23	16	16.67%
U.S.	2001	61	2.42%	89	16	16.67%
U.S.	2001	62	2.94%	91	16	16.67%
U.S.	2001	63	0.46%	71	16	16.67%
U.S.	2001	64	1.25%	80	16	16.67%
U.S.	2002	4	0.12%	32	15	15.63%
U.S.	2002	7	0.30%	59	15	15.63%
U.S.	2002	12	0.07%	16	15	15.63%
U.S.	2002	20	0.27%	56	15	15.63%
U.S.	2002	24	0.12%	33	15	15.63%
U.S.	2002	42	0.55%	72	15	15.63%
U.S.	2002	52	0.19%	45	15	15.63%
U.S.	2002	54	0.18%	44	15	15.63%
U.S.	2002	55	0.11%	30	15	15.63%
U.S.	2002	58	0.07%	17	15	15.63%
U.S.	2002	60	0.10%	27	15	15.63%
U.S.	2002	61	2.51%	89	15	15.63%
U.S.	2002	62	2.86%	90	15	15.63%
U.S.	2002	63	0.53%	71	15	15.63%
U.S.	2002	64	1.22%	81	15	15.63%
U.S.	2003	4	0.12%	33	15	15.63%
U.S.	2003	7	0.33%	60	15	15.63%
U.S.	2003	12	0.07%	17	15	15.63%
U.S.	2003	20	0.28%	57	15	15.63%
U.S.	2003	24	0.10%	28	15	15.63%
U.S.	2003	42	0.53%	71	15	15.63%
U.S.	2003	52	0.16%	42	15	15.63%
U.S.	2003	54	0.17%	44	15	15.63%
U.S.	2003	55	0.10%	29	15	15.63%
U.S.	2003	58	0.06%	15	15	15.63%
U.S.	2003	60	0.09%	26	15	15.63%
U.S.	2003	61	2.45%	88	15	15.63%
U.S.	2003	62	2.82%	90	15	15.63%
U.S.	2003	63	0.57%	72	15	15.63%
U.S.	2003	64	1.13%	80	15	15.63%
U.S.	2004	4	0.11%	32	16	16.67%
U.S.	2004	7	0.32%	59	16	16.67%
U.S.	2004	12	0.07%	20	16	16.67%

Country	Year	HS2 code	Proportion	Ranking	Quantity of tariff peak sectors	Proportion of tariff peak sectors
U.S.	2004	20	0.27%	57	16	16.67%
U.S.	2004	24	0.09%	26	16	16.67%
U.S.	2004	42	0.49%	71	16	16.67%
U.S.	2004	51	0.03%	7	16	16.67%
U.S.	2004	52	0.15%	40	16	16.67%
U.S.	2004	54	0.15%	41	16	16.67%
U.S.	2004	55	0.10%	27	16	16.67%
U.S.	2004	58	0.06%	15	16	16.67%
U.S.	2004	60	0.08%	21	16	16.67%
U.S.	2004	61	2.20%	88	16	16.67%
U.S.	2004	62	2.52%	90	16	16.67%
U.S.	2004	63	0.58%	72	16	16.67%
U.S.	2004	64	1.02%	78	16	16.67%
U.S.	2005	4	0.11%	31	16	16.67%
U.S.	2005	7	0.29%	58	16	16.67%
U.S.	2005	12	0.07%	19	16	16.67%
U.S.	2005	20	0.26%	57	16	16.67%
U.S.	2005	24	0.08%	23	16	16.67%
U.S.	2005	42	0.45%	69	16	16.67%
U.S.	2005	51	0.02%	7	16	16.67%
U.S.	2005	52	0.12%	32	16	16.67%
U.S.	2005	54	0.15%	41	16	16.67%
U.S.	2005	55	0.10%	29	16	16.67%
U.S.	2005	58	0.06%	17	16	16.67%
U.S.	2005	60	0.07%	21	16	16.67%
U.S.	2005	61	2.17%	87	16	16.67%
U.S.	2005	62	2.38%	90	16	16.67%
U.S.	2005	63	0.58%	72	16	16.67%
U.S.	2005	64	0.80%	75	16	16.67%
U.S.	2006	4	0.10%	29	16	16.67%
U.S.	2006	7	0.29%	60	16	16.67%
U.S.	2006	12	0.07%	21	16	16.67%
U.S.	2006	20	0.26%	57	16	16.67%
U.S.	2006	24	0.08%	22	16	16.67%
U.S.	2006	42	0.44%	69	16	16.67%
U.S.	2006	51	0.02%	5	16	16.67%
U.S.	2006	52	0.09%	26	16	16.67%
U.S.	2006	54	0.13%	38	16	16.67%
U.S.	2006	55	0.10%	31	16	16.67%
U.S.	2006	58	0.05%	15	16	16.67%
U.S.	2006	60	0.06%	18	16	16.67%
U.S.	2006	61	2.06%	87	16	16.67%
U.S.	2006	62	2.16%	88	16	16.67%
U.S.	2006	63	0.57%	71	16	16.67%
U.S.	2006	64	0.77%	74	16	16.67%
U.S.	2007	4	0.10%	30	16	16.67%
U.S.	2007	7	0.31%	62	16	16.67%

(*Continued*)

Appendix 2 (Continued)

Country	*Year*	*HS2 code*	*Proportion*	*Ranking*	*Quantity of tariff peak sectors*	*Proportion of tariff peak sectors*
U.S.	2007	12	0.08%	22	16	16.67%
U.S.	2007	20	0.30%	61	16	16.67%
U.S.	2007	24	0.08%	21	16	16.67%
U.S.	2007	42	0.38%	66	16	16.67%
U.S.	2007	51	0.02%	5	16	16.67%
U.S.	2007	52	0.08%	23	16	16.67%
U.S.	2007	54	0.13%	37	16	16.67%
U.S.	2007	55	0.10%	32	16	16.67%
U.S.	2007	58	0.04%	14	16	16.67%
U.S.	2007	60	0.05%	16	16	16.67%
U.S.	2007	61	2.08%	87	16	16.67%
U.S.	2007	62	2.06%	86	16	16.67%
U.S.	2007	63	0.56%	71	16	16.67%
U.S.	2007	64	0.93%	76	16	16.67%
U.S.	2008	4	0.10%	31	15	15.63%
U.S.	2008	7	0.30%	61	15	15.63%
U.S.	2008	12	0.10%	33	15	15.63%
U.S.	2008	20	0.31%	62	15	15.63%
U.S.	2008	24	0.08%	23	15	15.63%
U.S.	2008	42	0.45%	69	15	15.63%
U.S.	2008	52	0.06%	19	15	15.63%
U.S.	2008	54	0.11%	35	15	15.63%
U.S.	2008	55	0.09%	27	15	15.63%
U.S.	2008	58	0.04%	14	15	15.63%
U.S.	2008	60	0.04%	16	15	15.63%
U.S.	2008	61	1.85%	85	15	15.63%
U.S.	2008	62	1.81%	84	15	15.63%
U.S.	2008	63	0.51%	70	15	15.63%
U.S.	2008	64	0.84%	75	15	15.63%
U.S.	2009	4	0.12%	34	15	15.63%
U.S.	2009	7	0.39%	65	15	15.63%
U.S.	2009	12	0.11%	31	15	15.63%
U.S.	2009	20	0.37%	64	15	15.63%
U.S.	2009	24	0.10%	28	15	15.63%
U.S.	2009	42	0.41%	67	15	15.63%
U.S.	2009	52	0.06%	17	15	15.63%
U.S.	2009	54	0.11%	30	15	15.63%
U.S.	2009	55	0.09%	22	15	15.63%
U.S.	2009	58	0.04%	14	15	15.63%
U.S.	2009	60	0.05%	15	15	15.63%
U.S.	2009	61	2.25%	89	15	15.63%
U.S.	2009	62	2.14%	88	15	15.63%
U.S.	2009	63	0.65%	72	15	15.63%
U.S.	2009	64	0.98%	79	15	15.63%
U.S.	2010	4	0.10%	28	15	15.63%
U.S.	2010	7	0.38%	64	15	15.63%
U.S.	2010	12	0.09%	25	15	15.63%

Country	*Year*	*HS2 code*	*Proportion*	*Ranking*	*Quantity of tariff peak sectors*	*Proportion of tariff peak sectors*
U.S.	2010	20	0.32%	61	15	15.63%
U.S.	2010	24	0.08%	21	15	15.63%
U.S.	2010	42	0.43%	67	15	15.63%
U.S.	2010	52	0.07%	18	15	15.63%
U.S.	2010	54	0.11%	34	15	15.63%
U.S.	2010	55	0.09%	24	15	15.63%
U.S.	2010	58	0.04%	14	15	15.63%
U.S.	2010	60	0.04%	15	15	15.63%
U.S.	2010	61	2.03%	88	15	15.63%
U.S.	2010	62	1.91%	86	15	15.63%
U.S.	2010	63	0.63%	72	15	15.63%
U.S.	2010	64	1.05%	79	15	15.63%
U.S.	2011	4	0.10%	27	16	16.67%
U.S.	2011	7	0.37%	63	16	16.67%
U.S.	2011	12	0.10%	32	16	16.67%
U.S.	2011	20	0.33%	61	16	16.67%
U.S.	2011	24	0.07%	19	16	16.67%
U.S.	2011	42	0.44%	67	16	16.67%
U.S.	2011	51	0.01%	5	16	16.67%
U.S.	2011	52	0.07%	18	16	16.67%
U.S.	2011	54	0.11%	34	16	16.67%
U.S.	2011	55	0.09%	26	16	16.67%
U.S.	2011	58	0.04%	14	16	16.67%
U.S.	2011	60	0.04%	15	16	16.67%
U.S.	2011	61	1.98%	87	16	16.67%
U.S.	2011	62	1.79%	85	16	16.67%
U.S.	2011	63	0.57%	73	16	16.67%
U.S.	2011	64	0.89%	79	16	16.67%
U.S.	2012	4	0.12%	32	16	16.67%
U.S.	2012	7	0.35%	62	16	16.67%
U.S.	2012	12	0.11%	30	16	16.67%
U.S.	2012	20	0.32%	61	16	16.67%
U.S.	2012	24	0.09%	25	16	16.67%
U.S.	2012	42	0.52%	70	16	16.67%
U.S.	2012	51	0.02%	5	16	16.67%
U.S.	2012	52	0.06%	16	16	16.67%
U.S.	2012	54	0.11%	29	16	16.67%
U.S.	2012	55	0.08%	22	16	16.67%
U.S.	2012	58	0.04%	12	16	16.67%
U.S.	2012	60	0.05%	15	16	16.67%
U.S.	2012	61	1.93%	86	16	16.67%
U.S.	2012	62	1.75%	84	16	16.67%
U.S.	2012	63	0.54%	72	16	16.67%
U.S.	2012	64	0.98%	79	16	16.67%
U.S.	2013	4	0.11%	29	16	16.67%
U.S.	2013	7	0.40%	65	16	16.67%
U.S.	2013	12	0.14%	40	16	16.67%

(*Continued*)

Appendix 2 (Continued)

Country	*Year*	*HS2 code*	*Proportion*	*Ranking*	*Quantity of tariff peak sectors*	*Proportion of tariff peak sectors*
U.S.	2013	20	0.33%	61	16	16.67%
U.S.	2013	24	0.10%	28	16	16.67%
U.S.	2013	42	0.54%	70	16	16.67%
U.S.	2013	51	0.01%	5	16	16.67%
U.S.	2013	52	0.05%	15	16	16.67%
U.S.	2013	54	0.11%	30	16	16.67%
U.S.	2013	55	0.08%	21	16	16.67%
U.S.	2013	58	0.04%	11	16	16.67%
U.S.	2013	60	0.05%	14	16	16.67%
U.S.	2013	61	2.05%	87	16	16.67%
U.S.	2013	62	1.82%	85	16	16.67%
U.S.	2013	63	0.57%	72	16	16.67%
U.S.	2013	64	1.09%	80	16	16.67%
U.S.	2014	4	0.12%	31	16	16.67%
U.S.	2014	7	0.39%	64	16	16.67%
U.S.	2014	12	0.16%	40	16	16.67%
U.S.	2014	20	0.32%	59	16	16.67%
U.S.	2014	24	0.09%	24	16	16.67%
U.S.	2014	42	0.54%	70	16	16.67%
U.S.	2014	51	0.01%	5	16	16.67%
U.S.	2014	52	0.05%	14	16	16.67%
U.S.	2014	54	0.10%	28	16	16.67%
U.S.	2014	55	0.09%	22	16	16.67%
U.S.	2014	58	0.04%	10	16	16.67%
U.S.	2014	60	0.05%	13	16	16.67%
U.S.	2014	61	2.01%	87	16	16.67%
U.S.	2014	62	1.73%	84	16	16.67%
U.S.	2014	63	0.57%	72	16	16.67%
U.S.	2014	64	1.10%	80	16	16.67%

Note: tariff data is collected from the WTO-WITS database and a sector is defined as Tariff Peak Sector if the tariff level is above 15%. The ranking of a sector is ordered based on its values of average tariff level. For example, a sector's ranking corresponds to ten if its tariff level is ranked ten in an ascending order in all sectors.

Appendix 3 Characteristics of top ten lowest tariff products in China and the U.S. in 2000–2014

Country	*Year*	*HS code*	*Average tariff*	*Classification by BEC*	*Classification by elasticity of substitution*
China	2000	1	5.54	Intermediate good	High elasticity of substitution
China	2000	23	5.98	Intermediate good	High elasticity of substitution
China	2000	25	4.30	Intermediate good	Low elasticity of substitution
China	2000	26	1.85	Intermediate good	High elasticity of substitution
China	2000	31	5.00	Intermediate good	Low elasticity of substitution
China	2000	47	1.00	Intermediate good	High elasticity of substitution
China	2000	49	5.25	Final good	Low elasticity of substitution
China	2000	75	6.22	Intermediate good	High elasticity of substitution
China	2000	86	5.42	Intermediate good	Low elasticity of substitution
China	2000	88	3.47	Intermediate good	High elasticity of substitution
China	2001	25	3.77	Intermediate good	Low elasticity of substitution
China	2001	26	1.22	Intermediate good	High elasticity of substitution
China	2001	31	4.63	Intermediate good	Low elasticity of substitution
China	2001	47	1.00	Intermediate good	High elasticity of substitution
China	2001	49	4.91	Final good	Low elasticity of substitution
China	2001	75	5.28	Intermediate good	High elasticity of substitution
China	2001	78	5.25	Intermediate good	Low elasticity of substitution
China	2001	79	4.92	Intermediate good	High elasticity of substitution
China	2001	86	5.00	Intermediate good	Low elasticity of substitution
China	2001	88	3.47	Intermediate good	High elasticity of substitution
China	2002	25	3.71	Intermediate good	Low elasticity of substitution
China	2002	26	1.14	Intermediate good	High elasticity of substitution
China	2002	30	5.06	Final good	High elasticity of substitution

(*Continued*)

Appendix 3 (Continued)

Country	*Year*	*HS code*	*Average tariff*	*Classification by BEC*	*Classification by elasticity of substitution*
China	2002	47	0.00	Intermediate good	High elasticity of substitution
China	2002	49	3.39	Final good	Low elasticity of substitution
China	2002	75	4.87	Intermediate good	High elasticity of substitution
China	2002	78	4.93	Intermediate good	Low elasticity of substitution
China	2002	79	4.77	Intermediate good	High elasticity of substitution
China	2002	86	3.98	Intermediate good	Low elasticity of substitution
China	2002	88	2.21	Intermediate good	High elasticity of substitution
China	2003	25	3.70	Intermediate good	Low elasticity of substitution
China	2003	26	1.14	Intermediate good	High elasticity of substitution
China	2003	30	4.47	Final good	High elasticity of substitution
China	2003	47	0.00	Intermediate good	High elasticity of substitution
China	2003	49	2.76	Final good	Low elasticity of substitution
China	2003	75	4.87	Intermediate good	High elasticity of substitution
China	2003	78	4.79	Intermediate good	Low elasticity of substitution
China	2003	79	4.71	Intermediate good	High elasticity of substitution
China	2003	86	3.98	Intermediate good	Low elasticity of substitution
China	2003	88	2.13	Intermediate good	High elasticity of substitution
China	2004	25	3.69	Intermediate good	Low elasticity of substitution
China	2004	26	1.14	Intermediate good	High elasticity of substitution
China	2004	30	4.44	Final good	High elasticity of substitution
China	2004	44	4.61	Intermediate good	High elasticity of substitution
China	2004	47	0.00	Intermediate good	High elasticity of substitution
China	2004	49	2.76	Final good	Low elasticity of substitution
China	2004	78	4.65	Intermediate good	Low elasticity of substitution

Country	Year	HS code	Average tariff	Classification by BEC	Classification by elasticity of substitution
China	2004	79	4.65	Intermediate good	High elasticity of substitution
China	2004	86	3.98	Intermediate good	Low elasticity of substitution
China	2004	88	2.13	Intermediate good	High elasticity of substitution
China	2005	25	3.68	Intermediate good	Low elasticity of substitution
China	2005	26	1.14	Intermediate good	High elasticity of substitution
China	2005	30	4.43	Final good	High elasticity of substitution
China	2005	44	4.40	Intermediate good	High elasticity of substitution
China	2005	47	0.00	Intermediate good	High elasticity of substitution
China	2005	49	2.76	Final good	Low elasticity of substitution
China	2005	78	4.65	Intermediate good	Low elasticity of substitution
China	2005	79	4.65	Intermediate good	High elasticity of substitution
China	2005	86	3.98	Intermediate good	Low elasticity of substitution
China	2005	88	2.18	Intermediate good	High elasticity of substitution
China	2006	25	3.43	Intermediate good	Low elasticity of substitution
China	2006	26	1.14	Intermediate good	High elasticity of substitution
China	2006	30	4.44	Final good	High elasticity of substitution
China	2006	44	4.39	Intermediate good	High elasticity of substitution
China	2006	47	0.00	Intermediate good	High elasticity of substitution
China	2006	49	2.76	Final good	Low elasticity of substitution
China	2006	75	4.49	Intermediate good	High elasticity of substitution
China	2006	78	4.65	Intermediate good	Low elasticity of substitution
China	2006	79	4.65	Intermediate good	High elasticity of substitution
China	2006	86	3.98	Intermediate good	Low elasticity of substitution
China	2006	88	2.00	Intermediate good	High elasticity of substitution

(*Continued*)

Appendix 3 (Continued)

Country	*Year*	*HS code*	*Average tariff*	*Classification by BEC*	*Classification by elasticity of substitution*
China	2007	25	3.72	Intermediate good	Low elasticity of substitution
China	2007	26	1.14	Intermediate good	High elasticity of substitution
China	2007	30	4.49	Final good	High elasticity of substitution
China	2007	44	3.90	Intermediate good	High elasticity of substitution
China	2007	47	0.00	Intermediate good	High elasticity of substitution
China	2007	49	2.76	Final good	Low elasticity of substitution
China	2007	78	4.31	Intermediate good	Low elasticity of substitution
China	2007	79	4.50	Intermediate good	High elasticity of substitution
China	2007	86	3.94	Intermediate good	Low elasticity of substitution
China	2007	88	2.07	Intermediate good	High elasticity of substitution
China	2008	25	3.32	Intermediate good	Low elasticity of substitution
China	2008	26	1.14	Intermediate good	High elasticity of substitution
China	2008	27	4.17	Intermediate good	High elasticity of substitution
China	2008	30	4.12	Final good	High elasticity of substitution
China	2008	44	3.90	Intermediate good	High elasticity of substitution
China	2008	47	0.00	Intermediate good	High elasticity of substitution
China	2008	49	2.76	Final good	Low elasticity of substitution
China	2008	78	4.31	Intermediate good	Low elasticity of substitution
China	2008	86	3.94	Intermediate good	Low elasticity of substitution
China	2008	88	2.07	Intermediate good	High elasticity of substitution
China	2009	25	3.09	Intermediate good	Low elasticity of substitution
China	2009	26	1.14	Intermediate good	High elasticity of substitution
China	2009	27	4.17	Intermediate good	High elasticity of substitution
China	2009	30	4.23	Final good	High elasticity of substitution

Country	*Year*	*HS code*	*Average tariff*	*Classification by BEC*	*Classification by elasticity of substitution*
China	2009	44	3.90	Intermediate good	High elasticity of substitution
China	2009	47	0.00	Intermediate good	High elasticity of substitution
China	2009	49	2.76	Final good	Low elasticity of substitution
China	2009	78	4.31	Intermediate good	Low elasticity of substitution
China	2009	86	3.94	Intermediate good	Low elasticity of substitution
China	2009	88	2.07	Intermediate good	High elasticity of substitution
China	2010	25	3.13	Intermediate good	Low elasticity of substitution
China	2010	26	1.14	Intermediate good	High elasticity of substitution
China	2010	27	4.18	Intermediate good	High elasticity of substitution
China	2010	30	4.23	Final good	High elasticity of substitution
China	2010	44	3.90	Intermediate good	High elasticity of substitution
China	2010	47	0.00	Intermediate good	High elasticity of substitution
China	2010	49	2.76	Final good	Low elasticity of substitution
China	2010	78	4.31	Intermediate good	Low elasticity of substitution
China	2010	86	3.94	Intermediate good	Low elasticity of substitution
China	2010	88	2.07	Intermediate good	High elasticity of substitution
China	2011	25	3.10	Intermediate good	Low elasticity of substitution
China	2011	26	1.14	Intermediate good	High elasticity of substitution
China	2011	27	4.06	Intermediate good	High elasticity of substitution
China	2011	30	4.23	Final good	High elasticity of substitution
China	2011	44	3.90	Intermediate good	High elasticity of substitution
China	2011	47	0.00	Intermediate good	High elasticity of substitution
China	2011	49	2.76	Final good	Low elasticity of substitution
China	2011	79	3.78	Intermediate good	High elasticity of substitution

(*Continued*)

Appendix 3 (Continued)

Country	*Year*	*HS code*	*Average tariff*	*Classification by BEC*	*Classification by elasticity of substitution*
China	2011	86	3.94	Intermediate good	Low elasticity of substitution
China	2011	88	2.07	Intermediate good	High elasticity of substitution
China	2014	25	2.67	Intermediate good	Low elasticity of substitution
China	2014	26	1.08	Intermediate good	High elasticity of substitution
China	2014	27	3.89	Intermediate good	High elasticity of substitution
China	2014	30	4.21	Final good	High elasticity of substitution
China	2014	44	3.89	Intermediate good	High elasticity of substitution
China	2014	47	0.00	Intermediate good	High elasticity of substitution
China	2014	49	2.59	Final good	Low elasticity of substitution
China	2014	79	3.78	Intermediate good	High elasticity of substitution
China	2014	86	3.94	Intermediate good	Low elasticity of substitution
China	2014	88	2.07	Intermediate good	High elasticity of substitution
U.S.	2000	9	0.38	Final good	High elasticity of substitution
U.S.	2000	25	0.26	Intermediate good	Low elasticity of substitution
U.S.	2000	26	0.00	Intermediate good	High elasticity of substitution
U.S.	2000	27	0.16	Intermediate good	High elasticity of substitution
U.S.	2000	30	0.00	Final good	High elasticity of substitution
U.S.	2000	31	0.00	Intermediate good	Low elasticity of substitution
U.S.	2000	47	0.00	Intermediate good	High elasticity of substitution
U.S.	2000	49	0.35	Final good	Low elasticity of substitution
U.S.	2000	88	0.20	Intermediate good	High elasticity of substitution
U.S.	2000	97	0.00	Final good	Low elasticity of substitution
U.S.	2001	9	0.38	Final good	High elasticity of substitution
U.S.	2001	25	0.26	Intermediate good	Low elasticity of substitution

Country	*Year*	*HS code*	*Average tariff*	*Classification by BEC*	*Classification by elasticity of substitution*
U.S.	2001	26	0.00	Intermediate good	High elasticity of substitution
U.S.	2001	27	0.16	Intermediate good	High elasticity of substitution
U.S.	2001	30	0.00	Final good	High elasticity of substitution
U.S.	2001	31	0.00	Intermediate good	Low elasticity of substitution
U.S.	2001	47	0.00	Intermediate good	High elasticity of substitution
U.S.	2001	49	0.26	Final good	Low elasticity of substitution
U.S.	2001	88	0.20	Intermediate good	High elasticity of substitution
U.S.	2001	97	0.00	Final good	Low elasticity of substitution
U.S.	2002	9	0.38	Final good	High elasticity of substitution
U.S.	2002	25	0.24	Intermediate good	Low elasticity of substitution
U.S.	2002	26	0.03	Intermediate good	High elasticity of substitution
U.S.	2002	27	0.17	Intermediate good	High elasticity of substitution
U.S.	2002	30	0.00	Final good	High elasticity of substitution
U.S.	2002	31	0.00	Intermediate good	Low elasticity of substitution
U.S.	2002	47	0.00	Intermediate good	High elasticity of substitution
U.S.	2002	49	0.18	Final good	Low elasticity of substitution
U.S.	2002	88	0.20	Intermediate good	High elasticity of substitution
U.S.	2002	97	0.00	Final good	Low elasticity of substitution
U.S.	2003	25	0.24	Intermediate good	Low elasticity of substitution
U.S.	2003	26	0.03	Intermediate good	High elasticity of substitution
U.S.	2003	27	0.17	Intermediate good	High elasticity of substitution
U.S.	2003	30	0.00	Final good	High elasticity of substitution
U.S.	2003	31	0.00	Intermediate good	Low elasticity of substitution
U.S.	2003	47	0.00	Intermediate good	High elasticity of substitution

(*Continued*)

Appendix 3 (Continued)

Country	*Year*	*HS code*	*Average tariff*	*Classification by BEC*	*Classification by elasticity of substitution*
U.S.	2003	48	0.27	Intermediate good	High elasticity of substitution
U.S.	2003	49	0.09	Final good	Low elasticity of substitution
U.S.	2003	88	0.20	Intermediate good	High elasticity of substitution
U.S.	2003	97	0.00	Final good	Low elasticity of substitution
U.S.	2004	25	0.24	Intermediate good	Low elasticity of substitution
U.S.	2004	26	0.03	Intermediate good	High elasticity of substitution
U.S.	2004	27	0.17	Intermediate good	High elasticity of substitution
U.S.	2004	30	0.00	Final good	High elasticity of substitution
U.S.	2004	31	0.00	Intermediate good	Low elasticity of substitution
U.S.	2004	47	0.00	Intermediate good	High elasticity of substitution
U.S.	2004	48	0.00	Intermediate good	High elasticity of substitution
U.S.	2004	49	0.00	Final good	Low elasticity of substitution
U.S.	2004	88	0.20	Intermediate good	High elasticity of substitution
U.S.	2004	97	0.00	Final good	Low elasticity of substitution
U.S.	2005	25	0.24	Intermediate good	Low elasticity of substitution
U.S.	2005	26	0.03	Intermediate good	High elasticity of substitution
U.S.	2005	27	0.17	Intermediate good	High elasticity of substitution
U.S.	2005	30	0.00	Final good	High elasticity of substitution
U.S.	2005	31	0.00	Intermediate good	Low elasticity of substitution
U.S.	2005	47	0.00	Intermediate good	High elasticity of substitution
U.S.	2005	48	0.00	Intermediate good	High elasticity of substitution
U.S.	2005	49	0.00	Final good	Low elasticity of substitution
U.S.	2005	88	0.20	Intermediate good	High elasticity of substitution
U.S.	2005	97	0.00	Final good	Low elasticity of substitution

Country	*Year*	*HS code*	*Average tariff*	*Classification by BEC*	*Classification by elasticity of substitution*
U.S.	2006	25	0.24	Intermediate good	Low elasticity of substitution
U.S.	2006	26	0.03	Intermediate good	High elasticity of substitution
U.S.	2006	27	0.17	Intermediate good	High elasticity of substitution
U.S.	2006	30	0.00	Final good	High elasticity of substitution
U.S.	2006	31	0.00	Intermediate good	Low elasticity of substitution
U.S.	2006	47	0.00	Intermediate good	High elasticity of substitution
U.S.	2006	48	0.00	Intermediate good	High elasticity of substitution
U.S.	2006	49	0.00	Final good	Low elasticity of substitution
U.S.	2006	88	0.20	Intermediate good	High elasticity of substitution
U.S.	2006	97	0.00	Final good	Low elasticity of substitution
U.S.	2007	25	0.23	Intermediate good	Low elasticity of substitution
U.S.	2007	26	0.03	Intermediate good	High elasticity of substitution
U.S.	2007	27	0.17	Intermediate good	High elasticity of substitution
U.S.	2007	30	0.00	Final good	High elasticity of substitution
U.S.	2007	31	0.00	Intermediate good	Low elasticity of substitution
U.S.	2007	47	0.00	Intermediate good	High elasticity of substitution
U.S.	2007	48	0.00	Intermediate good	High elasticity of substitution
U.S.	2007	49	0.00	Final good	Low elasticity of substitution
U.S.	2007	88	0.21	Intermediate good	High elasticity of substitution
U.S.	2007	97	0.00	Final good	Low elasticity of substitution
U.S.	2008	25	0.23	Intermediate good	Low elasticity of substitution
U.S.	2008	26	0.03	Intermediate good	High elasticity of substitution
U.S.	2008	27	0.17	Intermediate good	High elasticity of substitution
U.S.	2008	30	0.00	Final good	High elasticity of substitution

(*Continued*)

Appendix 3 (Continued)

Country	*Year*	*HS code*	*Average tariff*	*Classification by BEC*	*Classification by elasticity of substitution*
U.S.	2008	31	0.00	Intermediate good	Low elasticity of substitution
U.S.	2008	47	0.00	Intermediate good	High elasticity of substitution
U.S.	2008	48	0.00	Intermediate good	High elasticity of substitution
U.S.	2008	49	0.00	Final good	Low elasticity of substitution
U.S.	2008	88	0.21	Intermediate good	High elasticity of substitution
U.S.	2008	97	0.00	Final good	Low elasticity of substitution
U.S.	2009	25	0.23	Intermediate good	Low elasticity of substitution
U.S.	2009	26	0.03	Intermediate good	High elasticity of substitution
U.S.	2009	27	0.17	Intermediate good	High elasticity of substitution
U.S.	2009	30	0.00	Final good	High elasticity of substitution
U.S.	2009	31	0.00	Intermediate good	Low elasticity of substitution
U.S.	2009	47	0.00	Intermediate good	High elasticity of substitution
U.S.	2009	48	0.00	Intermediate good	High elasticity of substitution
U.S.	2009	49	0.00	Final good	Low elasticity of substitution
U.S.	2009	88	0.21	Intermediate good	High elasticity of substitution
U.S.	2009	97	0.00	Final good	Low elasticity of substitution
U.S.	2010	25	0.23	Intermediate good	Low elasticity of substitution
U.S.	2010	26	0.03	Intermediate good	High elasticity of substitution
U.S.	2010	27	0.17	Intermediate good	High elasticity of substitution
U.S.	2010	30	0.00	Final good	High elasticity of substitution
U.S.	2010	31	0.00	Intermediate good	Low elasticity of substitution
U.S.	2010	47	0.00	Intermediate good	High elasticity of substitution
U.S.	2010	48	0.00	Intermediate good	High elasticity of substitution
U.S.	2010	49	0.00	Final good	Low elasticity of substitution

Country	Year	HS code	Average tariff	Classification by BEC	Classification by elasticity of substitution
U.S.	2010	88	0.21	Intermediate good	High elasticity of substitution
U.S.	2010	97	0.00	Final good	Low elasticity of substitution
U.S.	2011	25	0.23	Intermediate good	Low elasticity of substitution
U.S.	2011	26	0.03	Intermediate good	High elasticity of substitution
U.S.	2011	27	0.17	Intermediate good	High elasticity of substitution
U.S.	2011	30	0.00	Final good	High elasticity of substitution
U.S.	2011	31	0.00	Intermediate good	Low elasticity of substitution
U.S.	2011	47	0.00	Intermediate good	High elasticity of substitution
U.S.	2011	48	0.00	Intermediate good	High elasticity of substitution
U.S.	2011	49	0.00	Final good	Low elasticity of substitution
U.S.	2011	88	0.21	Intermediate good	High elasticity of substitution
U.S.	2011	97	0.00	Final good	Low elasticity of substitution
U.S.	2012	25	0.24	Intermediate good	Low elasticity of substitution
U.S.	2012	26	0.03	Intermediate good	High elasticity of substitution
U.S.	2012	27	0.17	Intermediate good	High elasticity of substitution
U.S.	2012	30	0.00	Final good	High elasticity of substitution
U.S.	2012	31	0.00	Intermediate good	Low elasticity of substitution
U.S.	2012	47	0.00	Intermediate good	High elasticity of substitution
U.S.	2012	48	0.08	Intermediate good	High elasticity of substitution
U.S.	2012	49	0.00	Final good	Low elasticity of substitution
U.S.	2012	88	0.21	Intermediate good	High elasticity of substitution
U.S.	2012	97	0.00	Final good	Low elasticity of substitution
U.S.	2013	25	0.24	Intermediate good	Low elasticity of substitution
U.S.	2013	26	0.03	Intermediate good	High elasticity of substitution

(Continued)

Appendix 3 (Continued)

Country	*Year*	*HS code*	*Average tariff*	*Classification by BEC*	*Classification by elasticity of substitution*
U.S.	2013	27	0.17	Intermediate good	High elasticity of substitution
U.S.	2013	30	0.00	Final good	High elasticity of substitution
U.S.	2013	31	0.00	Intermediate good	Low elasticity of substitution
U.S.	2013	47	0.00	Intermediate good	High elasticity of substitution
U.S.	2013	48	0.08	Intermediate good	High elasticity of substitution
U.S.	2013	49	0.00	Final good	Low elasticity of substitution
U.S.	2013	88	0.21	Intermediate good	High elasticity of substitution
U.S.	2013	97	0.00	Final good	Low elasticity of substitution
U.S.	2014	25	0.24	Intermediate good	Low elasticity of substitution
U.S.	2014	26	0.03	Intermediate good	High elasticity of substitution
U.S.	2014	27	0.17	Intermediate good	High elasticity of substitution
U.S.	2014	30	0.00	Final good	High elasticity of substitution
U.S.	2014	31	0.00	Intermediate good	Low elasticity of substitution
U.S.	2014	47	0.00	Intermediate good	High elasticity of substitution
U.S.	2014	48	0.08	Intermediate good	High elasticity of substitution
U.S.	2014	49	0.00	Final good	Low elasticity of substitution
U.S.	2014	88	0.21	Intermediate good	High elasticity of substitution
U.S.	2014	97	0.00	Final good	Low elasticity of substitution

Note: the BEC classification and concordance of BEC-HS1996 can be accessed via https://wits.worldbank.org/product_concordance.html, and data of elasticity of substitution is obtained from Broda and Weinstein (2006). A product is classified to the High Group if its elasticity of substitution is higher than the average level, to the Low otherwise.

Appendix 4 Characteristics of top ten highest tariff products in China and the U.S. in 2000–2014

Country	*Year*	*HS code*	*Average tariff (%)*	*Classification by BEC*	*Classification by elasticity of substitution*
China	2000	4	36.77	Final good	High elasticity of substitution
China	2000	8	30.09	Final good	High elasticity of substitution
China	2000	10	54.38	Intermediate good	Low elasticity of substitution
China	2000	11	44.53	Intermediate good	Low elasticity of substitution
China	2000	15	40.52	Intermediate good	High elasticity of substitution
China	2000	17	42.88	Intermediate good	High elasticity of substitution
China	2000	21	39.77	Final good	Low elasticity of substitution
China	2000	22	56.79	Final good	High elasticity of substitution
China	2000	24	56.67	Final good	High elasticity of substitution
China	2000	87	35.00	Intermediate good	High elasticity of substitution
China	2001	4	33.11	Final good	High elasticity of substitution
China	2001	8	28.42	Final good	High elasticity of substitution
China	2001	10	54.34	Intermediate good	Low elasticity of substitution
China	2001	11	43.48	Intermediate good	Low elasticity of substitution
China	2001	15	39.22	Intermediate good	High elasticity of substitution
China	2001	17	41.88	Intermediate good	High elasticity of substitution
China	2001	21	37.06	Final good	Low elasticity of substitution
China	2001	22	51.88	Final good	High elasticity of substitution
China	2001	24	49.33	Final good	High elasticity of substitution
China	2001	87	31.42	Intermediate good	High elasticity of substitution
China	2002	4	23.82	Final good	High elasticity of substitution
China	2002	8	23.24	Final good	High elasticity of substitution
China	2002	10	33.69	Intermediate good	Low elasticity of substitution

(*Continued*)

Appendix 4 (Continued)

Country	*Year*	*HS code*	*Average tariff (%)*	*Classification by BEC*	*Classification by elasticity of substitution*
China	2002	11	30.04	Intermediate good	Low elasticity of substitution
China	2002	17	33.55	Intermediate good	High elasticity of substitution
China	2002	20	22.81	Final good	High elasticity of substitution
China	2002	21	29.35	Final good	Low elasticity of substitution
China	2002	22	38.76	Final good	High elasticity of substitution
China	2002	24	39.33	Final good	High elasticity of substitution
China	2002	87	23.64	Intermediate good	High elasticity of substitution
China	2003	8	21.08	Final good	High elasticity of substitution
China	2003	10	32.08	Intermediate good	Low elasticity of substitution
China	2003	11	27.88	Intermediate good	Low elasticity of substitution
China	2003	17	30.35	Intermediate good	High elasticity of substitution
China	2003	20	21.28	Final good	High elasticity of substitution
China	2003	21	26.07	Final good	Low elasticity of substitution
China	2003	22	31.89	Final good	High elasticity of substitution
China	2003	24	34.44	Final good	High elasticity of substitution
China	2003	37	21.31	Intermediate good	Low elasticity of substitution
China	2003	67	21.50	Intermediate good	Low elasticity of substitution
China	2004	10	32.03	Intermediate good	Low elasticity of substitution
China	2004	11	26.83	Intermediate good	Low elasticity of substitution
China	2004	17	29.25	Intermediate good	High elasticity of substitution
China	2004	19	19.80	Final good	High elasticity of substitution
China	2004	20	19.82	Final good	High elasticity of substitution
China	2004	21	22.78	Final good	Low elasticity of substitution
China	2004	22	26.68	Final good	High elasticity of substitution

Country	Year	HS code	Average tariff (%)	Classification by BEC	Classification by elasticity of substitution
China	2004	24	30.67	Final good	High elasticity of substitution
China	2004	37	21.00	Intermediate good	Low elasticity of substitution
China	2004	67	21.50	Intermediate good	Low elasticity of substitution
China	2005	11	20.39	Intermediate good	Low elasticity of substitution
China	2005	17	23.00	Intermediate good	High elasticity of substitution
China	2005	19	19.41	Final good	High elasticity of substitution
China	2005	20	19.69	Final good	High elasticity of substitution
China	2005	21	22.36	Final good	Low elasticity of substitution
China	2005	22	22.93	Final good	High elasticity of substitution
China	2005	24	30.67	Final good	High elasticity of substitution
China	2005	64	19.66	Final good	High elasticity of substitution
China	2005	67	21.45	Intermediate good	Low elasticity of substitution
China	2005	96	19.77	Final good	Low elasticity of substitution
China	2006	10	30.47	Intermediate good	Low elasticity of substitution
China	2006	11	25.71	Intermediate good	Low elasticity of substitution
China	2006	17	27.38	Intermediate good	High elasticity of substitution
China	2006	20	19.70	Final good	High elasticity of substitution
China	2006	21	22.54	Final good	Low elasticity of substitution
China	2006	22	22.82	Final good	High elasticity of substitution
China	2006	24	28.78	Final good	High elasticity of substitution
China	2006	64	19.66	Final good	High elasticity of substitution
China	2006	67	21.50	Intermediate good	Low elasticity of substitution
China	2006	96	19.78	Final good	Low elasticity of substitution
China	2007	10	30.47	Intermediate good	Low elasticity of substitution

(*Continued*)

Appendix 4 (Continued)

Country	*Year*	*HS code*	*Average tariff (%)*	*Classification by BEC*	*Classification by elasticity of substitution*
China	2007	11	26.03	Intermediate good	Low elasticity of substitution
China	2007	17	27.38	Intermediate good	High elasticity of substitution
China	2007	20	19.70	Final good	High elasticity of substitution
China	2007	21	22.54	Final good	Low elasticity of substitution
China	2007	22	22.72	Final good	High elasticity of substitution
China	2007	24	30.67	Final good	High elasticity of substitution
China	2007	67	21.50	Intermediate good	Low elasticity of substitution
China	2007	92	19.64	Final good	Low elasticity of substitution
China	2007	96	19.68	Final good	Low elasticity of substitution
China	2008	10	30.47	Intermediate good	Low elasticity of substitution
China	2008	11	26.03	Intermediate good	Low elasticity of substitution
China	2008	17	27.38	Intermediate good	High elasticity of substitution
China	2008	20	19.68	Final good	High elasticity of substitution
China	2008	21	20.66	Final good	Low elasticity of substitution
China	2008	22	22.61	Final good	High elasticity of substitution
China	2008	24	30.67	Final good	High elasticity of substitution
China	2008	67	21.50	Intermediate good	Low elasticity of substitution
China	2008	92	19.64	Final good	Low elasticity of substitution
China	2008	96	19.36	Final good	Low elasticity of substitution
China	2009	10	30.47	Intermediate good	Low elasticity of substitution
China	2009	11	26.03	Intermediate good	Low elasticity of substitution
China	2009	17	27.38	Intermediate good	High elasticity of substitution
China	2009	20	19.69	Final good	High elasticity of substitution
China	2009	21	21.91	Final good	Low elasticity of substitution

Country	*Year*	*HS code*	*Average tariff (%)*	*Classification by BEC*	*Classification by elasticity of substitution*
China	2009	22	22.51	Final good	High elasticity of substitution
China	2009	24	30.67	Final good	High elasticity of substitution
China	2009	64	19.15	Final good	High elasticity of substitution
China	2009	67	21.50	Intermediate good	Low elasticity of substitution
China	2009	96	19.36	Final good	Low elasticity of substitution
China	2010	10	30.47	Intermediate good	Low elasticity of substitution
China	2010	11	26.03	Intermediate good	Low elasticity of substitution
China	2010	17	27.38	Intermediate good	High elasticity of substitution
China	2010	20	19.72	Final good	High elasticity of substitution
China	2010	21	22.41	Final good	Low elasticity of substitution
China	2010	22	21.27	Final good	High elasticity of substitution
China	2010	24	30.67	Final good	High elasticity of substitution
China	2010	64	19.15	Final good	High elasticity of substitution
China	2010	67	21.50	Intermediate good	Low elasticity of substitution
China	2010	96	19.36	Final good	Low elasticity of substitution
China	2011	10	30.47	Intermediate good	Low elasticity of substitution
China	2011	11	26.03	Intermediate good	Low elasticity of substitution
China	2011	17	27.38	Intermediate good	High elasticity of substitution
China	2011	20	19.72	Final good	High elasticity of substitution
China	2011	21	22.41	Final good	Low elasticity of substitution
China	2011	22	21.27	Final good	High elasticity of substitution
China	2011	24	30.67	Final good	High elasticity of substitution
China	2011	64	19.15	Final good	High elasticity of substitution
China	2011	67	21.50	Intermediate good	Low elasticity of substitution

(*Continued*)

Appendix 4 (Continued)

Country	*Year*	*HS code*	*Average tariff (%)*	*Classification by BEC*	*Classification by elasticity of substitution*
China	2011	96	19.38	Final good	Low elasticity of substitution
China	2014	11	21.38	Intermediate good	Low elasticity of substitution
China	2014	17	23.00	Intermediate good	High elasticity of substitution
China	2014	19	18.82	Final good	High elasticity of substitution
China	2014	20	19.59	Final good	High elasticity of substitution
China	2014	21	21.48	Final good	Low elasticity of substitution
China	2014	22	21.05	Final good	High elasticity of substitution
China	2014	24	29.72	Final good	High elasticity of substitution
China	2014	64	19.32	Final good	High elasticity of substitution
China	2014	67	21.45	Intermediate good	Low elasticity of substitution
China	2014	96	19.34	Final good	Low elasticity of substitution
U.S.	2000	4	12.66	Final good	High elasticity of substitution
U.S.	2000	20	10.64	Final good	High elasticity of substitution
U.S.	2000	24	204.17	Final good	High elasticity of substitution
U.S.	2000	54	11.29	Intermediate good	Low elasticity of substitution
U.S.	2000	55	11.88	Intermediate good	High elasticity of substitution
U.S.	2000	58	10.21	Intermediate good	High elasticity of substitution
U.S.	2000	60	11.97	Intermediate good	High elasticity of substitution
U.S.	2000	61	13.71	Final good	High elasticity of substitution
U.S.	2000	62	10.75	Final good	High elasticity of substitution
U.S.	2000	64	12.26	Final good	High elasticity of substitution
U.S.	2001	4	12.66	Final good	High elasticity of substitution
U.S.	2001	20	10.64	Final good	High elasticity of substitution
U.S.	2001	24	204.17	Final good	High elasticity of substitution

Country	*Year*	*HS code*	*Average tariff (%)*	*Classification by BEC*	*Classification by elasticity of substitution*
U.S.	2001	54	11.03	Intermediate good	Low elasticity of substitution
U.S.	2001	55	11.51	Intermediate good	High elasticity of substitution
U.S.	2001	58	9.75	Intermediate good	High elasticity of substitution
U.S.	2001	60	11.61	Intermediate good	High elasticity of substitution
U.S.	2001	61	13.40	Final good	High elasticity of substitution
U.S.	2001	62	10.53	Final good	High elasticity of substitution
U.S.	2001	64	12.26	Final good	High elasticity of substitution
U.S.	2002	4	12.66	Final good	High elasticity of substitution
U.S.	2002	12	10.02	Intermediate good	Low elasticity of substitution
U.S.	2002	20	10.91	Final good	High elasticity of substitution
U.S.	2002	24	204.17	Final good	High elasticity of substitution
U.S.	2002	54	10.76	Intermediate good	Low elasticity of substitution
U.S.	2002	55	11.17	Intermediate good	High elasticity of substitution
U.S.	2002	60	11.41	Intermediate good	High elasticity of substitution
U.S.	2002	61	13.15	Final good	High elasticity of substitution
U.S.	2002	62	10.32	Final good	High elasticity of substitution
U.S.	2002	64	12.25	Final good	High elasticity of substitution
U.S.	2003	4	12.66	Final good	High elasticity of substitution
U.S.	2003	12	10.03	Intermediate good	Low elasticity of substitution
U.S.	2003	20	10.83	Final good	High elasticity of substitution
U.S.	2003	24	204.17	Final good	High elasticity of substitution
U.S.	2003	54	10.49	Intermediate good	Low elasticity of substitution
U.S.	2003	55	10.81	Intermediate good	High elasticity of substitution
U.S.	2003	60	11.03	Intermediate good	High elasticity of substitution

(*Continued*)

Appendix 4 (Continued)

Country	*Year*	*HS code*	*Average tariff (%)*	*Classification by BEC*	*Classification by elasticity of substitution*
U.S.	2003	61	12.85	Final good	High elasticity of substitution
U.S.	2003	62	10.12	Final good	High elasticity of substitution
U.S.	2003	64	12.25	Final good	High elasticity of substitution
U.S.	2004	4	12.66	Final good	High elasticity of substitution
U.S.	2004	12	10.03	Intermediate good	Low elasticity of substitution
U.S.	2004	20	10.83	Final good	High elasticity of substitution
U.S.	2004	24	204.17	Final good	High elasticity of substitution
U.S.	2004	54	10.18	Intermediate good	Low elasticity of substitution
U.S.	2004	55	10.77	Intermediate good	High elasticity of substitution
U.S.	2004	60	10.66	Intermediate good	High elasticity of substitution
U.S.	2004	61	12.54	Final good	High elasticity of substitution
U.S.	2004	62	10.01	Final good	High elasticity of substitution
U.S.	2004	64	12.24	Final good	High elasticity of substitution
U.S.	2005	4	12.66	Final good	High elasticity of substitution
U.S.	2005	12	10.03	Intermediate good	Low elasticity of substitution
U.S.	2005	20	10.83	Final good	High elasticity of substitution
U.S.	2005	24	204.17	Final good	High elasticity of substitution
U.S.	2005	54	10.18	Intermediate good	Low elasticity of substitution
U.S.	2005	55	10.77	Intermediate good	High elasticity of substitution
U.S.	2005	60	10.66	Intermediate good	High elasticity of substitution
U.S.	2005	61	12.54	Final good	High elasticity of substitution
U.S.	2005	62	10.01	Final good	High elasticity of substitution
U.S.	2005	64	12.24	Final good	High elasticity of substitution
U.S.	2006	4	12.66	Final good	High elasticity of substitution

Country	*Year*	*HS code*	*Average tariff (%)*	*Classification by BEC*	*Classification by elasticity of substitution*
U.S.	2006	12	10.03	Intermediate good	Low elasticity of substitution
U.S.	2006	20	10.83	Final good	High elasticity of substitution
U.S.	2006	24	204.17	Final good	High elasticity of substitution
U.S.	2006	54	10.18	Intermediate good	Low elasticity of substitution
U.S.	2006	55	10.77	Intermediate good	High elasticity of substitution
U.S.	2006	60	10.66	Intermediate good	High elasticity of substitution
U.S.	2006	61	12.54	Final good	High elasticity of substitution
U.S.	2006	62	10.01	Final good	High elasticity of substitution
U.S.	2006	64	12.24	Final good	High elasticity of substitution
U.S.	2007	4	12.29	Final good	High elasticity of substitution
U.S.	2007	12	13.08	Intermediate good	Low elasticity of substitution
U.S.	2007	20	11.57	Final good	High elasticity of substitution
U.S.	2007	24	204.98	Final good	High elasticity of substitution
U.S.	2007	54	10.31	Intermediate good	Low elasticity of substitution
U.S.	2007	55	10.62	Intermediate good	High elasticity of substitution
U.S.	2007	60	10.70	Intermediate good	High elasticity of substitution
U.S.	2007	61	12.78	Final good	High elasticity of substitution
U.S.	2007	62	10.08	Final good	High elasticity of substitution
U.S.	2007	64	11.11	Final good	High elasticity of substitution
U.S.	2008	4	12.66	Final good	High elasticity of substitution
U.S.	2008	12	13.08	Intermediate good	Low elasticity of substitution
U.S.	2008	20	10.82	Final good	High elasticity of substitution
U.S.	2008	24	204.17	Final good	High elasticity of substitution
U.S.	2008	54	10.31	Intermediate good	Low elasticity of substitution

(*Continued*)

Appendix 4 (Continued)

Country	*Year*	*HS code*	*Average tariff (%)*	*Classification by BEC*	*Classification by elasticity of substitution*
U.S.	2008	55	10.62	Intermediate good	High elasticity of substitution
U.S.	2008	60	10.70	Intermediate good	High elasticity of substitution
U.S.	2008	61	12.78	Final good	High elasticity of substitution
U.S.	2008	62	10.08	Final good	High elasticity of substitution
U.S.	2008	64	11.11	Final good	High elasticity of substitution
U.S.	2009	4	12.66	Final good	High elasticity of substitution
U.S.	2009	12	13.08	Intermediate good	Low elasticity of substitution
U.S.	2009	20	10.82	Final good	High elasticity of substitution
U.S.	2009	24	204.17	Final good	High elasticity of substitution
U.S.	2009	54	10.31	Intermediate good	Low elasticity of substitution
U.S.	2009	55	10.62	Intermediate good	High elasticity of substitution
U.S.	2009	60	10.70	Intermediate good	High elasticity of substitution
U.S.	2009	61	12.78	Final good	High elasticity of substitution
U.S.	2009	62	10.08	Final good	High elasticity of substitution
U.S.	2009	64	11.11	Final good	High elasticity of substitution
U.S.	2010	4	12.66	Final good	High elasticity of substitution
U.S.	2010	12	13.08	Intermediate good	Low elasticity of substitution
U.S.	2010	20	10.82	Final good	High elasticity of substitution
U.S.	2010	24	204.17	Final good	High elasticity of substitution
U.S.	2010	54	10.31	Intermediate good	Low elasticity of substitution
U.S.	2010	55	10.62	Intermediate good	High elasticity of substitution
U.S.	2010	60	10.70	Intermediate good	High elasticity of substitution
U.S.	2010	61	12.78	Final good	High elasticity of substitution
U.S.	2010	62	10.08	Final good	High elasticity of substitution

Country	Year	HS code	Average tariff (%)	Classification by BEC	Classification by elasticity of substitution
U.S.	2010	64	11.11	Final good	High elasticity of substitution
U.S.	2011	4	12.66	Final good	High elasticity of substitution
U.S.	2011	12	13.08	Intermediate good	Low elasticity of substitution
U.S.	2011	20	10.82	Final good	High elasticity of substitution
U.S.	2011	24	204.17	Final good	High elasticity of substitution
U.S.	2011	54	10.31	Intermediate good	Low elasticity of substitution
U.S.	2011	55	10.62	Intermediate good	High elasticity of substitution
U.S.	2011	60	10.70	Intermediate good	High elasticity of substitution
U.S.	2011	61	12.78	Final good	High elasticity of substitution
U.S.	2011	62	10.08	Final good	High elasticity of substitution
U.S.	2011	64	11.11	Final good	High elasticity of substitution
U.S.	2012	4	12.66	Final good	High elasticity of substitution
U.S.	2012	12	10.55	Intermediate good	Low elasticity of substitution
U.S.	2012	20	11.17	Final good	High elasticity of substitution
U.S.	2012	24	204.17	Final good	High elasticity of substitution
U.S.	2012	54	10.31	Intermediate good	Low elasticity of substitution
U.S.	2012	55	10.62	Intermediate good	High elasticity of substitution
U.S.	2012	60	10.70	Intermediate good	High elasticity of substitution
U.S.	2012	61	12.78	Final good	High elasticity of substitution
U.S.	2012	62	10.08	Final good	High elasticity of substitution
U.S.	2012	64	10.49	Final good	High elasticity of substitution
U.S.	2013	4	12.66	Final good	High elasticity of substitution
U.S.	2013	12	10.55	Intermediate good	Low elasticity of substitution
U.S.	2013	20	10.79	Final good	High elasticity of substitution

(Continued)

Appendix 4 (Continued)

Country	*Year*	*HS code*	*Average tariff (%)*	*Classification by BEC*	*Classification by elasticity of substitution*
U.S.	2013	24	204.17	Final good	High elasticity of substitution
U.S.	2013	54	10.31	Intermediate good	Low elasticity of substitution
U.S.	2013	55	10.62	Intermediate good	High elasticity of substitution
U.S.	2013	60	10.70	Intermediate good	High elasticity of substitution
U.S.	2013	61	12.78	Final good	High elasticity of substitution
U.S.	2013	62	10.08	Final good	High elasticity of substitution
U.S.	2013	64	10.49	Final good	High elasticity of substitution
U.S.	2014	4	12.66	Final good	High elasticity of substitution
U.S.	2014	12	10.55	Intermediate good	Low elasticity of substitution
U.S.	2014	20	10.79	Final good	High elasticity of substitution
U.S.	2014	24	204.17	Final good	High elasticity of substitution
U.S.	2014	54	10.31	Intermediate good	Low elasticity of substitution
U.S.	2014	55	10.62	Intermediate good	High elasticity of substitution
U.S.	2014	60	10.70	Intermediate good	High elasticity of substitution
U.S.	2014	61	12.78	Final good	High elasticity of substitution
U.S.	2014	62	10.08	Final good	High elasticity of substitution
U.S.	2014	64	10.49	Final good	High elasticity of substitution

Note: the BEC classification and concordance of BEC-HS1996 can be accessed via https://wits.worldbank.org/product_concordance.html, and data of elasticity of substitution is obtained from Broda and Weinstein (2006). A product is classified to the High Group if its elasticity of substitution is higher than the average level, to the Low otherwise.

Appendix 5 Summary of additional tariff product lists of the three rounds of Sino-U.S. trade friction. Additional tariff product lists of the first round Sino-U.S. trade friction

China's additional tariff list against the U.S. (first round: came into effect on July 6, 2018)

HS chapter	*Chapter description*	*Number of products*	*Examples*
Chapter 2	Meat and Edible Meat Offal	48	Meat and edible offal of bovine animals, swine, sheep, or goats, fresh, chilled, or frozen; meat and edible offal of the poultry of heading, fresh, chilled, or frozen
Chapter 3	Fish and Crustaceans, Mollusks, and Other Aquatic Invertebrates	182	Live fish; fish, fresh or frozen; crustaceans; mollusks
Chapter 4	Dairy Products; Birds' Eggs; Natural Honey; Edible Products of Animal Origin, Not Elsewhere Specified or Included	21	Milk and cream; butter; cheese, etc.
Chapter 5	Products of Animal Origin, Not Elsewhere Specified or Included	1	Cold, frozen gizzard
Chapter 7	Vegetable Seeds; Edible Vegetables and Certain Roots and Tubers	93	Potatoes, tomatoes, onions, cabbages, carrots, and other vegetables, fresh or chilled; dried leguminous vegetables, manioc, etc.
Chapter 8	Edible Fruit and Nuts; Peel of Citrus Fruit or Melons	86	Coconuts, cashew nuts, walnuts, Chinese chestnuts, pineapples, mangoes, watermelons, etc.
Chapter 10	Cereals	14	Other durum wheat, other maize, brown rice, and polished rice
Chapter 11	Products of the Milling Industry; Malt; Starches; Inulin Wheat Gluten	5	Maize flour, rice fine powder, etc.
Chapter 12	Oil Seeds and Oleaginous Fruits; Miscellaneous Grains, Seeds and Fruit; Industrial or Medicine Plante; Straw and Fodder	4	Yellow soya beans, black soya beans
Chapter 14	Vegetable Plaiting Material; Vegetable Products Not	1	Cotton linters

(*Continued*)

Appendix 5 (Continued)

China's additional tariff list against the U.S. (first round: came into effect on July 6, 2018)

HS chapter	*Chapter description*	*Number of products*	*Examples*
	Elsewhere Specified or Included		
Chapter 16	Preparations of Meat, of Fish or of Crustaceans, Mollusks, or Other Aquatic Invertebrates	41	Prepared or preserved fish; endangered shark's fins, canned; crustaceans, mollusks, prepared or preserved.
Chapter 20	Preparations of Vegetables, Fruit, Nuts, or Other Parts of Plants	3	Cranberries, orange juices.
Chapter 22	Beverages, Spirits, and Vinegar	2	Ethyl alcohol of any strength and other spirits, whiskies
Chapter 23	Residues and Waste from the Food Industries; Prepared Animal Fodder	3	Dog and cat food, put up for resale
Chapter 24	Tobacco and Manufactures; Tobacco Substitutes	12	Tobacco, cigars, and cigarettes
Chapter 52	Cotton	1	Cotton, not carded or combed
Chapter 87	Vehicles Other Than Railway or Tramway Rolling-Stock, and Parts and Accessories Thereof	28	Racing cars and small passenger buses, with spark-ignition engines and hybrid power; full electric vehicles; trucks, with spark-ignition engines
Total		545 Items	

U.S. additional tariff list against China (first round: came into effect on July 6, 2018)

HS chapter	*Chapter description*	*Number of products*	*Examples*
Chapter 28	Inorganic Chemicals; Organic or Inorganic Compounds of Precious Metals, of Rare-Earth Metals, of Radioactive Elements of Isotopes	1	Those of heading No. 2844, other than heavy water and isotopes other than its compounds
Chapter 40	Rubber and Articles Thereof	2	New pneumatic tires of rubber, used on aircraft
Chapter 84	Nuclear Reactors, Boilers, Machinery and	417	Nuclear reactors, steam turbines, diesel engines, excavators, marine

China's additional tariff list against the U.S. (first round: came into effect on July 6, 2018)

HS chapter	*Chapter description*	*Number of products*	*Examples*
	Mechanical Appliances, Parts Thereof		drilling platform, combine harvesters, numerically controlled machine tool
Chapter 85	Electrical Machinery and Equipment and Parts Thereof; Sound Recorders and Reproducers, Television Image and Sound Recorders and Reproducers, and Parts and Accessories of Such Article	186	DC and AC motors, generating sets with wind-powered, radar apparatus, light emitting diode
Chapter 86	Railway or Tramway Locomotives, Rolling-Stock, and Parts Thereof; Railway or Tramway Track Fixtures and Fittings and Parts Thereof; Mechanical (Including Electronic Mechanical) Traffic Signaling Equipment of All Kinds	17	Rail locomotives, driven by motors, parts of railway or trainway locomotives
Chapter 87	Vehicles Other Than Railway or Tramway Rolling-Stock, and Parts and Accessories Thereof	41	Passenger buses, with diesel engine, motor vehicles for the transport of goods, motorcycles, fire fighting vehicles
Chapter 88	Aircraft, Spacecraft, and Parts Thereof	15	Helicopters, airplanes, and other aircraft; spacecraft; communications satellites
Chapter 89	Ships, Boats, and Floating Structures	10	Ferryboats, cargo ships, oil tankers, fishing vessels, floating drilling platforms
Chapter 90	Optical, Photographic, Cinematographic, Measuring, Checking, Precision, Medical, or Surgical Instruments and Apparatus; Parts and Accessories Thereof	129	Stereoscopic microscopies, electronic navigational instruments, and appliances, electro-cardiographs, thermostats
Total		818	

(*Continued*)

Appendix 5 (Continued)

China's additional tariff list against the U.S. (first round: came into effect on July 6, 2018)

HS chapter	*Chapter description*	*Number of products*	*Examples*
Additional tariff product lists of the second round Sino-U.S. trade friction			
China's additional tariff list against the U.S. (second round: came into effect on August 23, 2018)			
HS chapter	*Chapter description*	*Number of products*	*Examples*
Chapter 23	Residues and Waste from the Food Industries; Prepared Animal Fodder	1	Flours and meals of fish, of a kind used in animal feeding
Chapter 26	Ores, Slag, and Ash	3	Manganese slags, slags, dross, oxide scaling and other waste from the manufacture of iron or steel
Chapter 27	Mineral Fuels, Mineral Oils, and Products of Their Distillation; Bituminous Substances, Mineral Waxes	64	Anthracite, not agglomerated; coal gas, water gas, and similar gases; diesel and pitch, etc.
Chapter 29	Organic Chemicals	11	Ethylene, propylene, styrene, acrylonitrile
Chapter 34	Soap, Organic Surface-Active Agents, Washing Preparations, Lubricating Preparations, Artificial Waxes, Prepared Waxes, Polishing or Sourcing Preparations, Candles and Similar Articles, Modelling Pastes, "Dental Waxes" and Dental Preparations	3	Lubricants, nonionic surface-active agents
Chapter 35	Albuminoidal Substances; Modified Starches; Glues; Enzymes	1	Other adhesives based on rubber or plastic
Chapter 39	Plastics and Articles Thereof	13	Polypropylene in primary forms; other propylene copolymers, in primary forms
Chapter 40	Rubber and Articles Thereof	1	CIIR or BIIR, in plates, sheets, or strip
Chapter 44	Wood and Articles of Wood; Wood Charcoal	3	Wood pellets
Chapter 45	Cork and Articles or Cork	1	Waste cork

China's additional tariff list against the U.S. (first round: came into effect on July 6, 2018)

HS chapter	*Chapter description*	*Number of products*	*Examples*
Chapter 47	Pulp of Wood or of Other fibrous Cellulosic Material; Recovered (Waste and Scrap) Paper or Paperboard	4	Waste and scrap of paper or paper board made of mechanical wood pulps
Chapter 51	Wool, Fine or Coarse Animal Hair, Hose Hair Yarn and Woven Fabric	4	Waste of coarse hair of animals
Chapter 52	Cotton	3	Garneted stock and other cotton waste
Chapter 55	Man-made Staple Fibers	2	Waste of synthetic and artificial fibers
Chapter 63	Other Made-Up Textile Articles; Sets; Worn Clothing and Worn Textile Articles; Rags	2	Sorted rags of textile materials
Chapter 70	Glass and Glassware	1	Optical fiber preforms
Chapter 71	Natural or Cultured Pearls, Precious or Semi-Precious Stones, Precious Metals, Metals Clad with Precious Metal, and Articles Thereof; Imitation Jewelry; Coin	2	Gold and waste and scrap with gold
Chapter 72	Iron and Steel	7	Waste and scrap of cast iron and stainless steel
Chapter 73	Articles of Iron or Steel	2	Other articles of iron or steel, for technical use or not for technical use
Chapter 74	Copper and Articles Thereof	1	Waste and scrap of copper
Chapter 75	Nickel and Articles Thereof	1	Waste and scrap of nickel
Chapter 76	Aluminium and Articles Thereof	1	Waste and scrap of aluminium
Chapter 79	Zinc and Articles Thereof	1	Waste and scrap of zinc
Chapter 80	Tin and Articles Thereof	1	Waste and scrap of tin
Chapter 81	Other Base Metals; Cements Articles and Thereof	12	Waste and scrap of tungsten, tantalum, and magnesium; unwrought germanium and vanadium, etc.

(*Continued*)

Appendix 5 (Continued)

China's additional tariff list against the U.S. (first round: came into effect on July 6, 2018)

HS chapter	*Chapter description*	*Number of products*	*Examples*
Chapter 85	Electrical Machinery and Equipment and Parts Thereof; Sound Recorders and Reproducers, Television Image and Sound Recorders and Reproducers, and Parts and Accessories of Such Article	2	Connector for a voltage not exceeding 36 volts, other connectors
Chapter 87	Vehicles Other Than Railway or Tramway Rolling-Stock, and Parts and Accessories Thereof	178	Passenger busses, motor vehicles for the transport of persons, motor vehicles for the transport of goods, motorcycles, bicycles, etc.
Chapter 89	Ships, Boats, and Floating Structures	1	Vessels and other floating structures for breaking up
Chapter 90	Optical, Photographic, Cinematographic, Measuring, Checking, Precision, Medical, or Surgical Instruments and Apparatus; Parts and Accessories Thereof	7	Optical fibers, and optical fiber bundles, magnetic resonance imaging devices, other instruments and appliances for ophthalmology
Total		333	

U.S. additional tariff list against China (second round: came into effect on August 23, 2018)

HS chapter	*Chapter description*	*Number of products*	*Examples*
Chapter 27	Mineral Fuels, Mineral Oils and Products of Their Distillation; Bituminous Substances, Mineral Waxes	3	Petroleum oils and oils obtained from bituminous minerals
Chapter 34	Soap, Organic Surface-Active Agents, Washing Preparations, Lubricating Preparations, Artificial Waxes, Prepared Waxes, Polishing or Sourcing Preparations, Candles, and Similar Articles, Modelling Pastes,	3	Lubricating preparations and preparations of a kind used for the oil or grease treatment of textile materials, leather, furskins

China's additional tariff list against the U.S. (first round: came into effect on July 6, 2018)

HS chapter	*Chapter description*	*Number of products*	*Examples*
	"Dental Waxes" and Dental Preparations		
Chapter 38	Miscellaneous Chemical Products	2	Additives or oils obtained from bituminous minerals
Chapter 39	Plastics and Articles Thereof	146	Polymers of ethylene, polymers of propylene; tubes of plastic; other plates, sheets, foil of plastics, etc.
Chapter 70	Glass and Glassware	1	Unworked fused quartz tubes
Chapter 73	Articles of Iron or Steel	6	Bridges, bridge-sections, towers, and structures and parts of steels
Chapter 76	Aluminium and Articles Thereof	2	Stranded wire, cables of aluminium, not electrically insulated
Chapter 84	Nuclear Reactors, Boilers, Machinery and Mechanical Appliances, Parts Thereof	31	Machinery and apparatus for making up paper pulp, paper or paperboard; seeders; machines and apparatus for the manufacture of semiconductors and flat panel display
Chapter 85	Electrical Machinery and Equipment and Parts Thereof; Sound Recorders and Reproducers, Television Image and Sound Recorders and Reproducers, and Parts and Accessories of Such Article	36	DC or AC motors, accumulators, memories, electronic integrated circuits
Chapter 86	Railway or Tramway Locomotives, Rolling-Stock and Parts Thereof; Railway or Tramway Track Fixtures and Fittings and Parts Thereof; Mechanical (Including Electronic Mechanical) Traffic	13	Rail locomotives powered by electric accumulators, diesel-electric locomotives, railway passenger coaches and parts thereof, containers

(*Continued*)

Appendix 5 (Continued)

China's additional tariff list against the U.S. (first round: came into effect on July 6, 2018)

HS chapter	*Chapter description*	*Number of products*	*Examples*
	Signaling Equipment of All Kinds		
Chapter 87	Vehicles Other Than Railway or Tramway Rolling-Stock, and Parts and Accessories Thereof	19	Tractors, motor vehicles for the transport of goods, motorcycles and bicycles
Chapter 89	Ships, Boats, and Floating Structures	1	Refrigerated vessels and cargo ships
Chapter 90	Optical, Photographic, Cinematographic, Measuring, Checking, Precision, Medical, or Surgical Instruments and Apparatus; Parts and Accessories Thereof	16	Direction-finding compasses, thermometers, calibrating meters, multimeters
Total		279	

Additional tariff product lists of the third round Sino-U.S. trade friction

China's additional tariff list against the U.S. (came into effect on September 24, 2018)

HS chapter	*Chapter description*	*Number of products*	*Examples*
China imposed 10% additional tariff against the U.S.			
Chapter 1	Live Animals; Animal Products	2	Other horses, other live animals
Chapter 2	Meat and Edible Meat Offal	3	Meat of bovine animals and other meat and edible meat offal, dried, smoked or salted, in brine
Chapter 3	Fish and Crustaceans, Mollusks, and Other Aquatic Invertebrates	1	Smoked herrings, other than edible fish offal
Chapter 4	Dairy Products, Bird's Eggs; Natural Honey; Edible Products of Animal Origin, Not Elsewhere Specified or Included	3	Natural honey and other bee products
Chapter 5	Products of Animal Origin, Not Elsewhere Specified or Included	7	Hog casings, whole and pieces; shells and bone of coral, crustaceans, or echinoderms, feathers

China's additional tariff list against the U.S. (first round: came into effect on July 6, 2018)

HS chapter	*Chapter description*	*Number of products*	*Examples*
			and down of a kind used for stuffing
Chapter 6	Live Trees and Other Plants; Bulb, Roots and The Like; Cut Flowers and Ornamental Foliage	7	Other live plants not used for seeding; mosses and lichens, fresh; other edible fruits, nut trees and bushes
Chapter 7	Vegetable Seeds; Edible Vegetables and Certain Roots and Tubers	4	Peas, frozen; other leguminous vegetables, spinach, etc.
Chapter 8	Edible Fruit and Nuts; Peel of Citrus Fruit or Melons	4	Peel of citrus fruit or melons, frozen strawberries, etc.
Chapter 9	Edible Fruit and Nuts; Peel of Citrus Fruit or Melons	18	Coffee, scented tea, green tea, Oolong tea, pepper, etc.
Chapter 11	Products of the Milling Industry; Malt; Starches; Inulin Wheat Gluten	15	Wheat flour, power and flakes of potatoes, potato starch, wheat gluten, etc.
Chapter 12	Oil Seeds and Oleaginous Fruits; Miscellaneous Grains, Seeds, and Fruit; Industrial or Medicine Plante; Straw and Fodder	12	Ground-nuts, in shell; other sunflower seeds; plants of a kind used primarily in perfumery, fresh, chilled, frozen or dried, etc.
Chapter 13	Lac; Gums; Resins and Other Vegetable Saps and Extracts	9	Pectic substances, pectinates and pectates; agar; gum Arabic, etc.
Chapter 14	Vegetable Plaiting Material; Vegetable Products Not Elsewhere Specified or Included	2	Bamboos and other vegetable products
Chapter 15	Animal or Vegetable Fats and Oils and Their Cleavage Products, Prepared Animal Fats, Animal or Vegetable Waxes	29	Fish cod – liver oil and its fractions; crude linseed oil and its fractions, sesame oil and its fractions, etc.
Chapter 16	Preparations of Meat, of Fish or of Crustaceans, Mollusks, or Other Aquatic Invertebrates	5	Hams and cuts of swine, prepared or preserved; sausages and similar products with natural casing, etc.
Chapter 17	Sugars and Sugar Confectionery	10	Granulated sugar, chemically pure fructose, chewing gum, etc.

(*Continued*)

Appendix 5 (Continued)

China's additional tariff list against the U.S. (first round: came into effect on July 6, 2018)

HS chapter	*Chapter description*	*Number of products*	*Examples*
Chapter 18	Cocoa and Cocoa Preparations	8	Cocoa paste, not defatted; cocoa oil and fat, etc.
Chapter 19	Preparations of Cereals, Flour, Starch, or Milk; Pastrycooks' Products	15	Pasta, stuffed; formula milk power; waffles and community wafers, etc.
Chapter 20	Preparations of Vegetables, Fruit, Nuts, or Other Parts of Plants	45	Fruits, canned; mixed vegetable juice; mixed fruit juice
Chapter 21	Miscellaneous Edible Preparations	11	Active yeasts, ice cream, baking powder, etc.
Chapter 22	Beverages, Spirits, and Vinegar	24	Natural waters and aerated water, wine, spirits, vodka, etc.
Chapter 23	Residues and Waste from the Food Industries; Prepared Animal Fodder	4	Bran of maize, bran of wheat, and other residues
Chapter 25	Salt; Sulphur; Earths and Stone; Plastering Materials, Lime, and Cement	47	Edible salt, natural graphite, granite, quicklime, slaked lime, etc.
Chapter 26	Ores, Slag, and Ash	11	Iron, manganese, copper, nickel ores, and concentrates, etc.
Chapter 27	Mineral Fuels, Mineral Oils, and Products of Their Distillation; Bituminous Substances, Mineral Waxes	1	Liquefied natural gas
Chapter 28	Inorganic Chemicals; Organic or Inorganic Compounds of Precious Metals, of Rare-Earth Metals, of Radioactive Elements of Isotopes	118	Hydrogen, iodine, calcium, sulphuric acid, carbon dioxide, colloidal precious metals, etc.
Chapter 29	Organic Chemicals	187	Methanoic acid, methylamine, nitrogenous compounds, acetylene, aspartame, methanol, etc.
Chapter 30	Pharmaceutical Products	4	Adhesive plaster, contraceptive preparations based on hormones
Chapter 31	Fertilizers	12	Urea, sodium nitrate, sodium chloride, fertilizers containing the

China's additional tariff list against the U.S. (first round: came into effect on July 6, 2018)

HS chapter	Chapter description	Number of products	Examples
			two fertilizing elements phosphorus and potassium
Chapter 32	Dyeing Extracts; Tannins and Their Derivatives; Dyes, Pigments and Other Coloring Matter; Paints and Varnishes; Putty and Other Mastics; Inks	41	Quebracho extract, carotene, paints and varnishes, driers, etc.
Chapter 33	Essential Oils and Resinoids; Perfumery Cosmetic or Toilet Preparations	29	Perfumes and toilet waters, beauty or make-up preparations and preparations for the care of the skin, toothpastes, etc.
Chapter 34	Soap, Organic Surface-Active Agents, Washing Preparations, Lubricating Preparations, Artificial Waxes, Prepared Waxes, Polishing or Sourcing Preparations, Candles and Similar Articles, Modelling Pastes, "Dental Waxes" and Dental Preparations	10	Soap, synthetic detergents in power form, etc.
Chapter 35	Albuminoidal Substances; Modified Starches; Glues; Enzymes	3	Casein and other casein derivatives, etc.
Chapter 37	Photographic or Cinematographic Goods	17	PS plates, CTP plates, laser films, developed film in rolls, etc.
Chapter 38	Miscellaneous Chemical Products	34	Rosin, insecticides, oleic acid, activated carbon, etc.
Chapter 39	Plastics and Articles Thereof	77	Polyisobutene, polyvinyl chloride, furniture, and carriages of plastics, etc.
Chapter 40	Rubber and Articles Thereof	60	Natural rubber, pneumatic tires of rubber, articles of apparel of vulcanized rubber, etc.
Chapter 41		21	Raw skins of sheep or lambs; raw hides and

(Continued)

Appendix 5 (Continued)

China's additional tariff list against the U.S. (first round: came into effect on July 6, 2018)

HS chapter	*Chapter description*	*Number of products*	*Examples*
	Raw Hides and Skins (Other Than Furskins) and Leather		skins of bovine or equine animals; chamois leather, etc.
Chapter 42	Articles of Leather; Saddlery and Harness; Travel Goods, Handbags, and Similar Containers; Articles of Animal Gut (Other Than Silk-Worm Gut)	23	Saddle and harness; articles of apparel of leather or of composition leather; trunks or suit-cases with outer surface of plastics or textile
Chapter 43	Furskins and Artificial Fur; Manufactures Thereof	10	Raw furskins of mink, articles of apparel of furskin, articles of artificial fur, etc.
Chapter 44	Wood and Articles of Wood; Wood Charcoal	97	Wood charcoal, wood, wood floorboard, tools of wood, etc.
Chapter 45	Cork and Articles or Cork	5	Natural cork; corks, plates, sheets, and strips are pressed against cork
Chapter 46	Manufactures of Straw, of Esparto or of Other Plaiting Materials; Basketwarc and Wickerwork	5	Mats, matting, screens of bamboo
Chapter 47	Pulp of Wood or of Other fibrous Cellulosic Material; Recovered (Waste and Scrap) Paper or Paperboard	2	Pulps of fibers derived from recovered paper or paperboard
Chapter 48	Paper and Paperboard; Article of Paper Pulp, of Paper or of Paperboard Currency Paper (Water-Mark Bank Note Paper)	77	Newsprint; paper and paperboard, corrugated; envelopes, etc.
Chapter 49	Printed Books, Newspapers, Pictures and Other Products of the Printing Industry; Manuscripts, Typescripts and Plans	16	Calendars of all kind, printed; dictionaries and encyclopedias; maps, printed
Chapter 50	Silk	6	Unbleached or bleached silk machine fabrics
Chapter 51	Wool, Fine or Coarse Animal Hair, Hose Hair Yarn and Woven Fabric	22	Yarn of goats hair, woven fabrics of fine goats hair

China's additional tariff list against the U.S. (first round: came into effect on July 6, 2018)

HS chapter	*Chapter description*	*Number of products*	*Examples*
Chapter 52	Cotton	72	Cotton yarn, cotton sewing thread, woven fabrics of cotton
Chapter 53	Other Vegetable Textile Fibers; Paper Yarn and Woven Fabrics of Paper Yarn	5	Woven fabrics of flax; blended linen woven fabrics
Chapter 54	Man-made Filaments	70	Sewing thread of filaments; fabrics of nylon; blended fabrics of artificial filament
Chapter 55	Man-made Staple Fibers	71	Nylon; woven fabrics of artificial staple fibers; polyester fabrics, etc.
Chapter 56	Wadding, Felt and Nonwovens; Special Yarns, Twine, Cordage, Ropes and Cables and Articles Thereof	21	Cotton swaddle and swollen products, nonwovens of chemical fiber filaments, etc.
Chapter 57	Carpets and Other Textile Floor Coverings	17	Woven carpets, and other floor coverings of textile materials, etc.
Chapter 58	Special Woven Fabrics; Tufted Textile Fabrics; Lace; Tapestries; Trimmings; Embroidery	32	Woven pile fabrics; mechanically made lace of cotton; embroidery, etc.
Chapter 59	Impregnated, Coated, Covered or Laminated Textile Fabrics; Textile Articles of a Kind Suitable for Industrial Use	29	Painting canvas; artificial leather; textile wall coverings, etc.
Chapter 60	Knitted or Crocheted Fabrics	37	Long pile fabrics; knitted or crocheted fabrics of cotton, etc.
Chapter 61	Articles of Apparel and Clothing Accessories, Kitted or Crocheted	90	Men's or women's overcoats, wind jackets, garments of cotton or wool, etc.
Chapter 62	Articles of Apparel and Clothing Accessories Not Knitted or Crocheted	119	Overcoats padded with feathers or down, overalls, dresses, etc.
Chapter 63	Other Made Up Textile Articles; Sets; Worn	44	Blankets and travelling rugs; bed linen, etc.

(Continued)

Appendix 5 (Continued)

China's additional tariff list against the U.S. (first round: came into effect on July 6, 2018)

HS chapter	*Chapter description*	*Number of products*	*Examples*
	Clothing and Worn Textile Articles; Rags		
Chapter 64	Footwear, Gaiters and the Like; Parts of Such Articles	31	Waterproof footwear, footwear with outer soles of leather, and uppers of textile materials
Chapter 65	Headgear and Parts Thereof	8	Hats and other head gear, knitted or crocheted; safety headgear
Chapter 66	Umbrellas, Sun Umbrellas, Walking-Sticks, Seat-Sticks, Whips, Riding-Crops and Parts Thereof	5	Umbrella having a telescopic shaft, walking-sticks, etc.
Chapter 67	Prepared Feathers and Down and Articles Made of Feathers or of Down; Artificial Flowers; Articles of Human Hair	6	Wigs; flowers, foliage and fruit and parts thereof, of silk or spun silk, etc.
Chapter 68	Articles of Stone, Plaster, Cement, Asbestos, Mica or Similar Materials	35	Articles of marbles; articles of cement; other articles of carbon fibers, etc.
Chapter 69	Ceramic Products	22	Wall tiles, flooring blocks, ceramic floor tiles, ceramic baths, etc.
Chapter 70	Glass and Glassware	43	Float wired glass, sheets, or boards; clock or watch glasses; glassware, etc.
Chapter 71	Natural or Cultured Pearls, Precious or Semi-Precious Stones, Precious Metals, Metals Clad with Precious Metal, and Articles Thereof; Imitation Jewelry; Coin	49	Crystals; diamonds; articles of precious stones, or semiprecious stones, etc.
Chapter 72	Iron and Steel	140	Alloy pig iron, hot-rolled steel, cold-rolled steel, etc.
Chapter 73	Articles of Iron or Steel	89	Sheet piling of iron or steel; tubes, pipes and hollow profiles, seamless; domestic appliances of iron or steel, etc.
Chapter 74	Copper and Articles Thereof	55	Unrefined copper; refined copper plates, sheets and strips; sanitary ware and

China's additional tariff list against the U.S. (first round: came into effect on July 6, 2018)

HS chapter	*Chapter description*	*Number of products*	*Examples*
			parts thereof, of copper, etc.
Chapter 75	Nickel and Articles Thereof	9	Non alloy nickel; nickel plates, sheets, strips and foils, etc.
Chapter 76	Aluminium and Articles Thereof	31	Unwrought aluminum alloy, aluminium tubes, aluminium cans and containers, etc.
Chapter 78	Lead and Articles Thereof	3	Unwrought lead alloys, containing by weight antimony; lead and lead alloy sheets, etc.
Chapter 79	Zinc and Articles Thereof	6	Unwrought zinc, zinc and zinc alloy bars, rods, profiles and wire, etc.
Chapter 80	Tin and Articles Thereof	8	Tin and tin alloy plates, sheets and strip, etc.
Chapter 81	Other Base Metals; Cements Articles and Thereof	26	Wire of molybdenum; germanium and articles thereof; tubes or pipes of titanium, etc.
Chapter 82	Tools, Implements, Cutlery, Spoons and Forks, of Base Metal, Parts Thereof Base Metal	57	Picks, hoes, rakes, scissors, tailors' shears, etc.
Chapter 83	Miscellaneous Articles of Base Metal	20	Keys; fittings and brackets for construction of base metal; electrodes of base metal, etc.
Chapter 84	Nuclear Reactors, Boilers, Machinery and Mechanical Appliances, Parts Thereof	541	Steam boilers, distillation towers, cranes, machine tools for drilling or boring, printers, etc.
Chapter 85	Electrical Machinery and Equipment and Parts Thereof; Sound Recorders and Reproducers, Television Image and Sound Recorders and Reproducers, and Parts and Accessories of Such Article	327	Electric motors and generators, transformers, battery cells and primary batteries, mobile communication base stations, industrial robots, etc.

(*Continued*)

Appendix 5 (Continued)

China's additional tariff list against the U.S. (first round: came into effect on July 6, 2018)

HS chapter	*Chapter description*	*Number of products*	*Examples*
Chapter 86	Railway or Tramway Locomotives, Rolling-Stock and Parts Thereof; Railway or Tramway Track Fixtures and Fittings and Parts Thereof; Mechanical (Including Electronic Mechanical) Traffic Signaling Equipment of All Kinds	10	Railway or tramway tram axle; containers, etc.
Chapter 88	Aircraft, Spacecraft, and Parts Thereof	2	Gliders and hang gliders; balloons, dirigibles and other non-powered aircraft
Chapter 89	Ships, Boats, and Floating Structures	8	Sailboats; non-motorized vessels; other floating structures, etc.
Chapter 90	Optical, Photographic, Cinematographic, Measuring, Checking, Precision, Medical, or Surgical Instruments and Apparatus; Parts and Accessories Thereof	95	Camera lenses; telescopes; LCD panels; thermometers, etc.
Chapter 91	Clocks and Watches and Part Thereof	19	Wrist-watches, electrically operated; mechanical wrist watches; wall clocks, etc.
Chapter 92	Musical Instruments Parts and Accessories of Such Articles	15	Grand pianos, accordions, musical instruments played with a bow, etc.
Chapter 93	Arms and Ammunition; Parts and Accessories Thereof	1	Other firearms and similar devices
Chapter 94	Furniture; Bedding, Mattresses, Mattresses Supports, Cushions and Similar Stuffed Furnishings; Lamps and Lighting Fittings, Not Elsewhere Specified or Included; Illuminated Signs, Illuminated Name-Plates and the	43	Seats; electric table, desk, bedside or floor standing lamps; furniture of plastics, etc.

China's additional tariff list against the U.S. (first round: came into effect on July 6, 2018)

HS chapter	*Chapter description*	*Number of products*	*Examples*
	Like; Prefabricated Building		
Chapter 95	Toys, Games, and Sports Requisites; Parts and Accessories Thereof	31	Animal dolls, balls, skates, etc.
Chapter 96	Miscellaneous Manufactured Articles	52	Buttons, snap fasteners, ball point pens, pencils, etc.
Chapter 97	Works of Art, Collectors' Pieces, and Antiques	4	Stamps; original sculptures and statuary; hand-painted paintings, pastels, and other drawings; antiques of an age exceeding one hundred years, etc.
Total			3,571
China imposed 5% additional tariff against the U.S.			
Chapter 1	Live Animals; Animal Products	3	Other mammals, other reptiles, other insects
Chapter 4	Dairy Products; Birds' Eggs; Natural Honey; Edible Products of Animal Origin, Not Elsewhere Specified or Included	1	Other egg yolks
Chapter 5	Products of Animal Origin, Not Elsewhere Specified or Included	2	Other feathers or down; skins and other parts of birds, with their feathers or down
Chapter 7	Vegetable Seeds; Edible Vegetables and Certain Roots and Tubers	5	Potatoes, frozen; sweet corns, frozen, etc.
Chapter 9	Coffee, Tea, Mate, and Spices	2	Coffee husks and skins
Chapter 11	Products of the Milling Industry; Malt; Starches; Inulin Wheat Gluten	4	Flakes, meal and powder of potatoes; maize starch
Chapter 12	Oil Seeds and Oleaginous Fruits; Miscellaneous Grains, Seeds and Fruit; Industrial or Medicine Plante; Straw and Fodder	5	Ground-nuts, shelled; fruit stones or kernels of peaches, plums and prunes
Chapter 13	Lac; Gums; Resins and Other Vegetable Saps and Extracts	2	Saps and extracts of hops

(Continued)

Appendix 5 (Continued)

China's additional tariff list against the U.S. (first round: came into effect on July 6, 2018)

HS chapter	*Chapter description*	*Number of products*	*Examples*
Chapter 15	Animal or Vegetable Fats and Oils and Their Cleavage Products, Prepared Animal Fats, Animal or Vegetable Waxes	3	Cotton seed oil, linseed oil, bee wax
Chapter 16	Preparations of Meat, of Fish or of Crustaceans, Mollusks, or Other Aquatic Invertebrates	2	Meat, meat offal of turkeys; chicken breast
Chapter 17	Sugars and Sugar Confectionery	3	Anhydrous lactose
Chapter 18	Cocoa and Cocoa Preparations	1	Cocoa powder, containing added sugar or other sweetening matter
Chapter 19	Preparations of Cereals, Flour, Starch or Milk; Pastrycooks' Products	3	Rice vermicelli, bulgur wheat
Chapter 20	Preparations of Vegetables, Fruit, Nuts, or Other Parts of Plants	15	Tomatoes paste, in air tight containers; peanut butters, etc.
Chapter 21	Miscellaneous Edible Preparations	5	Tomato ketchup and other tomato sauces, etc.
Chapter 22	Beverages, Spirits, and Vinegar	2	Vermouth and other similar wines
Chapter 23	Residues and Waste from the Food Industries; Prepared Animal Fodder	6	Beet-pulp, bagasses and other waste of sugar manufacture; other preparations of a kind used in animal feeding
Chapter 25	Salt; Sulphur; Earths and Stone; Plastering Materials, Lime and Cement	21	Sea water, kieselguhr, wollastonite, etc.
Chapter 26	Ores, Slag, and Ash	4	Lead ores and concentrates; molybdenum ores and concentrates, etc.
Chapter 28	Inorganic Chemicals; Organic or Inorganic Compounds of Precious Metals, of Rare-Earth Metals, of Radioactive Elements of Isotopes	102	Manganese dioxide, heavy water, hydrogen chloride, etc.
Chapter 29	Organic Chemicals	157	Paraformaldehyde; vitamins and their deviants, unmixed; caffeine and salts of caffeine

China's additional tariff list against the U.S. (first round: came into effect on July 6, 2018)

HS chapter	*Chapter description*	*Number of products*	*Examples*
Chapter 30	Pharmaceutical Products	8	First-aid boxes and kits, cartridge bags; absorbent cotton, gauze, bandages
Chapter 31	Fertilizers	7	Ammonium sulphate; organic-inorganic compound fertilizer
Chapter 32	Dyeing Extracts; Tannins and Their Derivatives; Dyes, Pigments and Other Coloring Matter; Paints and Varnishes; Putty and Other Mastics; Inks	20	Titanium dioxide, pigment of a kind used in the manufacture of paints, water-based inkjet ink
Chapter 33	Essential Oils and Resinoids; Perfumery Cosmetic or Toilet Preparations	14	Essential oils of lemon; extracted oil resins
Chapter 34	Soap, Organic Surface-Active Agents, Washing Preparations, Lubricating Preparations, Artificial Waxes, Prepared Waxes, Polishing or Sourcing Preparations, Candles and Similar Articles, Modelling Pastes, "Dental Waxes" and Dental Preparations	14	Polishes and creams for glass or metal; candles and similar articles
Chapter 35	Albuminoidal Substances; Modified Starches; Glues; Enzymes	14	Alkaline lipase; gelatin and gelatin derivatives
Chapter 36	Explosives; Pyrotechnic Products; Matches; Pyrophoric Alloys; Certain Combustible Preparations	6	Fireworks, firecrackers; signaling flares, rain rockets, fog rockets
Chapter 37	Photographic or Cinematographic Goods	26	Flexographic printing plates; films for color photography
Chapter 38	Miscellaneous Chemical Products	44	Artificial graphite; disinfectants; preparations and charges for fire-extinguishers
Chapter 39	Plastics and Articles Thereof	55	Hoses of plastics; windows, doors of plastics, etc.
		42	

(*Continued*)

Appendix 5 (Continued)

China's additional tariff list against the U.S. (first round: came into effect on July 6, 2018)

HS chapter	*Chapter description*	*Number of products*	*Examples*
Chapter 40	Rubber and Articles Thereof		Articles of hard rubber; pneumatic tires of rubber
Chapter 41	Raw Hides and Skins (Other Than Furskins) and Leather	6	Raw hides and skins of swines; whole raw hides and skins of bovine animals
Chapter 43	Furskins and Artificial Fur; Manufactures Thereof	1	Whole raw furskins of other animals
Chapter 44	Wood and Articles of Wood; Wood Charcoal	12	Poplar boards; inlaid woods
Chapter 47	Pulp of Wood or of Other Fibrous Cellulosic Material; Recovered (Waste and Scrap) Paper or Paperboard	12	Mechanical wood pulp; chemical wood pulp
Chapter 48	Paper and Paperboard; Article of Paper Pulp, of Paper or of Paperboard Currency Paper (Water-Mark Bank Note Paper)	23	Kraft paper, self-copy paper
Chapter 49	Printed Books, Newspapers, Pictures and Other Products of the Printing Industry; Manuscripts, Typescripts and Plans	8	Children's picture, drawing or coloring books; globes, celestial globes
Chapter 52	Cotton	4	Cotton sewing thread
Chapter 54	Man-made Filaments	19	Synthetic multi-filament single yarn
Chapter 55	Man-made Staple Fibers	13	Polyacrylonitrile filament tow
Chapter 56	Wadding, Felt and Nonwovens; Special Yarns, Twine, Cordage, Ropes and Cables and Articles Thereof	14	Wadding made of chemical fibers; twine, cordage, rope, or cable of polyethylene or polypropylene
Chapter 57	Carpets and Other Textile Floor Coverings	4	Carpets of nylon, tufted, and floor coverings of other textile materials, tufted
Chapter 58	Special Woven Fabrics; Tufted Textile Fabrics; Lace; Tapestries; Trimmings; Embroidery	7	Chenille fabrics of cotton; woven fabrics of silk or spun silk
Chapter 59	Impregnated, Coated, Covered or Laminated Textile Fabrics; Textile	9	Textile hose piping and similar textile tubing

China's additional tariff list against the U.S. (first round: came into effect on July 6, 2018)

HS chapter	*Chapter description*	*Number of products*	*Examples*
	Articles of a Kind Suitable for Industrial Use		
Chapter 60	Knitted or Crocheted Fabrics	3	Knitted or crocheted fabrics of rubber thread
Chapter 61	Articles of Apparel and Clothing Accessories, Kitted or Crocheted	2	Knitted or crocheted sockets and other socks
Chapter 62	Articles of Apparel and Clothing Accessories Not Knitted or Crocheted	1	Garments made up of textile materials or nonwovens
Chapter 63	Other Made Up Textile Articles; Sets; Worn Clothing and Worn Textile Articles; Rags	13	Electric blankets; curtains of cotton, knitted, etc.
Chapter 64	Footwear, Gaiters and the Like; Parts of Such Articles	2	Other footwear with uppers of leather, incorporating a protective metal toe-cap
Chapter 65	Headgear and Parts Thereof	4	Headgear of furskins; headgear of rubber or of plastics
Chapter 66	Umbrellas, Sun Umbrellas, Walking-Sticks, Seat-Sticks, Whips, Riding-Crops and Parts Thereof	1	Garden or similar umbrellas
Chapter 67	Prepared Feathers and Down and Articles Made of Feathers or of Down; Artificial Flowers; Articles of Human Hair	4	Flowers, foliage and fruit and parts thereof, of plastics
Chapter 68	Articles of Stone, Plaster, Cement, Asbestos, Mica or Similar Materials	21	Abrasive paper; building blocks and bricks of articles of cement
Chapter 69	Ceramic Products	10	Ceramic wares for laboratory, chemical or other technical uses
Chapter 70	Glass and Glassware	38	Rearview mirrors for vehicles; toughened safety glass for vehicles; glass wool and articles thereof
Chapter 71	Natural or Cultured Pearls, Precious or Semi-Precious Stones, Precious Metals, Metals Clad with Precious Metal, and	17	Synthetic diamonds; silversmiths' wares and parts thereof

(Continued)

Appendix 5 (Continued)

China's additional tariff list against the U.S. (first round: came into effect on July 6, 2018)			
HS chapter	*Chapter description*	*Number of products*	*Examples*
	Articles Thereof; Imitation Jewelry; Coin		
Chapter 72	Iron and Steel	19	Powders of alloy steel; flat-rolled stainless steel, hot-rolled
Chapter 73	Articles of Iron or Steel	47	Casing and tubing of a kind used in drilling for oil or gas, of stainless steel; products of stainless wire, for industrial use; nuts
Chapter 74	Copper and Articles Thereof	16	Net, grating, mesh and sheet of copper wire
Chapter 75	Nickel and Articles Thereof	10	Nickel alloy plates, sheets, strip, foil, tubes
Chapter 76	Aluminium and Articles Thereof	20	Aluminium alloy bars, rods, wires and profiles
Chapter 78	Lead and Articles Thereof	4	Lead and lead alloy bars, rods, wires and profiles
Chapter 79	Zinc and Articles Thereof	3	Zinc plates, sheets, strip and foil
Chapter 80	Tin and Articles Thereof	2	Tin and tin alloy tubes, pipes and tube or pipe fittings
Chapter 81	Other Base Metals; Cements Articles and Thereof	26	Molybdenum and articles thereof; bars, rods, profiles and profile shapes, of titanium, etc.
Chapter 82	Tools, Implements, Cutlery, Spoons and Forks, of Base Metal, Parts Thereof Base Metal	25	Axes, billhooks and similar hewing tools; razors
Chapter 83	Miscellaneous Articles of Base Metal	15	Central control door lock, of a kind used for motor vehicles; flexible tubing of iron or steel
Chapter 84	Nuclear Reactors, Boilers, Machinery and Mechanical Appliances, Parts Thereof	193	Spark-ignition aircraft engines, of an output not exceeding 298kW; pulley tackle, powered by electric motor, and lifting machinery; machine tools for polishing; milking machines, etc.
Chapter 85	Electrical Machinery and Equipment and Parts Thereof; Sound Recorders and Reproducers, Television	132	Digital telephone exchanger; long distance telephone exchanger; telegraph exchanger; optical fiber cable; electrical lighting

China's additional tariff list against the U.S. (first round: came into effect on July 6, 2018)

HS chapter	*Chapter description*	*Number of products*	*Examples*
	Image and Sound Recorders and Reproducers, and Parts and Accessories of Such Article		equipment for motor vehicles
Chapter 86	Railway or Tramway Locomotives, Rolling-Stock and Parts Thereof; Railway or Tramway Track Fixtures and Fittings and Parts Thereof; Mechanical (Including Electronic Mechanical) Traffic Signaling Equipment of All Kinds	4	Containers of 20 feet; other diesel-electric locomotives
Chapter 87	Vehicles Other Than Railway or Tramway Rolling-Stock, And Parts and Accessories Thereof	91	Pedestrian controlled tractors; special purpose motor vehicles; parts and accessories of motor vehicles
Chapter 88	Aircraft, Spacecraft and Parts Thereof	7	Small and medium planes and other aircrafts; helicopters of an unladen weight not exceeding 7 kg
Chapter 89	Ships, Boats and Floating Structures	3	Motor boats; inflated vessels for pleasure or sports; inflatable raft
Chapter 90	Optical, Photographic, Cinematographic, Measuring, Checking, Precision, Medical, or Surgical Instruments and Apparatus; Parts and Accessories Thereof	113	Lasers; ultraviolet and infrared ray devices, B-ultrasonic diagnostic equipment, etc.
Chapter 91	Clocks and Watches and Part Thereof	3	Time registers, time recorders
Chapter 92	Musical Instruments Parts and Accessories of Such Articles	7	Brass-wind musical instruments; percussion musical instruments
Chapter 93	Arms and Ammunition; Parts and Accessories Thereof	5	Parts of shotgun cartridges and air gun pellets; military swords, cutlasses, bayonets, lances and similar arms and parts thereof

(*Continued*)

Appendix 5 (Continued)

China's additional tariff list against the U.S. (first round: came into effect on July 6, 2018)

HS chapter	*Chapter description*	*Number of products*	*Examples*
Chapter 94	Furniture; Bedding, Mattresses, Mattresses Supports, Cushions and Similar Stuffed Furnishings; Lamps and Lighting Fittings, Not Elsewhere Specified or Included; Illuminated Signs, Illuminated Name-Plates and the Like; Prefabricated Building	13	Mattress, fitted with spring; seats of a kind used for motor vehicles
Chapter 95	Toys, Games, and Sports Requisites; Parts and Accessories Thereof	15	Video games, operated by coins; playing cards; treadmill
Chapter 96	Miscellaneous Manufactured Articles	13	Medicine capsules; infant diapers
Chapter 97	Works of Art, Collectors' Pieces and Antiques	4	Reproductions of paintings, drawings and pastels
Total			1,636

U.S. additional tariff list against China (came into effect on September 24, 2018)

HS chapter	*Chapter description*	*Number of products*	*Examples*
Chapter 2	Meat and Edible Meat Offal	7	Meat of swine, fresh, chilled or frozen
Chapter 3	Fish and Crustaceans, Mollusks, and Other Aquatic Invertebrates	264	Live fish; fish, fresh or chilled; fish, frozen; crustaceans; mollucs, etc.
Chapter 4	Dairy Products; Birds' Eggs; Natural Honey; Edible Products of Animal Origin, Not Elsewhere Specified or Included	20	Whey; butter; birds' eggs; natural honey, etc.
Chapter 5	Products of Animal Origin, Not Elsewhere Specified or Included	14	Pigs', hogs' or boars' bristles and hairs; horse hair and waste horse hair, etc.
Chapter 7	Vegetable Seeds; Edible Vegetables and Certain Roots and Tubers	143	Onions, shallots, garlic, cabbages, cauliflowers, fresh or chilled; vegetables, frozen; dried vegetables, etc.

China's additional tariff list against the U.S. (first round: came into effect on July 6, 2018)

HS chapter	*Chapter description*	*Number of products*	*Examples*
Chapter 8	Edible Fruit and Nuts; Peel of Citrus Fruit or Melons	90	Coconuts, Brazil nuts and cashew nuts, fresh or dried; bananas, apples, pears, fresh or dried, etc.
Chapter 10	Cereals	22	Wheat and maslin; barley; oats; maize for seed; grain sorghum, etc.
Chapter 11	Products of the Milling Industry; Malt; Starches; Inulin Wheat Gluten	38	Wheat flour; flour of potatoes; malt; starches, etc.
Chapter 12	Oil Seeds and Oleaginous Fruits; Miscellaneous Grains, Seeds and Fruit; Industrial or Medicine Plante; Straw and Fodder	48	Soya beans; ground nuts; linseed; rape seeds; hops, etc.
Chapter 14	Lac; Gums; Resins and Other Vegetable Saps and Extracts	8	Vegetable materials of a kind used primarily for plaiting
Chapter 15	Vegetable Plaiting Material; Vegetable Products Not Elsewhere Specified or Included	8	Fats and oils and their fractions, of fish or marine mammals; wool grease, etc.
Chapter 16	Animal or Vegetable Fats and Oils and Their Cleavage Products, Prepared Animal Fats, Animal or Vegetable Waxes	90	Prepared or preserved fish, crustaceans, mollusks, etc.
Chapter 17	Preparations of Meat, of Fish or of Crustaceans, Mollusks, or Other Aquatic Invertebrates	5	Cane or beet sugar and chemically pure sucrose, in solid form; sugar confectionary, not containing cocoa
Chapter 19	Preparations of Cereals, Flour, Starch or Milk; Pastrycooks' Products	6	Malt extract; pasta; bread, biscuits, pastry, etc.
Chapter 20	Preparations of Vegetables, Fruit, Nuts or Other Parts of Plants	140	Vegetables, fruits, nuts and other edible parts of plants prepared or preserved by vinegar or acetic acid, etc.
Chapter 21	Miscellaneous Edible Preparations	3	Sauces; mixed condiments, etc.
Chapter 22	Beverages, Spirits and Vinegar	20	Mineral waters, aerated water; beer; wine, etc.
		21	

(*Continued*)

Appendix 5 (Continued)

China's additional tariff list against the U.S. (first round: came into effect on July 6, 2018)

HS chapter	*Chapter description*	*Number of products*	*Examples*
Chapter 23	Residues and Waste from the Food Industries; Prepared Animal Fodder		Preparations of a kind used in animal feeding
Chapter 24	Tobacco and Manufactures; Tobacco Substitutes	46	Tobacco, cigars and cheroots, etc.
Chapter 25	Salt; Sulphur; Earths and Stone; Plastering Materials, Lime and Cement	65	Salt; Sulphur; marble; granite, etc.
Chapter 26	Ores, Slag and Ash	33	Iron, nickel, lead, uranium or thorium, titanium ores and concentrates
Chapter 27	Mineral Fuels, Mineral Oils and Products of Their Distillation; Bituminous Substances, Mineral Waxes	59	Coal; coal gas; crude oils and extracts; bitumen, etc.
Chapter 28	Inorganic Chemicals; Organic or Inorganic Compounds of Precious Metals, of Rare-Earth Metals, of Radioactive Elements of Isotopes	231	Sulphuric acid; nitric acid; nitrites; sulphides; carbides, etc.
Chapter 29	Organic Chemicals	693	Acyclic hydrocarbons; cyclic hydrocarbons; acyclic alcohols; phenols; amine-function compounds; sugars, chemically pure, etc.
Chapter 31	Fertilizers	24	Animal or vegetable fertilizers; mineral or chemical fertilizers, nitrogenous; mineral or chemical fertilizers, phosphatic; mineral or chemical fertilizers, potassic, etc.
Chapter 32	Dyeing Extracts; Tannins and Their Derivatives; Dyes, Pigments and Other Coloring Matter; Paints and Varnishes; Putty and Other Mastics; Inks	102	Coloring matters; paints; ink, etc.
Chapter 33	Essential Oils and Resinoids; Perfumery	25	Essential oils; odoriferous substances; perfumes and toilet waters; beauty or

China's additional tariff list against the U.S. (first round: came into effect on July 6, 2018)

HS chapter	*Chapter description*	*Number of products*	*Examples*
	Cosmetic or Toilet Preparations		make-up preparations and preparations for the care of the skin; preparation for use on the hair, etc.
Chapter 34	Soap, Organic Surface-Active Agents, Washing Preparations, Lubricating Preparations, Artificial Waxes, Prepared Waxes, Polishing or Sourcing Preparations, Candles and Similar Articles, Modelling Pastes, "Dental Waxes" and Dental Preparations	33	Soap, detergents, lubricants, artificial waxes, etc.
Chapter 35	Albuminoidal Substances; Modified Starches; Glues; Enzymes	10	Albumins; enzymes, etc.
Chapter 36	Explosives; Pyrotechnic Products; Matches; Pyrophoric Alloys; Certain Combustible Preparations	1	Ferro-cerium and other pyrophoric alloys
Chapter 37	Photographic or Cinematographic Goods	37	Photographic film, sensitized; photographic film plates and film; cinematographic film, chemical preparation for photographic use
Chapter 38	Miscellaneous Chemical Products	142	Insecticides; preparations and charges for fire-extinguishers; activated carbon, etc.
Chapter 39	Plastics and Articles Thereof	53	Polymers of ethylene; tubes of plastic; plastic products for transport or packaging, etc.
Chapter 40	Rubber and Articles Thereof	124	Natural rubber; synthetic rubber; rubber tires, etc.
Chapter 41	Raw Hides and Skins (Other Than Furskins) and Leather	85	Leather of bovine and equine animals; leather of sheep and lambs, etc.
Chapter 42	Articles of Leather; Saddlery and Harness; Travel Goods, Handbags, and Similar Containers; Articles of Animal Gut	86	Saddlery; articles of apparel and clothing accessories, of leather or of composition leather

(*Continued*)

Appendix 5 (Continued)

China's additional tariff list against the U.S. (first round: came into effect on July 6, 2018)

HS chapter	*Chapter description*	*Number of products*	*Examples*
	(Other Than Silk-Worm Gut)		
Chapter 43	Furskins and Artificial Fur; Manufactures Thereof	15	Articles of apparel of furskin; artificial fur and articles thereof
Chapter 44	Wood and Articles of Wood; Wood Charcoal	180	Wood charcoal; log wood boards; wooden tool cases, etc.
Chapter 45	Cork and Articles or Cork	19	Natural cork, articles of natural cork, agglomerated cork, etc.
Chapter 46	Manufactures of Straw, of Esparto or of Other Plaiting Materials; Basketware and Wickerwork	48	Products of plaiting materials
Chapter 47	Pulp of Wood or of Other fibrous Cellulosic Material; Recovered (Waste and Scrap) Paper or Paperboard	21	Mechanical wood pulp; chemical wood pulp; waste and scrap paper and paperboards
Chapter 48	Paper and Paperboard; Article of Paper Pulp, of Paper or of Paperboard Currency Paper (Water-Mark Bank Note Paper)	222	Newsprint; toilet papers; copying papers, kraft papers; paper stationery, etc.
Chapter 50	Silk	13	Raw silk; silk yarn; woven fabric of silk or spun silk, etc.
Chapter 51	Wool, Fine or Coarse Animal Hair, Hose Hair Yarn and Woven Fabric	101	Wool; yarn of wool or of fine animal hair; woven fabrics of wool or fine animal hair
Chapter 52	Cotton	230	Cotton; cotton sewing thread; woven fabrics of cotton
Chapter 53	Other Vegetable Textile Fibers; Paper Yarn and Woven Fabrics of Paper Yarn	30	Flax; abaca; woven fabrics of flax, etc.
Chapter 54	Man-Made Filaments	129	Sewing thread of chemical filaments; synthetic filament yarn; artificial filament yarn, etc.
Chapter 55	Man-made Staple Fibers	130	Synthetic staple fibers, sewing thread of chemical staple fibers, etc.

China's additional tariff list against the U.S. (first round: came into effect on July 6, 2018)

HS chapter	*Chapter description*	*Number of products*	*Examples*
Chapter 56	Wadding, Felt and Nonwovens; Special Yarns, Twine, Cordage, Ropes and Cables and Articles Thereof	55	Twine, cordage, rope and cables; knotted netting of twine, cordage or rope, etc.
Chapter 57	Carpets and Other Textile Floor Coverings	48	Carpets and other textile floor coverings, woven, etc.
Chapter 58	Special Woven Fabrics; Tufted Textile Fabrics; Lace; Tapestries; Trimmings; Embroidery	68	Woven pile fabrics; toweling; embroidery, etc.
Chapter 59	Impregnated, Coated, Covered or Laminated Textile Fabrics; Textile Articles of a Kind Suitable for Industrial Use	58	Textile wall coverings, textile hose pipping, transmission or conveyor belts, etc.
Chapter 60	Knitted or Crocheted Fabrics	55	Pile fabrics, knitted or crocheted
Chapter 65	Headgear and Parts Thereof	26	Hat-forms, hat bodies, and hoods; hats, knitted or crocheted, etc.
Chapter 67	Prepared Feathers and Down and Articles Made of Feathers or of Down; Artificial Flowers; Articles of Human Hair	2	Feathers, part of feathers, down and articles thereof
Chapter 68	Articles of Stone, Plaster, Cement, Asbestos, Mica or Similar Materials	65	Articles of cement, of concrete, or of artificial stone; articles of plaster; articles of bitumen; asbestos-cement, etc.
Chapter 69	Ceramic Products	50	Bricks, blocks, tiles and other ceramic goods of siliceous fossil meals; ceramic tableware, kitchenware; tableware, kitchen ware, of porcelain or china, etc.
Chapter 70	Glass and Glassware	110	Float glass sheets; safety glass, consisting of toughened or laminated glass; glassware
Chapter 71	Natural or Cultured Pearls, Precious or Semi-Precious Stones, Precious Metals, Metals Clad with Precious Metal, and	48	Pearls, natural or cultured; diamonds; silver, gold, articles of precious metal, etc.

(*Continued*)

Appendix 5 (Continued)

China's additional tariff list against the U.S. (first round: came into effect on July 6, 2018)

HS chapter	*Chapter description*	*Number of products*	*Examples*
	Articles Thereof; Imitation Jewelry; Coin		
Chapter 72	Iron and Steel	38	Pig iron; ferro-alloys; flat-rolled products of iron and non-alloy steel; stainless steel; other alloy steel, etc.
Chapter 73	Articles of Iron or Steel	134	Tubes and pipes, seamless of iron or steal; sheet piling of iron or steel; containers of iron or steel; stoves, ranges and similar non-electric domestic appliances of iron or steel; sanitary ware of iron or steel, etc.
Chapter 74	Copper and Articles Thereof	87	Refined copper and copper alloys; copper plates; copper foil; copper tubes and pipes, etc.
Chapter 75	Nickel and Articles Thereof	28	Unwrought nickel; nickel plates, sheets, strip and foil; nickel tubes, pipes and tube or pipe fittings, etc.
Chapter 76	Aluminium and Articles Thereof	21	Aluminium powders and flakes; aluminium structures and parts of structures; aluminium containers; aluminum household articles and parts thereof
Chapter 78	Lead and Articles Thereof	9	Unwrought lead; lead plates, sheets, strip, etc.
Chapter 79	Zinc and Articles Thereof	7	Unwrought zinc; zinc bars, rods, plates, etc.
Chapter 80	Tin and Articles Thereof	2	Other articles of tin
Chapter 81	Other Base Metals; Cements Articles and Thereof	37	Tungsten, molybdenum, magnesium, titanium, manganese and articles there of; cermets and articles thereof
Chapter 82	Tools, Implements, Cutlery, Spoons and Forks, of Base Metal, Parts Thereof Base Metal	94	Spades, shovels, mattocks and similar tools; hand tools and machine tools; knives with cutting blades, etc.
Chapter 83	Miscellaneous Articles of Base Metal	36	Padlocks and locks, of base metal; mirrors of base metal, etc.
		196	

China's additional tariff list against the U.S. (first round: came into effect on July 6, 2018)

HS chapter	*Chapter description*	*Number of products*	*Examples*
Chapter 84	Nuclear Reactors, Boilers, Machinery and Mechanical Appliances, Parts Thereof		Steam turbines; internal combustion piston engines and parts thereof; pumps for liquid; airs or vacuum pumps; cranes; fork-lift trucks; printing machinery; weaving machines; machine-tools for processing; calculating machines; machines for offices, etc.
Chapter 85	Electrical Machinery and Equipment and Parts Thereof; Sound Recorders and Reproducers, Television Image and Sound Recorders and Reproducers, and Parts and Accessories of Such Article	213	Electric motors and generators; electrical transformers; electro-magnets; primary cells and primary batteries; wire telephones; loudspeakers; wireless telephones; television reception apparatus; incandescent bulbs; thermionic tubes, wires, cables, etc.
Chapter 86	Railway or Tramway Locomotives, Rolling-Stock and Parts Thereof; Railway or Tramway Track Fixtures and Fittings and Parts Thereof; Mechanical (Including Electronic Mechanical) Traffic Signaling Equipment of All Kinds	1	Non-electric rail locomotives
Chapter 87	Vehicles Other Than Railway or Tramway Rolling-Stock, And Parts and Accessories Thereof	125	Chassis for the moto vehicles; bodies, for the motor vehicles; parts of the motor vehicles; bicycles and other cycles, not motorized; trailers and semi-trailers
Chapter 88	Aircraft, Spacecraft, and Parts Thereof	1	Parachutes and rotachutes, and parts thereof
Chapter 89	Ships, Boats, and Floating Structures	8	Vessels for pleasure or sports and other vessels; other floating structures
Chapter 90	Optical, Photographic, Cinematographic, Measuring, Checking, Precision, Medical, or	71	Optical fibers; cameras; cinematographic cameras and projectors; image projectors; compound

(*Continued*)

Appendix 5 (Continued)

China's additional tariff list against the U.S. (first round: came into effect on July 6, 2018)

HS chapter	*Chapter description*	*Number of products*	*Examples*
	Surgical Instruments and Apparatus; Parts and Accessories Thereof		optical microscopes; surveying instruments, etc.
Chapter 91	Clocks and Watches and Part Thereof	17	Instrument panel clocks for vehicles, aircraft, spacecraft, or vessels; time recorders, etc.
Chapter 94	Furniture; Bedding, Mattresses, Mattresses Supports, Cushions, and Similar Stuffed Furnishings; Lamps and Lighting Fittings, Not Elsewhere Specified or Included; Illuminated Signs, Illuminated Name-Plates and the Like; Prefabricated Building	77	Seats; other furniture and parts thereof; mattress, fitted with spring; other lamps and lighting fittings; prefabricated buildings
Chapter 96	Miscellaneous Manufactured Articles	24	Buttons, snap fasteners, etc.
Total			5,745

Note: product lists are obtained from the Official Announcements Chinese Customs Tariff Commission of the State Council, the Office of the United States Trade Representative (USTR), and other public media materials. We count the number of products within each HS chapter by hand in this table, based on the description of each product in the list.

Index

For Product Safety Concerns and Information please contact our EU representative GPSR@taylorandfrancis.com
Taylor & Francis Verlag GmbH, Kaufingerstraße 24, 80331 München, Germany

www.ingramcontent.com/pod-product-compliance
Ingram Content Group UK Ltd.
Pitfield, Milton Keynes, MK11 3LW, UK
UKHW022020180926
475701UK00005B/939
9780367707064